An Encyclopedia of Political Record Labels

AN ENCYCLO-PEDIA OF POLITICAL RECORD LABELS

3rd Edition

Josh MacPhee

Common Notions
Brooklyn, NY
2019

An Encyclopedia of Political Record Labels
Josh MacPhee

ISBN: 978-1-942173-11-3
LCCN: 2019942336

Common Notions
314 7th Street
Brooklyn, NY 11215
commonnotions.org
info@commonnotions.org

Pound the Pavement
c/o Josh MacPhee
314 7th Street
Brooklyn, NY 11215
poundthepavementpress.com
josh@justseeds.org

Cover and internal design by Josh MacPhee/Antumbradesign.org
The type is set in Berthold Akzidenz Grotesk, originally produced in the late 19th century,
explicitly *not* for book design. Ooops.

The music is not a threat: Action that music inspires *can* be a threat.
—Chumbawamba, 1985

The term "protest song" is no longer valid because it is ambiguous and has been misused. I prefer the term "revolutionary song."
—Victor Jara, 1969

Who no know go know.
—Fela Kuti, 1975

CONTENTS

ACKNOWLEDGEMENTS

Thank you to Monica Johnson and Asa Michigan for putting up with my piles of weird records and supporting all my crazy endeavors, Malav Kanuga and all at Common Notions for taking this project on, including Erika Biddle, Morgan Buck, Neelufar Franklin, Ash Goh, Julia Judge, and Natsumi Paxton, Jack Marchesi for doing such a thorough copy editing of the manuscript from the second edition, Michael McCanne for tossing ideas around and being so supportive, Ganzeer for helping me with the Arabic, Mike Andrews for pushing, pulling, and kicking the manuscript into its final shape, and Nicki Kattoura and Ilan Friedland for doing the last bit of fine-tooth combing.

I'd also like to thank Jon Active, AK Press, Book Thug Nation, Half Letter Press, Justseeds, Left Bank Books, Marc Pawson, Printed Matter, Quimby's (Chicago and New York), Red Emma's, and all the other stores and distributors who helped make the initial two editions so successful. I owe a big debt to Richard Alexander, Tim Devin, Alec Dunn, Marc Fischer, Eric Kjensrud, Mohamed Mehdi, June Julien Misserey, Skot Oh!, Anthony Romero, Stefan Szczelkun, and Erin Yahnke—all of whom tipped me off to great labels to include, as well as photographing labels and giving feedback on the early editions. Christian Brandt, formerly of Reckless Records in Chicago, was a great help when I started collecting political vinyl for Interference Archive back in 2015, and Johanna Halbeisen and the New Song Library were an amazing last minute resource, filling in a lot of gaps.

INTRODUCTION

Thanks for picking up this book, the third edition of *An Encyclopedia of Political Record Labels*. This project developed out of my semi-obsessive need to organize and catalog things, mixed with a deep love of logo design and political graphics. I grew up enmeshed in the do-it-yourself punk music scene of the late eighties and early nineties. Some of the first artworks I mass-produced were record covers for friends' bands, and I felt a deep connection between art-making and the apparatus around music and vinyl record production–whether designing flyers for shows, or hurriedly screen-printing album covers for a band in their van before we got to the next stop on tour. By the early 2000s my love of music had largely been crushed, primarily through a disillusionment with the potentials of political punk, but in part because of the seeming end of the vinyl record. I loved cassettes, and tolerated CDs, but the MP3 is the most soulless form of audio transport, and for me, listening to a hard drive of songs rotating via algorithm and playing through tinny computer speakers sucked all the life out of music.

In 2014, while helping Silvia Federici sort and clean out her files, she passed along a series of 7″ records put out by political groups in Italy in the sixties and seventies. This re-sparked my interest in music, and started a new fascination with folk music from around the world, something that was contraband during my days as an austere anarchist punk. I realized that not only did I know nothing about folk music–it was all kumbaya to me–but I had completely misunderstood its political import, particularly in other parts of the world. This led me to help organize the exhibition *If a Song Could Be Freedom...* at Interference Archive in Brooklyn in the summer of 2015. Working on the show opened up an amazingly expansive world of music to me, not just political folk from Italy, but anti-imperialist chants from Eritrea, revolutionary Afrocentric dub from Jamaica, communist fado from Portugal, and Black liberation jive from South Africa.

Rather than merely scratching the itch, the exhibition launched me into a not-entirely-healthy collecting spree of political albums and singles released around the world. Nowadays, often to my partner's chagrin, very little of the music I listen to is Western pop, and I've been playing all kinds of stuff to my toddler to see what he gravitates to and finds the most fun to dance to. This interest in socially conscious music has reengaged all the record-collecting switches in my head and relaunched all the tricks of scouring liner notes for clues to other records, mapping out the connections between musicians, and tracking down exciting new groups because they share a label with a favorite act.

Encyclopedia

In the title of this book, the name "encyclopedia" might be a slight misnomer. Instead of making a formal claim to historical fact, what I present is my research, very much in process. Much is drawn directly from the records (including 95 percent of the logos), with large amounts of help from the websites Discogs, Wikipedia, and Google Translate. Even though I've expanded the entries from 142 (first edition) to 230 (second edition) to 789 (the third edition you are reading now), this list is still by no means complete, nor likely 100 percent correct. It's pieced together from clues on the backs of record covers and in the footnotes of websites, tips from friends, advertisements in *Sing Out!* (a quarterly journal of folk music), flyers slipped into album sleeves, and my own extrapolation from music-related Wikipedia entries in a dozen different languages.

That said, it is organized as a reference book. It's not intended to be read from cover to cover, but to be bounced around in; each time you pick it up, I hope it provides a new nugget of useful or fascinating information. There were infinite ways that this book could have been organized, but I eventually decided on alphabetical order as the most simple and straightforward. There is a alphabet guide on the far right of each page spread to help you get around. While in the English language we tend to put modifiers after nouns (i.e., Cobblestone Records), in other languages the modifiers come first (i.e., Disques Pavé). I've alphabetized based on how the label is written in its own language; so in the previous example, Disques Pavé is under D. If a label didn't tend to use the modifier, I didn't either. For instance, Discos Pentagrama was a small Mexican folk label active in the eighties, but its name is almost always written simply as "Pentagrama," so I've placed it under P. I've used the same logic for acronyms. If a label is primarily known by its acronym–such as EGREM from Cuba– I've left it as such. If not, I've written out the full name. Lastly, just as in English the articles "the" and "a" are ignored when alphabetizing things, I've done the same with foreign-language articles (e.g., "el/la" and "un/una" in Spanish).

While not intended to be read front to back, this book should still be interesting to read in chunks, where you can really start to see patterns and overlapping information. If you simply use it as a reference, you might not get to see just how many European Communist parties released records to support electoral campaigns, or how many labels across the globe released Chilean music as an act of solidarity after the fascist coup in the country in 1973. It is through this macro lens that some really compelling political ideas take shape, which is why the index (new to this edition) is so important. Give it a skim to see just how many people, movements, and ideas overlap and are connected to multiple labels.

Political

I'm profoundly interested in the roles that culture plays in social movements, and the actions of people organizing to transform their lives and their worlds. Until recently, most of that interest was channeled into the visual realm, studying political posters and graphics. (See *Signs of Change: Social Movement Cultures 1960s to Now*, AK Press, 2010, for more on this.) Researching the movements against the dictatorship in

Chile and against apartheid in South Africa has given me a profound appreciation for the roles that music can play in social struggles. But I'm not an ethnomusicologist, and actually know very little about music on the level of sound. So I'm very much approaching this project by looking at the apparatus *around* music and its production and distribution, as much or more than its sonic qualities. And because this is ultimately a study of politics and social movements, you will find that much in here does not focus on music per se, but instead on field recordings, political speeches, and other forms of recorded sound. I'm not interested solely in music, but also in questions about who performs the sound, how it's recorded, how it's distributed, how it's packaged, and who designs the packaging. That is why this book is a collection of "labels," not musicians or recording artists. But more on that later.

Like "encyclopedia," the term "political" in the title of this book is also a bit misleading. Technically, this is a compendium of labels that would all fall somewhere on the spectrum of "left." I've actively excluded highly politicized and ideological recordings from the center and right. Believe me, they exist, and many are just as interesting as those included here from a musical, design, and materialist perspective (for example, see releases from the John Birch Society's Key Records, or Detroit's white supremacist Resistance Records—not to be confused with the two labels of the same name included in this book). But this project needed limits, and I'm most familiar with left movements and how they function, so keeping things reigned in by defining the politics this way made sense. In addition, while I might have kept out the Right, there is certainly no ideological consistency within this collection. It is extremely ecumenical: European anarchists rub shoulders with African nationalists, Latin American communists share pages with militant defenders of minority languages and suppressed nationalities. I also in no way support much of the politics here. I am no more excited by the homophobia of some of the early Black nationalist records than I am by the Stalinism of some of the New Communist parties that emerged in the seventies. But outside of some extreme examples (for instance, I have excluded the Rassemblement du Peuple Togolais—a political party that ruled Togo for over forty years, which released a number of cool records with the word "revolutionary" in the title—because although loudly anti-imperialist, it was also brutally antidemocratic and anticommunist), I've largely included labels and groups because they self-defined as part of a progressive political project, be that socialist, communist, or nationalist.

I have largely focused on smaller, independent labels with some dedication to political music or social struggles. I have excluded major labels, even if they put out political records, because it is far from their mission. I feel confident in saying that a small Danish label that put out a six-pack of Chilean politicized folk records after the 1973 coup has some sense of solidarity or connection to that struggle, while Epic Records, which put out *Sandinista!* by The Clash, surely never gave a shit about the Nicaraguan revolution. At the same time, I have included a number of state-sponsored labels, such as Melodiya from the Soviet Union, which is the Eastern Bloc equivalent of a major label, because the politics of the state hewed to an explicitly communist and anti-imperialist line.

While cutting out corporate music makes a lot of sense when looking at political music from the production end, it has some unfortunate side effects. Hip-hop, a musical style that became massively popular almost at the point of its conception, lived almost entirely under a corporate umbrella until the explosion of an underground scene in the late nineties. It thus falls outside the purview of this project. This means that labels such as Raptivism—founded in 1998—are not included, and rap and hip-hop are largely, and conspicuously, absent in the book. Similarly, there are extremely interesting politics embedded in the club and house music scenes, but I haven't found a way to access this social engagement through the lens of the record label.

I initially gravitated towards recordings released by anarchist, socialist, and communist outfits, but this encyclopedia also articulates a lot about the intersection of music, sound recordings, and nationalism, although I didn't start out with this intention. While much of the scholarship on the development of modern nationalist movements focuses on print culture (for example, see Benedict Anderson's writing), one can glean from the entries included here that audio recording and the vinyl record have also been important components of preserving and articulating nationalism. A couple dozen labels included here focus specifically on minority linguistic and cultural groups fighting for sovereignty within larger national states. Armenian, Basque, Breton, Catalan, Corsican, Gaelic, and Welsh all make appearances, never mind unique dialects of larger language groups. In addition, some of the labels represent identity groups that transcend current borders (for instance Berbers), as well as those that are fighting for their traditional territories and homelands, such as Catholics in Northern Ireland, the Québécois, Palestinians, and various groups in the Western Sahara.

The gaps in the nationalist narrative contained in these pages are just as interesting as the presences. There are highly organized, popular, and militant struggles that aren't visible in this landscape of music and record labels. For example, a couple of the most active and mass-based political movements over the past fifty years have been the Kurdish struggle and the Naxalites and other Maoist peasant struggles in India. But neither of these struggles shows up much on vinyl. All of the Kurdish recordings available are presented as ethnographic and anthropological. When politics is present in the music and lyrics, it tends to be glossed over or ignored by the liner notes and presentation of the music by the record label. The situation is similar in India. There is a massive music infrastructure in the country, where major British companies such as His Master's Voice had large-scale pressing plants, yet there is no discernible dissident music culture captured on record. Requests for information to multiple experts in this field have come up empty, and while there is a robust culture of politicized Bollywood soundtracks, they are all put out by major record companies. Similar situations seem to hold for Tibet as well as the Tamil struggle in Sri Lanka. Music was and is important to these struggles, which is clear from the development of cassette and CD-R labels in places like Sri Lanka and the Western Sahara—the Tamil Tigers and the Polisario Front both began producing and distributing a flood of cassettes and CD-Rs in the mid-nineties. But I could find nothing by these groups released on vinyl.

So what this project documents is a product of the uneven access to pressing plants, or even record players, across different regions of the globe. Most of South America decolonized in the nineteenth century, and developed a robust middle-class in the period after WWII; as a result, during the heyday of vinyl people there had access to both vinyl production and the means to distribute, purchase, and listen to the records. In comparison, most of Africa didn't decolonize until the late 1950s and early sixties, and then much of southern and Portuguese Africa not until the seventies. After independence, very few of these countries had vinyl pressing plants, and if they did, it was based on the whims of the previous colonial power. For instance, Portugal had built plants in both Angola and Mozambique, but not in Cape Verde or Guinea-Bissau, leading cultural militants in the latter locales to press records in Europe and import them back into Africa. While the British had situated plants in Nigeria and Kenya, as far as I've been able to research, the French didn't build any outside of Algeria, so that Francophone Africa had to produce their records in France. The location of the largest music production, distribution, and consumption infrastructures on the continent was in South Africa, but because of the apartheid regime, it was certainly not used to press much with overt left political content. In fact, South African anti-apartheid organizations like the African National Congress were banned in the country, forcing them to release records through solidarity organizations across Europe and smuggle them back into South Africa.

Meanwhile, back in South America, dissident musicians and political organizations in Argentina, Chile, Peru, Uruguay, and Venezuela were able to access pressing plants with relative ease, and often build large-scale music labels (until they were suppressed by military dictatorships in the 1970s–but that's a different story). In the early seventies the region is practically lousy with "nueva canción" (new song) labels, which were pressing a truly popular and mass-based form of political music. So not only was the vinyl record affordable to most middle-class and many working-class communities, but people also had access to record players in their homes. Within much of Latin America, the vinyl record, as both an archive of sound and a commodity, was seen as a viable way to distribute political ideas from below. Musicians developed their own regional takes on nueva canción, yet many also helped build the infrastructure that allowed musicians from across the continent to tour and have their records pressed locally. DICAP in Chile and Ayuí in Uruguay were just two of many musician-driven labels.

The Caribbean presents another situation where the majority of music lovers–be it reggae, soca, calypso, or steel bands–were extremely poor and likely didn't have record players. But they did have transistor radios, which they listened to extensively. So any musician who wanted to bring their music to the people had to press records, and then get them into the hands of popular radio DJs. Ideally, records would then also end up in the collections of the people who ran the local sound systems–mobile collectives of DJs, sound techs, and "toasters" (MCs) who rove around ghettos on trucks loaded up with massive stacks of speakers. These two forms of consuming music collectively meant that there was little need for individual record ownership.

By contrast, in East Asia the dominant form of political musical production was from above, with centralized state record labels producing music and recordings in direct support of their regimes. The Chinese Communist Party founded China Records (Zhongguo Changpian) in 1954, only five years after taking power, and by the mid-sixties had put out hundreds of records for both internal use and export. Their Vietnamese and Laotian Communist Party counterparts (which created the Dihavina and Dislaohaksat labels, respectively) inherited countries without pressing plants (the pressing plant in Vietnam was in the south, so the Communists couldn't access it until after they won the war), so they had to turn to the Soviet block to get records made; in addition, a much smaller proportion of their populations had access to record players.

Because many movements in the Global South had limited access to pressing plants, producing records for these struggles could become, for supporters in the North, a multifaceted act of solidarity. While a 7″ single was literally impossible to make in Portuguese-controlled Guinea-Bissau, it was not particularly difficult in the Netherlands; in fact, five hundred or a thousand copies could be pressed for pennies each, a simple printed sleeve barely adding to the cost. So when the Amsterdam-based Angola Comité released several records in the seventies in support of political groups from southern Africa and the Portuguese African colonies, it could sell them inexpensively and still make a decent amount of money, which would be turned around and donated right back to those struggles. In addition, the records themselves became tools for education–covered with information about anticolonialism–and vehicles for musicians in Africa to get their music heard across the globe.

Non-nationalist minority identity also fueled record production. The feminist and lesbian movements in particular vigorously took up the form of the vinyl record. Not only did most of the broad left labels from around the world (see Demos, Expression Spontanée, Plateselskapet Mai) release records dedicated to feminist and/ or lesbian folk and pop music, but many individual musicians and small communities of artists created their own labels (Carolsdatter, Hexensaite, Index). Lesbians in the US even created their own distribution system for records, with Olivia Records acting as a clearinghouse for a number of smaller lesbian-focused labels. Interestingly, I've found no parallel to this amongst the gay male community, and although AIDS activism created one of the most impactful social movements of the twentieth century, it is strangely absent in the cosmology of the vinyl record.

Over the historical arc of the rise and fall of the vinyl record, we also see the volatile transformation of the popular understanding of politics: from a process of collective action undertaken through political groups, parties, and unions, to one rooted in the individual as the dominant social actor. The late fifties through the sixties witnessed the pressing to vinyl of thousands of versions of popular workers' songs, such as "L'Internationale" and "Bella Ciao." Each version may have varied slightly, but they all hewed closely enough to the traditional version to function as rallying cries for the working class. By the late sixties, this starts to change. Instead, we see a competition between different understandings of what constitutes "the people's music." On the one hand, a resurgent folk music redefines "popular" to denote not much commercial viability, but quite literally *of the people*. On the other, we see the development of thriving youth cultures across the globe, most identifying themselves in direct opposition to the status quo (and by extension, previous generations). This leads to the conception of "people's music" as dissident music, as a rejection of the folk music of the past in favor of something seen as fresh, new, and potentially liberatory. This takes different forms in different places, but the most intense and widespread examples are free jazz, experimental sound, prog rock, and eventually punk and hip-hop. While still rooted in specific communities, each of these genres eschews a desire for a mass audience, instead attempting to speak to individuals embedded in self-organized subcultures. This migration of political music from mass to subculture warrants much further exploration, but unfortunately there isn't room for it here.

Record

For this project, "record" is defined as a vinyl record. During the second half of the twentieth century, this object played an outsized role in the life of recorded sound: it was the primary form of both its distribution and commodification. While shellac and then early vinyl records in 16 and 78 rpm formats had existed since the 1880s, it wasn't until the late 1950s and early sixties that the 12" long-playing albums and 7" "singles" we recognize today came to dominate the music market. In the early 1930s, both RCA Victor and Columbia Records introduced $33^{1/3}$ rpm vinyl records; RCA Victor's version was 12" in diameter (or, to be more exact, thirty centimeters), while Columbia's version was 10" in diameter. But these experiments crashed with the economy during the Great Depression. Then in 1948, Columbia introduced the contemporary $33^{1/3}$ rpm 12" record. In 1949, RCA Victor released the 45 rpm 7" in competition; while this format spun faster and thus held less music than Columbia's format, RCA Victor bet that the eventual development of technology to enable the automatic playing of multiple records in a row would obviate the need for consumers to get up and change the records themselves. By 1956, the two systems would almost completely control the recorded music market, with the 12" for albums and the 7" for singles.

The significant crossover between recorded music and political movements begins with the Civil Rights Movement in the United States. The movement was extremely savvy with its use of emerging communication technologies, staging some of the first actions to be captured by news crews and broadcast live on television. The movement also took full advantage of the vinyl record. The Congress of Racial Equality released *Sit-In Songs: Songs of the Freedom Riders* in 1962. The Student Nonviolent Coordinating Committee's Freedom Singers quickly followed, releasing their first single and album–both titled *We Shall Overcome*–in 1963. Over two dozen recordings of Martin Luther King, Jr. were released on vinyl in the sixties. Even major labels got in on the act, with Mercury, Motown, Atlantic, and Buddah releasing Civil Rights Movement LPs. Folkways Records released field recordings of people marching, singing, and giving speeches at demonstrations. While Alan Lomax had been making invaluable recordings and eventually vinyl records of African American religious, labor, and prison songs, they feel like anthropological documents of a culture being subsumed by modern ways of life. In contrast, these movement records felt like just that, movement–they were documents of people in transition and struggle, and made the listener feel like they were there. Buying the records was a way to support the movement, and spread its message.

While the rise of the vinyl record tracks neatly with the explosion of the Civil Rights Movement, by an odd turn of history, the end of its heyday is roughly 1990–the year that Nelson Mandela is released from prison in South Africa, marking the turning point in the last of the great political struggles of the twentieth century. Just as the format of the vinyl phonograph record is eclipsed by the compact disc, we see the end of a twenty-year-plus flow of recordings focused on ending apartheid, crushing colonialism in southern Africa, and securing Mandela's release.

This overlap of time streams between vinyl and the modern social movement gives me a comfortable time frame to work with. I have focused almost entirely on labels most active during the two decades between 1970 and 1990.

By cutting things off by the mid-nineties, not only do I avoid most CD-oriented labels (although plenty are political); I also exclude a significant number of political labels that came out of the punk and other countercultural scenes of the late nineties and early 2000s. While much of the music produced by these labels was political, it could be argued that is was more *about* politics than *of* it, with musicians expressing political opinions more than actively participating in or supporting mass-based social struggles.

Because vinyl records are relatively complicated and expensive to produce, they carry with them a level of intentionality. The creation and crafting of vinyl records is a way to distribute not only music, but also design, art, and ideas, including lyrics, political and historical background, solidarity information, and more. The record was challenged by the cassette tape in the seventies and eighties, and finally superseded by the compact disc in the nineties. CDs themselves have been replaced by purely digital formats—MP3s, MP4s, WAV and FLAC files. But the vinyl record has reemerged, not only because people are nostalgic, but because it is an extremely stable—if analog—form of data storage. People also have a renewed appreciation for the very excess of its form—the brightly colored gatefold picture sleeves, lyric sheets, and poster inserts. So the word "record" in the title of this book also means record cover or sleeve, as this was as much the medium of political information as the music itself.

While the budgets of political bands and labels couldn't compete with, for example, the extreme lavishness of peak-era corporate prog rock—with its gatefold covers exploding with a rainbow of obsessively detailed paintings of organic machinery, its full-color inner sleeves, and its fold-out posters—an amazing amount of information (and often artfulness) was present in the packaging of many of the labels mentioned here. Italian folk label I Dischi del Sole packaged its 7" singles in clean, high-modernist gatefold sleeves, and French label Le Chant du Monde often packaged LPs in giant three-part covers that unfolded into three-foot-long posters jammed with lyrics, graphics, and information. Paredon Records in the US almost always included a twelve to twenty-four page booklet, chock-full of information about the music and its political context—which was quite important, since 90 percent of the label's output was of music directly connected to political struggles around the world.

A record's sleeve also has the potential to tell us more than what was originally printed on it. Almost all the records I have from Africa—plus a large portion of those from Southern Europe, especially Portugal—have a former owners name written on the cover, and often even on the vinyl labels themselves. The lesson here is not that Africans are more possessive of their property than Germans, but that in the time period covered by this book, records were comparatively expensive and hard to come by. When you got one, you held onto it fiercely. This preciousness of the record as an object added to its political value, as the owner tended not only keep the record, but absorb every aspect of it. While a political flyer or pamphlet might be discarded, a vinyl record rarely was. Because records were rare, you played them with friends, and they became social objects. In turn, the community built around listening to the music could be the foundation for discussing the politics. I distinctly remember having these kinds of discussions about the content of music as a teenager with my friends.

Labels

Like every other term in this book's title, I'm also being loose with "label." While many of the entries in this book concern professional entities organized for the purpose of producing vinyl records, many do not. I've purposely stretched the term "label" to include citizen's initiatives, labor unions, theaters, churches, and political parties that released records (as well as musical groups that self-released their records). I find this broad engagement with record production and distribution quite compelling.

Record collectors often call these releases on nontraditional labels "private press" records. That's a real misnomer here, as much of this output was created with wide distribution in mind, and with the intention of making the issues addressed by the releases far more public and social, rather than private and personal. In this book I use the word "ad hoc" instead, making clear that some of these records might have been one-offs, but this didn't make them marginal. Stories abound of activist musicians pressing five hundred copies of a 7" in support of a cause, only to sell out within weeks and re-pressing it three or four times.

While pressing a vinyl record isn't profoundly difficult, it is certainly more complex than printing a newsletter or poster. Not only is it more expensive; you also need to work with people who know how to mix sound recordings and create master tapes from which the vinyl will be pressed. Today one can do this at home on a laptop, but in 1972 you needed a recording studio, or at least a series of machines to record and mix onto metallic tape. I would have thought this would be a pretty significant barrier to entry, but given that there are over three hundred examples of political groupings and community entities included here, all of which released vinyl records as part of their activist work, its safe to say that this was a relatively common tactic in the political toolbox, and likely seen as effective enough to overcome the technical complications.

When I started this project, I was also interested in the intersection of music, politics, and design. One of the things that initially sparked my imagination was looking at the variety of logos and icons that different labels used, some riffing off common musical or political themes (vinyl record shapes, fists, peace doves, etc.); some entirely generic, as if their makers were still finding their ideological leanings; still others excitingly weird (see the mascot for Belgium's Agitat label).

As work on this book has progressed, I've been less and less focused on the graphics, and more on collecting and distilling the information and history. But the logos are still a very important part of this project, and hopefully for you, the reader, a very enjoyable one. I've been able to produce them in color in this edition, so they can really shine. Other than a very small number of examples where actual records were impossible for me to find, all the logos here have been photographed or scanned directly from the records and their sleeves (either by myself or friends). I've gotten a little creative with some of the icons, especially when labels themselves didn't appear to have a logo beyond their name displayed in a standard font, even as their covers were rich with imagery. In other words, some of these might not be "official" logos, but they all are derived from the records in one way or another.

Conclusion

Once the compact disc eclipsed the vinyl record in the late eighties, record companies quickly began to scale back vinyl production and heavily promote CDs. The reason wasn't simply because they were following sales trends. A CD costs a fraction of what a vinyl record costs to produce (less than 50¢ per unit, including the packaging, as opposed to $2–$5 for a vinyl record, depending on volume); record companies could sell CDs for the same retail price as vinyl, thus drastically increasing profits. In the late nineties, the rise of peer-to-peer file sharing software was the coup de grace for vinyl, with major labels now convinced that their future lay in music as digital files, not physical objects. By this time, most vinyl pressing plants in the US had been shut down because their primary customers, the major labels, stopped producing vinyl. The trend spread globally, with only a few significantly sized plants left in the world by 2005.

Whether it's rooted in nostalgia, a need for something material to come with one's consumption, or a real desire to hear the physicality of music crackling off a needle and through speakers, there is no question that vinyl has returned. Sales of vinyl records continue to rise, with 16.8 million LPs sold in the US in 2018, up 14.6 percent compared to 2017, and a massive 94.6 percent compared to 2006. Because the major labels forcibly closed so many pressing plants in the nineties, there is now a huge backlog for pressing vinyl at the remaining plants and at new boutique ones that have started in the past decade. It is not uncommon for a small band or label to have to wait six months to have a record pressed.

Vinyl records have also returned to bookstores—you can now by a copy of Black Sabbath's *Master of Reality* at Barnes and Noble. Vinyl has even begun showing up at Whole Foods. But the strangest new development is the return of the "record club." Well over a dozen vinyl subscription services have started up over the past couple years, one of the most popular being Vinyl Me, Please. An evolution of the record and tape clubs of old, here you sign up and have a new vinyl record sent to you every month. These are a mix of old and new recordings; most are lavishly packaged in gatefold sleeves, with colored vinyl, and other "unique to the club" perks. But the strangest thing about almost all these clubs is that you have no control over the content of the records, so one month you get a re-press of a classic prog rock album, and the next you get the new Taylor Swift LP.

All of this is to say, while vinyl has returned, it feels strangely hollow without a concomitant connection to movements, unions, community groups, and music acts that privilege content over stardom. I hope this little love letter to the potentials of the vinyl record can help reconnect it to its roots as a key tool in the Civil Rights Movement—a medium for improving our communities and world, not simply our personal consumption and listening experiences.

THE LABELS

1 in 12 Records
UK

The 1 in 12 Club is a music venue and social center in the small northern UK city of Bradford. Founded in 1981, it is organized collectively along anarchist lines—and in addition to putting on music events like the annual Mayday festival, the project has also published books and pressed records. Since its 1984 inception, the club's record label has put out eighteen records, the majority of which are compilations of local punk and indie bands.

3rd Street Records
USA

Named after its office location in Philadelphia, this label released a single LP, 1977's *Rebirth Cycle* by Mtume. James Mtume, who was Miles Davis's drummer in the seventies, released this LP of Afrocentric jazz improvisation just before formalizing Mtume into a politicized jazz/funk project that would sign to Epic Records in 1978. James Mtume had also recorded *Alkebu-Lan: Land of the Blacks* (Strata-East, 1972), another Black-nationalist jazz classic released with his group Mtume Umoja Ensemble.

7:84 Theatre Company
UK

Founded in 1971 in Scotland by David MacLennan, Elizabeth MacLennan, and John McGrath, 7:84 was a leftist theater troupe that produced travelling shows focused on political

issues within the UK. The name is taken from an economic statistic from 1966 claiming that 7 percent of the UK's population owned 84 percent of its wealth. In 1973 the group split into separate English and Scottish groups, and throughout the seventies and into the eighties both groups released recordings of their productions. The English section put out a 7″ with Robert Wyatt in 1985 (released by TUC) and the theater's most notable musical product was the lefty a cappella group, The Flying Pickets (all of whom had been part of 7:84, and many of whom had participated in miners' strikes in the seventies).

A&B Records
Antigua

Short for Antigua and Barbados, A&B Records is the home of calypso singer King Short Shirt and his band The Ghetto Vibes. Short Shirt (aka Mclean Emanuel) was a prolific singer whose songs usually featured social commentary, touching on Caribbean liberation (support for the revolution in Grenada and independence for Belize), Black Power, and antirepression. A&B released about fifty records between the early seventies and 1989.

ABR Productions
France

The label of political chanson singer Rosalie Dubois (aka Jeanine Rolleau) and her husband Bernard Berger. Throughout the seventies, Dubois released a series of five LPs of French revolutionary songs on this label, each volume focused on a different historical period in the country. The LP I have is titled *Chants Révolutionnaires de notre Histoire: De la Victoire au Front Populaire (1920–1938)*. It contains a dozen songs from the period of the

Popular Front government in France, between the end of the First World War and the invasion of the Nazis in 1940. Dubois also later released an LP on DOM/Expression Spontanée collecting songs from the various volumes.

acousti-yuri korolkoff

Acousti – Yuri Korolkoff
France

Yuri Korolkoff was a sound engineer who worked at Acousti Studio in Paris. This label name was used to release a 7″ of field recordings made by Korolkoff during the May '68 protests, originally captured as part of a film coordinated by Guy Chalon.

Action Records
Scotland

A Glasgow-based label that released a half dozen records in the sixties. The focus was on Scottish folk, especially working-class songs. In addition, Action released an LP of songs from the Iona Community, an ecumenical Christian sect (similar to the Quakers) committed to peace and social justice.

AD Records
UK

AD is the label of The African Dawn, a London-based band made up of musicians from Africa, the Caribbean, and Latin American. Over the four LPs released by the label and band between 1983 and 1989, they covered a lot of political ground, with songs such as "Africa Must Be Free," "El Salvador," "Intifaada," "Lewisham," "Questions—To Brecht With Love," and "Sharpeville Aftermath."

A Disc
Sweden

A Disc—also known as Arbetarrörelsens Skivbolag—was the record label of the Swedish labor movement. It ran for about a decade, roughly 1975–84, before it was shut down due to financial difficulties. Its fifty or so releases run the gamut of late-seventies political music: folk, nueva canción, early punk, Cuban bands, and bands expressing solidarity with the anti-apartheid movement.

Ad Libitum
Portugal

A small label that released a handful of 7″s in the mid-seventies, with half of them featuring postrevolution Portuguese folk or anticolonial African music.

African Methodist Episcopal Church
USA

The African Methodist Episcopal Church (AME) is one of the historically Black churches that has played an important activist role in civil rights struggles in the US, as well as in fighting oppression more broadly. It released a mid-sixties documentary record called *Pioneers of Protest*, featuring excerpts from Martin Luther King, Jr.'s presentation at the 1964 AME conference, as well as commentary by Roy Wilkins from the NAACP, A. Phillip Randolph from the Brotherhood of Sleeping Car Porters, and Daisy Bates, an activist central to the school integration struggle in Little Rock, Arkansas.

African National Congress
South Africa/UK

The African National Congress (ANC) was one of the major anti-apartheid organizations in South Africa for most of the twentieth century. After being banned and exiled by the South African government in the sixties, it began to style itself as a government-in-exile (with offices in multiple countries, but largely in the UK), including an armed wing, Umkhonto we Sizwe (or MK), but also multiple cultural units, such as the musical acts Amandla and Mayibuye. These groups released albums on various labels and with multiple solidarity organizations (A Disc, Afrogram, Angola Comité, Melodiya, Pläne, VARAgram) throughout the eighties. Many of these records were listed as co-releases, distributed or produced by the ANC even if it didn't press them.

Afrikan Poetry Theatre Records
USA

The label used to release an anti-apartheid 12″– *Kuulula y Azania*–by the Afrikan Poetry Theatre Ensemble in 1985. The Afrikan Poetry Theatre is an Afrocentric cultural center that has been based in Jamaica, Queens in New York City since its founding in 1976. The Theatre is, and has been, home to a wide array of cultural activities, including open-mic poetry nights, film festivals, African history classes, acting workshops, and educational tours to West Africa. *Kuulula y Azania* is the only vinyl record by the label, under the moniker APT Records.

AFRIKINGS
RECORDS

Afrikings
USA

Afrikings is the label name used to release a single LP by the popular Ghanaian highlife group African Brothers Band. The album, *Oh! No! Apartheid*, is one of the most overtly political of the group's fifty-plus LPs. The moniker "Afrikings" is likely a politicized version of one of the band's house labels, Afribros; the New York City address on the back cover of the Afrikings album is the same one found on the band's Afribros releases.

AFRO

Afro Records
USA

Afro Records was the name used to release the initial 1965 pressing of Malcolm X's *Message to the Grass Roots*. The album cover alternatively lists the label as Grass Roots L.P. Co., based in Detroit. The recording is of X's 1963 speech at the Northern Negro Grass Roots Leadership Conference, so it is possible that people involved in the conference were connected to the label. Later re-pressings were produced by Charisma and Paul Winley Records, the former owned by All Platinum Records (one of Sylvia Robinson's companies, who also owned Sugar Hill Records), and the latter known best for its extensive catalog of releases by early hip-hop pioneer Afrika Bambaataa.

Afro-American Museum, Inc.
USA

The International Afro-American Museum was founded by Charles H. Wright in 1965 in his house in Detroit. In the seventies, the museum released an LP of a live recording of Paul Robeson, *At the*

Peace Arch Park—1953. The concert had not been previously released, and the museum used the LP as a fundraiser. In 1978, Detroit leased a plot of downtown land to the museum, and in 1985 it was renamed the Museum of African American History.

Afrogram
Sweden

The back of the *Amandla Live* LP on this label states, "Afrogram is the record label of the Africa Groups of Sweden (AGS)." The AGS formed in 1974 as a national coordinating organization of local groups dedicated to fighting colonialism across southern Africa. As the seventies turned into the eighties, it focused on the struggle against apartheid in South Africa. In addition to putting out a least two records (both by the ANC cultural troupe Amandla), AGS also published regular bulletins, magazines, and books. In many ways it was the Swedish equivalent of the North America–based Liberation Support Movement.

Afro Som
Mozambique

A small label that released a half dozen 7"s between 1973 and 1975, some with a pro-FRELIMO bent (Frente de Libertação de Moçambique, or Mozambique Liberation Front).

AFSCME
USA

AFSCME is the American Federation of State and County Municipal Employees, and the largest union of public employees in the US. The union released two LPs with labor folk singer Joe Glazer, 1967's *AFSCME Sings with Joe Glazer*, and an early eighties LP, *Singing About Our Union: An Evening with Joe Glazer*. Both albums feature labor classics by Pete Seeger, Joe Hill, and others, as well as some songs specific to AFSCME's history and struggles (such as "On Our Way with AFSCME"). In 1971, Glazer remastered and rereleased *AFSCME Sings with Joe Glazer* under the title *Joe Glazer Sings Labor Songs* on his own Collector Records label.

Agitat
Belgium

A far-left Belgian label releasing records in the Dutch language in the seventies. I've found very little information about it, but the few releases I've tracked down are an eclectic mix of punk, political pop, and a great SWAPO benefit 7" of freedom songs from Namibia (then South West Africa).

Agitpop
Denmark

Agitpop was a political folk-rock band from Copenhagen, connected to Røde Mor (Red Mother) and the Demos scene. They released a half dozen records under the Agitpop label, all distributed by Demos. The band was led by Benny Holst, who also had an extensive solo career and recorded a number of albums with Povl Dissing (another popular and politically committed Danish folk musician).

Agit-Prop
UK

The house label of the British anarchist punk-turned-pop band Chumbawamba. They ran it from 1985 to 1992, putting out about twenty releases. The vast majority were Chumbawamba records, but they also did a couple compilations, the great Thatcher on Acid LP *Frank*, and a 12″ by the political hip-hop group Credit to the Nation. See also Sky & Trees (another label run by Chumbawamba).

AIDS Action Committee
USA

The AIDS Action Committee is a health nonprofit founded in Boston in the mid-eighties to address the AIDS epidemic. As part of its work in the late eighties and early nineties, it released a AIDS awareness hip-hop 12″ by the Positive Force Posse, "It's Not Who You Are, It's What You Do" b/w "Can We Do This." The record was released under the label name Foxtron, which appears to have been an ad hoc name used for this 12″ only.

Aksie Latin Amerika
Netherlands

Netherlands-based Latin American solidarity group that released two LPs of political nueva canción by Bolivian singer-songwriter Victor Hugo Cabrera. Both came with large booklets compiling information about exploitation and imperialism in Latin America, as well as resistance to it. Also known as Aktiegroep Latijns Amerika.

AKTIEKOMITEE ..NEEN aan de 30MILJARD..

Aktiegroep: „Neen aan de 30 Miljard"
Belgium

A political action group that pressed a 1975 7″ by the Belgian polit-folk act Het Cirkus Van Vuile Mong & Zijn Vieze Gasten. The group/label name translates to "No to the 30 Billion," which is a reference to protests against the mid-seventies purchase of thirty billion francs worth of combat aircraft by the Belgian state.

„AKTIONSKOMITEE CHILE"

"Aktionskommitee Chile" Köln
West Germany

A solidarity organization that released a joint German-Chilean LP featuring Salvador Allende, Wolf Biermann, Heinrich Böll, Victor Jara, Pablo Neruda, and Quilapayún. Proceeds were directed to Amnesty International's work around Chile. The record was manufactured by the classical label AULOS-Schallplatten.

Alacran

Alacran Productions
USA

The name used by the San Diego–based band Los Alacranes Mojados to release their 1979 LP, *Rolas de Aztlan*, a collection of songs focused on Chicano power. The band has long been popular locally and with Chicano movement activists, with songs mass distributed via CDs and file sharing, but their vinyl records are incredibly scarce.

Albatros
Italy

One of a series of politicized sublabels of Milan-based Vedette Record Company (along with I Dischi dello Zodiaco, Way Out, etc.). Each nominally had a genre-specific identity, although there was a lot of overlap. Albatros was intended as the outlet for global folk music, similar in many ways to Monitor in the US, with a heavy list of nueva canción chilena (Victor Jara, Violeta Parra, Juan Capra), American political folk (Woody Guthrie, Pete Seeger), a slew of Italian regional folk albums, lots of US blues records (including at least three LPs of prison songs), and a series of "African Rhythms and Instruments" LPs. The Albatros name was used from the late sixties until 1992, when Vedette folded. About two hundred albums are attributed to Albatros, although the exact dates and numbers are difficult to suss out because the label was never given its own catalog numbering system; instead, the records carry standard Vedette catalog numbers (i.e., VPA 8133).

Alcatraz
West Germany

Alcatraz is a krautrock band from Hamburg that has been active for forty-five years. Their initial LP was released on Philips, but since then they have put out a steady stream of records on their own label, also called Alcatraz. The most relevant here is one of the earliest, a 1978 concept LP titled *Energie Programm In Rock*, a sprawling forty-minute critique of nuclear power.

Alliance
UK

Alliance was an ad hoc label name used to release a 1982 double LP, *An Evening of International Poetry*, featuring tracks by nineteen Third Worldist authors including Okot p'Bitek and Edward Kamau Brathwaite. The recording was made on March 30, inaugurating the first International Book Fair of Radical Black and Third World Books, and was compiled and edited by Linton Kwesi Johnson and John La Rose. La Rose was a London-based Pan-Africanist who had emigrated from Trinidad and founded the Afro-Caribbean publishing company and bookshop New Beacon.

ALTERNATIVE ENERGY RECORDS

Alternative Energy
Ireland

A label created to release one record, *Anti-Nuclear*, a 12″ single from 1979 featuring and produced by the Irish folk singer Christy Moore (from the Moving Hearts) and his younger brother Barry Moore (aka Luka Bloom).

Alternative Tentacles
USA

Long-running San Francisco punk label started in 1979 by Jello Biafra of the Dead Kennedys. Its first years saw the release of mostly California-based politically charged punk (Dead Kennedys, Black Flag, 7 Seconds, MDC, early TSOL), as well as Vancouver's D.O.A. and Lansing, Michigan's Crucifucks. By the mid-eighties, Alternative Tentacles became a broad-spectrum punk label, though it continued to release highly political records by the Dead Kennedys, The Dicks, Amebix, and the Beatnigs. The label is still running, and has put out some five hundred releases.

Amalthea
Sweden

Based in Malmö, Amalthea initially pressed politicized folk and progg, then eventually became a more general rock label. It released late-seventies records by political theater troupes Musikteatergruppen Oktober and Tidingsteatern, and an album by Chilean protest folk duo Amerindos. In the eighties, it put out a double LP of Swedish rock musicians playing against apartheid, an LP of Jan Hammarlund and Kjerstin Norén playing Swedish renditions of songs by Italy's Cantacronache group, as well as Billy Bragg's LPs for the Scandinavian market. The label's releases were distributed by Plattlangarna.

American Civil Liberties Union
USA

The American Civil Liberties Union is best known for its legal work protecting free speech rights in the United States, but in 1973 the San Francisco chapter released a compilation LP of local street musicians recorded live on the street—*San Francisco Street Musicians and Their Music*. I would expect this to have been released as part of a campaign to support the right of street musicians to perform in public, but the record and cover are largely devoid of context.

AMERICANTO

Americanto
USA

A New York City–based label releasing political groups from Latin America. Its records bear little info about the label, as does the internet. It was active in the mid-seventies, and put out at least six albums, including vinyl by Victor Jara (Chile), Silvio Rodríguez and Noel Nicola (a live LP of these Cuban nueva trova musicians performing in the Dominican Republic), Jatari (Ecuador), a compilation of Argentine songs, and a documentary LP of testimony from torture victims of the Pinochet regime in Chile. The label had a relationship with the Center for Cuban Studies (which co-released some of the LPs) and likely with Paredon Records as well.

Amicale des Algériens en Europe
France

Amicale des Algériens en Europe (AAE), or Friends of Algeria in Europe, is a French cultural and social-service organization that supports Algerians living in France. It put out an LP in 1982 titled *Hyme à L'indépendance*, celebrating twenty years of Algerian independence. It's a deluxe production, with a gatefold sleeve and extensive liner notes, all assembled by the youth wing of AAE's cultural group.

AMIGA
GDR

The popular music (rock and jazz) sublabel of Deutsche Schallplatten Berlin, which was the state label of the German Democratic Republic (GDR, or East Germany). AMIGA began in the forties with a rather staid list of pop and light jazz, but by the late sixties it branched out into political folk and rock (Oktoberklub, Isabel Parra, Omega), free jazz (Berliner Improvisations-Quartett), and a broad range of African American musicians (from Billy Holiday to Max Roach). But don't get too excited; out of the thousands of records AMIGA put out, only a small number are both political and listenable!

"Amilcar-Cabral Gesellschaft e.V."

Amilcar Cabral Gesellschaft
West Germany

The name used by a German solidarity organization to release a double LP set of pro-independence songs from Guinea Bissau in 1977 titled *Luca Cata Maina* (The Fight Goes On), which includes very early tracks from the popular political group Super Mama Djombo. Sadly, this record is quite rare, and the music isn't available anywhere else.

Amnesty International
International

One of the largest human rights organizations in the world, Amnesty has used music as a tool in its work since the sixties. Most of the records related to the organization are benefit compilations produced by other labels—initially small labels such as Messidor and TVD, and eventually major labels like Island, which it partnered with for its well-known *The Secret Policeman's Ball* LPs. But Amnesty itself has also produced a number of records under its own name. Amnesty is interesting because it has bridged the gap between two very different styles of music activism: small-scale concert benefits by independent bands in support of specific campaigns, and "We Are the World"-style major spectacles with corporate backing.

Angola Comité

Angola Comité
Netherlands

A political solidarity group rather than a label, Angola Comité (sometimes called Angola Comité/ Mondlane Stichting) helped produce at least a half dozen records, mostly of field recordings of political songs from the liberation movements in southern Africa. The group not only supported Angola, but the struggles in Mozambique, Namibia, Zimbabwe, and South Africa as well. It's hard to nail down an exact discography because the records were generally not released with a clear label name or catalog numbers. The proceeds from all of their records were sent to multiple political organizations supporting African liberation; one of the most frequent recipients was the Medisch Komitee Angola.

Antagon
West Germany

A Hamburg-based polit-folk label, similar in output to the April, Schneeball, and Eigelstein labels. Its highest-profile act was Malicorne, with Schmetterlinge being the most prolific and explicitly political band on the label.

Anti-Apartheids Beweging Nederland
Netherlands

A Netherlands-based South African solidarity organization founded in 1971 that released a single LP in 1978, Jabula's *In Amsterdam*.

Anti-Corporate Speak Records
USA

The name for the private-press operation of Charles "Rick" Kelly, a protest singer who released a string of cassettes (including the amazingly named *3 Mile Island Blues and Other Hummable Ditties for the 80's*) and at least one 7" record (produced in 1980); the latter includes critiques of suburbia ("Sprawl") and corporations ("Don't Profit From Death").

Antiimperialistisches Solidaritätskomitee
West Germany

A political group that used record production as part of their organizing, Antiimperialistisches Solidaritätskomitee (ASK) was founded in 1973 and based in Frankfurt. ASK functioned as an antiracist, internationalist solidarity organization, which worked with other left groups in West Germany to spread information about national liberation movements in the Global South and to organize direct financial support. ASK folded in 1990, soon after the fall of the Berlin Wall.

Anti-War Action
Netherlands

Also known as AWA, Anti-War Action was a Dutch political organization focused on ameliorating the humanitarian disaster that followed the dissolution of Yugoslavia and the Balkan wars in the nineties. It released a 1993 benefit LP of political punk songs called *The Dignity of Human Being Is Vulnerable*, featuring The Ex, MDC, Born Against, De Kift, and eleven more bands. It followed this up with a 1996 CD, *Sperminator*, collecting punk protest songs (by Chumbawamba, Wat Tyler, Mecca Normal, Dog Faced Hermans, and nineteen more) in support of women's organizations in the former Yugoslavia.

Apir
Canada

The personal label of Alberto Kurapel, a Chilean leftist exiled to Canada after the 1973 coup in Chile. He released several LPs on this label, including 1986's *Guerrilla*, which features a song for Che based on a poem by Roque Dalton.

April
West Germany

An independent label formed as a cooperative in 1976 by a small group of German krautrock and prog bands, including Ton Steine Scherben, Embryo, and Sparifankal. As "April" was a music publishing name used by CBS, the group was pressured to change the name, which they did in 1977. The new name for the label was Schneeball.

Aquifer Records
USA

The personal label of politicized folk musician Fred Small. Before going on to release a string of records on Rounder and Flying Fish, he used Aquifer for his first releases in 1981 and 1982, including a 7" featuring a reworking of a Lou Reed song now called "Walk on the Supply Side" b/w "Dig a Hole in the Ground, or, How to Prosper During the Coming Nuclear War."

Arauco
Venezuela

It has been hard to find much info about this label. It's named after a city in the middle western coast of Chile that was the site of a large-scale Indigenous revolt, the Mapuche Uprising of 1598. The label's logo contains a hatchet, which is itself borrowed from the logo of the Partido Socialista de Chile, overthrown by Pinochet's fascist coup (see also CA de RE). A Chilean label in exile, its most important release was a compilation document of Salvador Allende's radio broadcasts from September 11, 1973, the day of the coup.

Arbeidernes Opplysningsforbund i Norge
Norway

Arbeidernes Opplysningsforbund i Norge, or AOF, was the record label of the Workers' Association of Norway (and translates as "Workers' Information Society in the North"). It released a half dozen records throughout the seventies. The one I have is a compilation of march chants and folk songs celebrating the seventy-fifth anniversary of the Arbeidernes Ungdomsfylking, or Norwegian Workers' Youth League. Also known as Arbeidernes Opplysningsforbund i Norden.

Arbeiterkampf
West Germany

An activist-rooted, Hamburg-based label (the name translates to "Workers Struggle") which operated in the seventies and put out a handful

of records, including a José Afonso 7″ in support of a Portuguese land co-op, a couple of records by the Chilean exiles Karaxu—who supported the Movimiento de Izquierda Revolucionaria, or MIR (the underground Chilean political party that attempted to carry out an armed struggle against the Pinochet regime)—and a compilation of German folk and rock bands active in the struggle against nuclear power.

Arbejderkultur KA (M-L)
Denmark

The label of the political group Kommunistisk Arbejderparti M-L (the Communist Labor Party, a small Maoist organization), which released one LP in 1975 by the group De Røde Raketter (The Red Rockets), featuring members of Røde Mor (Red Mother).

Arbejdernes Oplysningsforbund
Denmark

Record label of the Danish Workers' Educational Organization, or Arbejdernes Oplysningsforbund (AOF). Same initials, but distinct from the Norwegian AOF. Most of the output appears to have been records by the AOF in-house folk group, AOF's Sang-Og Musikgruppe. The publishing wing of the AOF also released records, sometimes under the label AOF's Forlag.

Arbetarkonferensen
Sweden

Label created after a 1974 Swedish labor conference of the same name to release an LP documenting the music performed at the event, most of which was folk and progg with a dose of political theater (including groups like Narren and Oktober).

 **Arbetarkultur**

Arbetarkultur
Sweden

A label used to release a 7″ in 1972—*Unga Gardet* (Young Guard)—by Röda Kapellet (Red Chapel), a folk band connected to multiple communist youth groups.

Arbetarrörelsens Bokcafé med Tidens Bokhandel
Sweden

The Workers' Movement's Book-Café and Publisher, based in the small city of Örebro; it released two LPs, almost a decade apart, which are both records in solidarity with Chile.

Arc
UK

Arc was the label name Lindsay Cooper used to release her experimental 1980 LP *Rags*, about women garment workers' living and working conditions in the factories of London in the mid-nineteenth century. Cooper had been a member of political prog group Henry Cow, as well as cofounder of the Feminist Improvising Group (which self-released a cassette in 1979, but never anything on vinyl).

Archalouiss
France

A small label likely run by the band Les Armenian's Sunshine, a folk/chanson outfit dedicated to maintaining Armenian folk traditions.

Archivi Sonori
Italy

From 1969 to 1975, this Milan-based label—a project of the Istituto Ernesto de Martino and Edizioni del Gallo—released a dozen albums true to the name "Sound Archives": field recordings from sites of social struggle. Recordings highlight the efforts of the Venezuelan guerrilla movement (FALN), the People's Movement for the Liberation of Angola (MPLA) before independence, workers occupying factories in Milan, and the 1968 International Congress of Anarchist Federations in Carrara, Tuscany, and more.

Ardkor Records
UK

The personal label of Crisis, a short-lived Trotskyist punk band from South East England. Formed in 1977, they released three 7″s and an LP, then broke up in 1980. Crisis's lyrics are ultraleft—with songs addressing racism, fascism, the Holocaust, the Cold War, and armed struggle—and their visual aesthetic draws heavily from the posters produced by the Ateliers Populaire in Paris during the May '68 revolt. They regularly played gigs in support of both Rock Against Racism and the Anti-Nazi League. This makes it all the more strange that two of the core members, Douglas Pearce and Tony Wakeford, went on to form Death in June, a band whose flirtations with the aesthetics and content of historical fascism have, for almost thirty years, provoked accusations of white supremacy and far-left calls for boycotts.

Areito
Cuba

A subsidiary of the Cuban state record company, EGREM, Areito was the country's main pop, Latin, and jazz label. It is well known as a producer of samba, son cubano, and Afro-Cuban music, along with Latin music more generally. By nature of being Cuban, the label additionally released a significant body of political music, including songs of the Cuban Revolution, nueva trova records (Silvio Rodríguez, Pablo Milanés, Sara Gonzalez), and memorial albums to Che Guevara and Jose Martí.

ARF Shant
USA

An Armenian label based in Los Angeles that put out a single LP of classical Armenian folk: 1977's *ARF Dashnaktsutyun 1890-1977* by the singer Karnig Sarkissian. "Dashnaktsutyun" is the Armenian name for the Armenian Revolutionary Federation (ARF), a political party founded in 1890 that is part of the Socialist International. As an interesting sidenote, Sarkissian spent time in prison after being convicted of participating in the 1982 attempted bombing of the Turkish consulate in Philadelphia, organized by the armed group, Justice Commandos of the Armenian Genocide.

ARGUMENT-Verlag

Argument-Verlag
West Germany

Founded in 1959, Argument is a Kreuzberg-based leftist publishing house focusing on criticism, politics, and the humanities. It pressed at least one record, a 7″ by the Hanns Eisler Chor, which was recorded at a seventy-fifth birthday concert for Eisler held in Berlin in 1973. The 7″ accompanied a book on the musician.

Ar(i)ston
Czechoslovakia

A short-lived label founded by Czech author and film director Josef Henke in 1968, in the wake of the Prague Spring. In 1969, Ar(i)ston released a memorial record to Jan Palach—*Kde Končí Svět (Na pamět' Jana Palacha)* (Where the World Ends [Jan Palach's memory])—which was extremely popular, with almost twenty-thousand copies pressed. Jan Palach was a twenty-year-old student who immolated himself to protest the Soviet occupation of Czechoslovakia and the end of the political thaw of the Prague Spring. The record was banned and eventually led to the suppression of the label. Henke also faced personal repression; in 1971 he was removed from his position at Czechoslovakia State Radio.

Arphone
Morocco

Arphone was the label of the band Izanzaren. Founded in 1974, the label released a series of the band's cassettes, and then in 1978 and 1979, a suite of self-titled LPs. Izanzaren is a Amazigh/Berber band that mixes poetry with plaintive banjo playing to describe the movement of people from rural to urban life in Morocco. Influenced by similar groups such as Nass El Ghiwane and Jil Jilala, they became an important voice for the intersection of longstanding traditions with the rush of contemporary life.

Ars Pro Femina
USA

Roberta Kosse and Jenny Malmquist's 1977 feminist choral and chamber music concept LP *The Return of the Great Mother* was released under the label name Ars Pro Femina. Kosse had previously played with lesbian folk singer Alix Dobkin.

Artists Against Apartheid
UK

Not a label, but a network of mostly British musicians supporting the UK Anti-Apartheid Movement, and in particular, the cultural boycott of South Africa. The impact of the Anti-Apartheid Movement on the UK music scene in the late eighties and early nineties was massive, and can be measured in part by the number of otherwise apolitical bands that added this logo to their record covers.

Arzobispado de Santiago
Chile

At the time of the far-right coup in 1973, the archbishop of the Catholic Church in Chile

was left-leaning and practiced a loose form of liberation theology. The Church provided space and programming for families of those assassinated and disappeared by the regime, and worked to publicize the human rights abuses of the Chilean state. It also created this record label to release a compilation LP titled *Cantata de los Derechos Humanos* (Songs of Human Rights), using nueva canción as a vehicle to deliver biblical parables as a critique of the Pinochet regime. The musicians on the record were from Ortiga, a Chilean group in exile in West Germany that also recorded LPs for Pläne.

ASCENSION
RECORDS

Ascension Records
USA

The label of the Kim and Reggie Harris Group, a folk/gospel act whose music revolved around the history of the Underground Railroad and the abolition of slavery. The label released a couple of records, the most widely distributed being 1984's *Music and the Underground Railroad*, with extensive liner notes about the history of opposition to slavery in the US.

Asch Recordings

Asch Records
USA

The original record label founded in 1938 by Moses Asch, almost ten years before he started Folkways. Most of the releases are from the forties, including a number of Woody Guthrie albums, and 10"s of songs from the Spanish Civil War. But for a period from about 1966 to 1970, the label name was revived to release a couple dozen recordings, including a number of African folk albums, and the Nancy Dupree LP, *Ghetto Reality*.

ASHA Recording Co.
USA

ASHA was jazz flutist Lloyd McNeill's label, which he used to release three albums in 1969 and 1970. All three are documents of the Black community in Washington, DC, with songs such as "Home Rule" and "Black Mayor." One of the LPs—1969's *Tanner Suite*—is dedicated to early twentieth-century African American painter Henry Ossawa Tanner, who was also an ardent antiracist activist.

AsianImprov Records
Asian Improv
USA

A San Francisco–based free jazz and improvisational music label started in 1987, focusing largely on Asian-American jazz musicians. Featured artists included the explicitly leftist Fred Houn (Ho) and Jon Jang. Sadly, after five years and six or seven vinyl releases, the label began to release music on CD only.

Aske Globus International
Czech Republic

One of the first record labels set up in the Czech Republic after the collapse of Soviet rule. Comprised of Družstvo ASKE (ASKE Cooperative) and Globus International (which would spin off to become the most important rock label in the Czech Republic in the nineties). The first releases on the label were from Czech rock bands (many connected to The Plastic People of the Universe, the dissident rock band that organized against the Communist regime), including the initial 7″, a compilation titled *Sanitka pro Rumunsko*

(Ambulance for Romania), featuring the band Echt! covering a Fugs song.

HỘI PHỤ NỮ VIỆT NAM TẠI PHÁP
Association des Femmes Vietnamiennes en France

Association des Femmes Vietnamiennes en France
France

The Association des Femmes Vietnamiennes en France was a women's organization set up in the mid-twentieth century by Vietnamese immigrants. It was connected to the nationalist and anticolonial coalition of the Vietminh, which launched the Vietnamese war of independence from both France and Japan. The group released at least one album, titled *Nhớ Bác, Kỷ Niệm 85 Nam Ngay Sinh Bac Ho* (roughly "Thanks To Uncle Ho, On His Eighty-Fifth Birthday") released in 1975 to celebrate what would have been Ho Chi Minh's eighty-fifth birthday.

Association des Stagiaires et Etudiants des Comores
Comoros

The Association des Stagiaires et Etudiants des Comores/ASEC (Association of Interns and Students of Comoros) is a political student group from the Union of Comoros, a small archipelago of islands nestled between Madagascar and the Eastern African coast. It released an LP and 7″ of student protest songs, distributed (and likely produced) by Le Kiosque d'Orphée in France.

Ateliers du Zoning
Belgium

A short-lived label set up to produce a series of anti-Eurovision records in 1979 (the year the contest was held in Jerusalem), including two compilation LPs and a Misty In Roots album recorded at the Counter Eurovision concert in Brussels. In addition to these, the label released an LP of Palestinian folk by Mustapha El Kurd and a 7″ of environmental protest songs by chanson singer Claude Semal.

AURORA

Aurora
GDR

Aurora was a sublabel of Deutsche Schallplatten Berlin—the official record label of East Germany—dedicated solely to Ernst Busch's output. Busch was a famous German actor, dedicated Communist, and singer who recorded hundreds of interpretations of political songs, including partisan songs, pieces from the Spanish Civil War, and compositions by Eisler, Weill, and Brecht. Aurora released about three dozen of his records between 1963 and 1989.

Auteurs Vereniging Proloog
Netherlands

A house label for the Dutch political theater collective Toneelwerkgroep Proloog. Their songs and productions were antiwar, class conscious, feminist, and pro-gay liberation.

Autonomy
Japan

Label of the post-punk/new wave band, Commune, which released a 7″ as well as a cassette-only album. This album in particular,

titled *Reality*, is pointedly political (with the songs "Fuck," "System," "Life," and "Capitalism"). The band shared members with the much more popular Japanese new wave band Aunt Sally.

Avanti
Sweden

A Gothenburg-based progg label that released politicized folk, rock, and polit-theater; active throughout the second half of the seventies. Avanti had connections with the Kommunistisk Ungdom (a Communist youth group) and released a couple records by Röda Kapellet. Additional releases include a document of the Swedish "supergroup" Canta Lucha playing at the 1978 Cuban Song Festival. The band featured Francisco Roca, a Chilean exile, and Pierre Ström, a prolific guitarist who was also part of the Kommunistisk Ungdom.

ATTF

Avrupa Türkiyeli Toplumcular Federasyonu
West Germany

Avrupa Türkiyeli Toplumcular Federasyonu (Socialist Federation of Turkey in Europe) was a European front group connected to the Turkish Communist Party (TKP). It had a Workers' Chorus (Avrupa Türkiyeli Toplumcular Federasyonu Işçi Korosu) that released an LP in 1974 and a 7″ in 1981 (dedicated to Nâzim Hikmet). Little information about the organization, label, or group is available in English, but the songs on the LP are a mix of originals, Brecht-Eisler tunes, traditional working-class songs ("L'Internationale"), and tunes penned by Hikmet himself.

Axum
UK

Axum was a small London-based roots reggae label that pressed around a half dozen 7″s in the late seventies and early eighties. The label was run by the Charles brothers, who made up the socially conscious band Zabandis (which also recorded for the label People Unite).

Ayuí/Tacuabé
Uruguay

A twinned record label set up in 1971 by musicians Daniel Viglietti, Los Olimareños, and Coriún Aharonián (an influential Uruguayan musicologist and composer). The Ayuí wing of the label released more popular music (including the specific form of nueva canción called "canto popular uruguayo"), while the Tacuabé wing focused on classical and experimental music and sounds.

Azwaw
France

A French label, run by the Berber musician Idir, that released exclusively North African music from Algeria and Morocco, most from Berber musicians. The dozen or so acts on its roster include a number of political and resistance musicians, such as Matoub Luones (who plays the Kabyle style of music), Cheb Khaled (who plays raï music), Groupe Berbere Agraw (militant Kabyle), and the band Nass El Ghiwane. The latter released a concept album

on Azwaw entitled *El Maana*, which documents the Israeli massacre of Palestinians in the Sabra and Shatila refugee camps in Lebanon in 1982.

Balkanton
Bulgaria

The Bulgarian state record label, also known as Балкантон. Like most Eastern Bloc labels, it released a slew of Communist martial and marching records, as well as a smattering of nueva canción, Cuban music, international folk, and even some Eastern European prog rock. In general, the output was more staid and less politically adventurous than its GDR (AMIGA/ETERNA) or even Soviet (Melodiya) equivalents.

Bamboo Records
USA

An ad hoc label created to release the band Yokohama, California's self-titled 1977 LP, a languid jazz-folk record and one of the earliest in a series of Asian-American-focused LPs released in the wake of *A Grain of Sand* on Paredon Records. The band's moniker comes from the novel of the same name, written by Toshio Mori and first published in 1949. It is believed to be the first novel published by a Japanese American.

Barlovento Discos
Catalonia

A small label focused on Catalan "nova cançó" (nueva canción). Artists included Gabriel Salinas,

Luis Pastor, and Elisa Serna. It ran from 1969 to 1973, and was owned by the Barcelona-based Discos Als 4 Vents.

Batuque
Angola

A 7″ label that released a couple dozen records, many featuring politicized semba and merengue-style folk music recorded around the time of Angolan independence.

Befria Südern
Sweden

The house label of the Swedish Vietnam solidarity musical group Freedom Singers/FNL-Grupperna. This anti-imperialist folk act put out an album of songs in support of the Vietnamese National Liberation Front (NLF) annually from 1968 to 1974. The records are well-designed, and each contains a booklet with lyrics, photographs, and information about Vietnam. Befria Südern means "Free the South."

Belgische Socialistische Partij
Belgium

The record label of the Belgian Socialist Party (BSP), it released a handful of 7″s on vinyl and flexi disc in the late sixties and early seventies—most to coincide with the electoral campaigns of its candidates. The two I have both feature renditions of "L'Internationale."

Better Youth Organization
USA

An early Los Angeles punk label started by members of Youth Brigade, infused with the ethos that "every generation has a responsibility to change what they feel is wrong in the world." The label's lasting contribution to political music is a slew of releases by the positive, or "posi," punk band 7 Seconds.

Biafra Choral Society
UK

The Biafra Choral Society was a London-based music organization that compiled a 1968 LP (*Birth of a Nation: Biafra*) of songs and speeches to benefit the Biafra Refugee Fund. From 1967 to 1970, Biafra attempted to secede from Nigeria. Biafra makes up a large piece of Southeastern Nigeria, contains most of Nigeria's oil reserves, and is composed of a number of ethnic groups, the largest being the Igbo. The Nigerian government set a blockade against Biafra, leading to almost two million deaths by starvation before the end of hostilities in 1970. A number of aid and relief organizations to help Biafra were set up around the world. This particular record was released without a label, but carries a catalog number from the pressing plant, Lyntone, one of Europe's largest producers of flexi discs.

Big Crossing Records
USA

This is the label name used to release *Land of*

the Free, Victor McManemy and Tom Dufelmeier's 1983 lefty folk-rock LP, featuring songs they wrote in support of the antinuclear movement ("Let's Stop the Tridents" and "Big Rock Point's On the Line") and against Indigenous genocide ("Land of the Free").

Big Toe
USA

An ad hoc label name used to release Abbie Hoffman's (of Yippie! fame) 1971 album *Wake Up, America!* The sprawling mess of an LP is a mix of political rants, radio call-ins, Dixieland jazz, and scrappy folk.

Black Artists Group
USA

Black Artists Group, or BAG, was a St. Louis-based arts collective that was an important part of the Black Arts Movement, and an early progenitor of the merging of free jazz and experimental theater. BAG ran from 1968 to 1972, and included a number of important free jazz players—Hamiet Bluiett, Joseph Bowie, Ronnie Burrage, Julius Hemphill, and Charles "Bobo" Shaw. After the project disbanded, many of the musicians left for Paris, and while there they released a single LP, *In Paris, Aries 1973*.

Black Australia
Australia

Label name used to release the soundtrack to the film *Wrong Side of the Road*, a split LP by two Aboriginal rock bands, No Fixed Address and Us Mob. Most Aboriginal protest and youth music was released on cassette or CD; this is one of only a dozen or so vinyl records produced, and one of the few not on a larger label (although this album was distributed by EMI Australia).

Blackbeard Records
USA

This was an ad hoc label name used to release a 7" by the eighties pop-funk-rock group The May Day Singers, who were the music wing of the Communist Workers' Party (CWP), a Maoist New Communist group led by Jerry Tung. The B side of the record, "Five Alive," is a song about and dedicated to the five CWP members killed by the Ku Klux Klan in Greensboro, North Carolina in 1979.

Black Family Records
USA

This label was set up by the Nation of Islam to release an LP of Minister Louis Farrakhan's speech on May 27, 1974, or Black Family Day. Multiple editions of this LP were released, some carrying the label and/or distributor name, 7 Speeches.

Black Fire
USA

Washington, DC-based funk and jazz label founded by radio DJ Jimmy Gray. The majority of the label's output was records by Oneness of Juju (also known simply as Juju), an Afrocentric soul-jazz band with revolutionary politics. Their music was always shifting from jazz to funk to disco, but they consistently supported African liberation movements and also recorded with Brian Jackson (Gil Scott-Heron's primary collaborator).

Black Forum
USA

A short-lived (1970–73) political experiment by Motown Records' Berry Gordy. Black Forum released eight LPs and one 7″, including spoken word albums by Stokely Carmichael, Langston Hughes, and Margaret Danner; Black Liberation soul and jazz by Amiri Baraka and Elaine Brown (of the Black Panther Party); and an album of field recordings titled *Guess Who's Coming Home: Black Fighting Men Recorded Live in Vietnam*.

Black Jazz Records
USA

Founded in Los Angeles in 1971, this label focused on its namesake, with about two dozen releases of funk-tinged Afrocentric jazz. Artists included Doug Carn, Henry Franklin (of the Creative Arts Ensemble, which recorded with Nimbus West Records), Gene Russell (who also founded the label), Chester Thompson (who went on to play in Tower of Power), and the band The Awakening.

Blackthorne
UK

Based in Kent, Blackthorne was Peggy Seeger

and Ewan MacColl's personal label. It ran roughly from 1976 through 1988, releasing close to twenty records, including a significant body of Seeger's explicitly feminist songs. A number of the label's releases were re-pressed by other labels, such as Folkways and Rounder.

Blue Records
South Africa

Although otherwise releasing records on major labels, the South African pop band Bright Blue self-released a 7″ for the songs "Yesterday Night" and "Weeping" in 1987 while between labels. "Weeping" became an anti-apartheid anthem, receiving extensive radio play, and with its extensive sampling of the ANC anthem "Nkosi Sikelel I'Afrika," provided backdoor access to a song otherwise banned by the government.

Bola Press
USA

The house label of poet and jazz vocalist Jayne Cortez; it released a half dozen of her free jazz/poetry albums, as well as a number of her chapbooks. Cortez was a key member of the Black Arts Movement and was married to Ornette Coleman for a decade.

Boží Mlýn Productions
Canada

Boží Mlýn was the record label of the dissident Czech rock group, The Plastic People of the

Universe. It was founded in 1977 by Paul Wilson, a Canadian who had helped translate Plastic People lyrics into English, and who served as the band's lead singer from 1970 to 1972. Plastic People was formed by Milan Hlavsa in 1968 as part of the counterculture that blossomed during the Prague Spring. In 1974 the Communist regime began suppressing the group, leading to their 1976 arrest and a series of prison sentences for multiple members. Wilson left Czechoslovakia and returned to Canada, where he released the groups records between 1978 and 1987.

Bread and Roses
USA

The cultural wing of District 1199 of the National Health Care Workers' Union (which became part of the Service Employees Internal Union/ SEIU in the early eighties), Bread and Roses organized art shows, poster series, and an annual calendar for the union, as well as pressing an LP titled *Take Care: A Musical Review of Life In the Hospitals*. Released in 1980, the album was a recording of a forty-five-minute musical show that Bread and Roses toured across the East and Midwest of the US. Bread and Roses released an additional record, *Ossie and Ruby and Bread and Roses* (by Ossie Davis and Ruby Dee), but there is no date anywhere on the album or sleeve. See also Local 1199 Drug and Hospital Union.

Broadside
USA

The label of *Broadside* magazine, one of the most important promoters of the US folk revival in the early sixties. The label released LPs of many of the musicians that wrote for or were discussed in the

magazine, including Pete Seeger, Tuli Kupferberg (The Fugs's first couple records were released on Broadside), Phil Ochs, Mikis Theodorakis, and the Rev. Frederick Douglass Kirkpatrick. In addition, compilations and field recording projects such as *Poems for Peace* and *We Shall Overcome! (Documentary Of The March On Washington)* were undertaken by the label. In many ways Broadside was a sister project to Folkways, and when the label folded at the end of the seventies, many of their records were re-pressed by Folkways.

BROADSIDE VOICES

Broadside Voices
USA

This is the name used to release Don L. Lee's Black nationalist poetry album *Rappin' & Readin'*. The label was based in Detroit and was also an active publisher of chapbooks by Black poets (although I believe this is its only vinyl release). Lee lived in Chicago, where he cofounded the Institute of Positive Education in 1969, and would change his name to Haki R. Madhubuti in 1974 and found Third World Press, the largest Black-owned publishing house in the US.

BROTHERHOOD

Brotherhood Records
USA

At first glance, this is just one of the many labels created to release albums related to Martin Luther King, Jr.—in this instance, pressing multiple versions of the services given at his funeral on April 9, 1968. But this one is worthy of note because it appears to be the record label of the Brotherhood Jaycees, a civic organization based at Graterford Maximum Security Prison in Graterford, Pennsylvania. Beyond releasing MLK's services, the label pressed an annual soul 7″ of Christmas songs, as well as at least one single by Power of Attorney, a funk band made up of prisoners at Graterford.

Bruksskivor
Sweden

The label of the political theater group Bruksteatern (Operating Theater, or Working Theater). In 1976 they released an LP documenting a performance in solidarity with Palestine (*Palestina Mitt Blod Min Väg Mitt Land*) on the label Oktober, and then in 1977 re-pressed it on their own label. They released an additional LP on Oktober of Brecht and Eisler songs, but *Palestina* appears to be the only record they put out themselves.

BT Klubben
Denmark

The ad hoc label name used for a split 7″ (Jan Toftlund and Faellesakkorden/Den Røde Lue) released in solidarity with Danish typographers and designers on strike in 1977. BT Klubben was the name of their union.

Bull Records
Italy

A label run by avant-garde classical and improvisational jazz composer Gaetano Liguori. The label was used to put out his own, as well as other,

avant-garde recordings in the eighties, including free jazz records dedicated to the revolutions in Eritrea and Nicaragua. In addition, a "Folk Line" sublabel released a small number of albums, including a phenomenal LP of pro–Polisario Front/ sahrawi music by the group Chahid El Wal-Li.

BUND DEMOKRATISCHER JUGEND/RBJ

Bund Demokratischer Jugend
West Germany

The label of the Federation of Democratic Youth, a West German communist group. They released one LP in 1975–*Kämpfende Jugend: Hoch die internationale Solidarität* (Fighting Youth: Long live international Solidarity)–featuring a collection of largely cover songs by the Democratic Youth Chorus. These include songs originally by Mikis Theodorakis, Hans Eisler, Pino Masi (of Lotta Continua), and Karaxu. Also known as Ring Bündischer Jugend.

Bürgeraktion Küste
Germany

A German political action group that released a single LP of antinuclear songs in 1976, *Atomanlagen In Liedern Und Gedichten Ihrer Norddeutscher Gegner*. The record is unique because it features songs written and sung in protest of four different nuclear plants, and was accompanied by a thick songbook as well as additional antinuclear literature.

Bürgerinitiative Kraftwerk Oberhavel/Oberjägerweg
West Germany

A citizens' initiative to shut down the Oberhavel nuclear power plant. It released a 1977 protest folk LP by Christian & Fred called *Beton oder Grün* (Concrete or Green), which included information about the campaign as well as a petition supporting the plant's closure.

Bürgerinitiative Westtangente Berlin
West Germany

A community organization founded in 1974 in West Berlin focused on stopping the construction of the Westtangente highway. Along with exhibitions, street fairs, bicycle events, and community meetings, the group released an LP in 1980 called *Stop dem Autobahnbau* (Stop the Highway Construction). The record features a range of music, with the expected polit-folk but also some nice blues-rock numbers, kids' songs, and speeches.

CA de RE
Netherlands

The house label for the band Lautaro, made up of a revolving group of Chilean musicians exiled in the Netherlands. Each of their two LPs (released in 1978 and 1979) was also published by the

Stichting Salvador Allende (Salvador Allende Foundation). In all likelihood, the band took it's name from Patricio Lautaro Weitzel Perez, a twenty-six-year-old antifascist militant tortured and killed by the Pinochet regime in October 1973. Although I'm unsure what the label name means, the logo of the hatchet also references the Partido Socialista de Chile, Allende's party, which was overthrown by the 1973 fascist coup.

Canadian Communist League (M-L)
Canada

The CCL (M-L) was founded in Montreal in 1975, one of many splits and reformations of the New Communist movement in North America. A small Maoist sect which took a hard anti-imperialist, pro-national liberation political line, they released a couple LPs in the late seventies. One of them, *Long Live International Solidarity!/ Vive La solidarité Internationale!,* is a compilation coproduced with a half-dozen like-minded Third Worldist groups, and consists of fifteen songs from ten countries (Canada, Guinea-Bissau, Haiti, India, Indonesia, Iran, Spain, Uruguay, Kampuchea, and Zimbabwe).

Candy-Ass Records
USA

Candy-Ass was a Portland, Oregon–based punk and pop label founded in 1992 in part by Jody Bleyle (who would help start the riot grrrl band Team Dresch a year later). It released a handful of riot grrrl records, but for the purposes of this project, the most important release was *Free to Fight!*, a double LP and book from 1995 focused on self-defense for women and girls. The album mixes songs by feminist and queer acts (Fifth Column, Cheesecake, Heavens to Betsy) with spoken word pieces discussing sexual assault and audio interludes providing self-defense instruction. The label intended to continue the project with a series of Free to Fight 7"s, but only one was released (in 1998), a split single by Sleater-Kinney and Cypher in the Snow.

Canzoniere delle Lame
Italy

Canzoniere delle Lame was a long-running political folk group from Bologna. They released a slew of singles on their own (or with local political groupings), but most of their albums were released on the label I Dischi dello Zodiaco. Although the logo above isn't for a specific label, it was used on many of the band's releases.

Cantares del Mundo
Uruguay

The label of communist singer and songwriter Alfredo Zitarrosa, one of the main proponents of "cantata del pueblo," Uruguay's unique variant of nueva canción. In addition to a handful of Zitarrosa's records, the label also released other politicized Latin American folk, such as Chile's Quilapayún. It appears as if the label folded when Zitarrosa went into exile in 1976.

Canzoniere il Contemporaneo
Italy

The self-run label of Canzoniere il Contemporaneo, an Italian political folk act from the seventies. The group performed political songs from Chile, Cuba, Greece, Vietnam, and Italy, as well as their own compositions.

Canto Libre
France

One of the many offshoots of the DICAP label, which went into European exile after the 1973 coup in Chile. This branch released Victor Jara, Inti-Illimani, and the Parra family for French audiences. Some of the records were produced jointly with Le Chant du Monde.

Canzoniere Internazionale
Italy

A popular and political folk group from the seventies, they primarily released records on I Dischi dello Zodiaco or Cetra (including LPs of Italian anarchist songs and nueva canción chilena), but they also self-released a solidarity 7" titled *Libertà per Angela Davis*.

Caracola
Argentina

Label name used to release *España Canta a la Libertad*, a sixties collection of songs and poems by Spanish communists, including Raimon (one of the key musicians in the Catalan nova cançó movement) and Chicho Sánchez Ferlosio, whose freedom songs were also released in Sweden by both the Oktober and Clarté labels.

Caravan/คาราวาน
Thailand

Caravan is one of the first Thai bands to merge folk sounds with rock elements and politics, a genre which has come to be known as "*phleng pheua chiwit*" (songs for life). Born out of the 1973 democracy movement, the band self-released its first 7" and LP, คนกับควาย (People with Buffalo), in 1975, and the LP was re-pressed for a US audience by Paredon Records in 1978 under the title *Thailand: Songs for Life*. The band was highly critical of US imperialism, following up its first album with 1976's อเมริกันอันตราย (American Danger), which became an important part of a successful campaign to drive the US military base U-Tapao out of Thailand. Most of Caravan's releases were similarly connected to popular struggles. Many were originally released on cassette or CD only—as well as almost exclusively for a Thai audience, so their vinyl LPs are coveted and quite rare.

Carolsdatter Productions

Carolsdatter Productions
USA

Carolsdatter is the label of Kristin Lems, a feminist-movement folk singer who was based in Urbana, Illinois. Under the name, she released three albums and two singles between 1977 and 1980, including the *Ballad of the ERA* 7" (Equal Rights Amendment) and the LP *We Will Never Give Up*.

CASA DE LAS AMERICAS

Casa de las Américas
Cuba

A sublabel of the Cuban state record company EGREM. Casa de las Américas is a popular cultural institution which supports novelists, essayists, and poets from the Global South. Its primary output has been in book form, but it has also released a series of nueva trova records, as well as various vinyl collections of political spoken word and poetry. These include speeches by key Latin American liberation figures (Pedro Albizu Campos), poets (Edward Kamau Brathwaite, Pablo Neruda), and novelists (Alejo Carpentier).

casi

CASI
Belgium

CASI was the label of the Centro di Azione Sociale Italiano Università Operaia (Italian Social Action Center, Worker's University) in Brussels, and in the seventies it released a series of three collections of songs about and by Italian migrant workers in Europe, performed by the singing group of the school.

Cassandra Records

Cassandra Records
USA

The record label of Malvina Reynolds, one of the grandmothers of the sixties folk revival. She is best know for her song "Little Boxes," but a wide variety of her songs—about issues ranging from nuclear war to labor organizing to civil rights—have been popularized and performed by Joan Baez, Devendra Banhart, Harry Belafonte, Elvis Costello, Death Cab for Cutie, Pete Seeger, and The Seekers. Reynolds used the label to release five of her LPs between 1972 and 1980, as well as a number of 7″ singles.

Catch 22
UK

A British label created to release a 7″—*Part of the Union!*—in support of the 1983 strike at the Hindle Gears plant in Bradford. The band—the Hindle Pickets—was made up in part of the striking workers themselves.

C B

C B
France

I'm unclear what the initials "C B" stand for, but this was the label name used to release a solidarity record with Breton political prisoners titled *Skoazell Vreizh* (which I believe roughly translates as "Help Brittany"). The Bretons are an ethnically Celtic population who live in Brittany, in northwest France, and their language was officially suppressed until 1951. A political struggle for both the maintenance of the Breton language and culture, as well as political independence, has been waged on and off for five hundred years. Although culturally conservative, much of Brittany has strong socialist and communist political sympathies.

CDA
Angola

Companhia de Discos de Angola was one of the main Angolan labels, running from 1972 (before independence in 1975) through the mid-eighties. It was key in creating a body of recordings of the uniquely Angolan form of guitar-driven merengue, often sung in Kikongo and other native languages. Many of the musicians, swept up in the excitement of independence, sung about popular political themes like education, women's liberation, and the guerrilla struggle. One of the label's highlights, David Zé, actually fought for the armed wing of the MPLA (Movimento Popular de Libertação de Angola, or People's Movement for the Liberation of Angola), and was killed in the South Africa- and US-driven civil wars that racked the country after 1975. Movimento and Merengue are other labels which were produced and distributed in Angola by CDA.

CEAL
Belgium

A DICAP-related label that released a couple LPs of nueva canción chilena in 1974 for the Franco-Belgian market.

Ceibo
Uruguay

Ceibo was an eighties Latin American folk and late nueva canción label. Founded in 1983, it emerged just as Uruguay was transitioning from military dictatorship back to civilian government. One of the label's most important releases was *Si Éste No Es El Pueblo* by Los Olimareños. The LP documents a live concert from May 18, 1984 that marked the triumphant return of the band to their home country of Uruguay after being in exile in Spain. The group played for the first time in a decade to an audience of fifty thousand.

Celluloid
France/USA

In the late seventies, Celluloid was formed by three partners in France. Shortly after, founding member Jean Karakos split and moved to New York City, taking the main Celluloid name with him. Karakos worked closely with experimental musician and producer Bill Laswell to develop an eclectic list of genre-hopping music. The globetrotting label produced records from sub-Saharan Africa (Fela, Youssou N'Dour, Francis Bebey), North Africa (Cheb Khaled, one of the main artists to popularize raï music beyond North Africa), Northern Ireland (political punks Stiff Little Fingers), and the US (The Last Poets). It also released strange (sometimes failed) experiments like Afrika Bambaataa's electro band Time Zone. In 1988, the label went bankrupt after releasing some five hundred LPs and singles. The name was bought and has continued on in multiple forms.

------

the Center for the Study of Comparative Folklore and Mythology, University of California

Center for the Study of Comparative Folklore and Mythology
USA

A department at the University of California, Los Angeles, the Center was involved in the publication of a wide range of books, and also in the recording of folk, blues, and roots music. It only released a couple LPs under its name: 1976's *Las Voces de los Campesinos*, a document by Francisco Garcia, Pablo Saludado, and Juanita Saludado collecting corridos by and about farm workers and the United Farm Workers union; and The Farr Brothers' 1978 LP *Texas Crapshooter*. But recordings made at the Center were released by a number of other labels.

Centerns Ungdomsförbund
Sweden

Centerns Ungdomsförbund (CUF) is the youth wing of the Centre Party, which began in the early twentieth century as a rural socialist party in Sweden. In the late seventies, however, it swung to the right, becoming staunchly neoliberal and aligning with the Christian Democrats. The youth wing is known for being far more green than the parent party, and the group released a couple of records in the seventies that called for development and public infrastructure to be democratically decided and for it to support all of Sweden, not just the urban centers. A 7″ titled *Framtid-Decentralisering* (Future Decentralization) demands that trains, public transit, and employment opportunities be available across the entire country.

Cercle du Disque Socialiste
France

Fully named "International Studies and Documentation—Socialist Records Circle," CDS was a short-lived sixties experiment in documenting expressly socialist and communist song. The ten 7″s the label released are a broad exercise in internationalism, with records by Luis Cilia (Portugal), Juan Capra (Chile), Carlos Puebla (Cuba), Aşık Nesimi (Turkey), and Judith Reyes (Mexico).

Chainsaw Records
USA

A Portland, Oregon label started by Donna Dresch in the early nineties, focusing on queer punk bands from the Pacific Northwest. The label released about two dozen records (only half on vinyl) by bands such as Excuse Seventeen, The Need, Sleater-Kinney, Team Dresch, and Third Sex.

Le Chant du Monde
France

Le Chant du Monde, which translates to "The Singing of the World," is the French equivalent of the US-based Folkways label. It produced a sprawling and far-reaching catalog of folk music and field recordings from around the world, with records representing a hundred countries in almost as many languages. Many of the records were licensed from—or to—similar labels in other countries, including the aforementioned Folkways, as well as Monitor, Paredon, I Dischi dello Zodiaco, and Pläne. Le Chant du Monde is also notable for having well-designed and illustrated triple gatefold covers on many of its releases, and for not shying away from politics, both with its Le Nouveau Chansonnier International sublabel and with liberation-themed experimental records by Collete Magny and the theater group Compagnie Jose Valverde.

CHEBEL RECORDS

Chebel Records
UK

Chebel released one record, a 7″ put together in 1975 by the Manchester office of the Campaign for Homosexual Equality. The A side was recorded by Tom, Rose, and Annie, with the "Tom" here being Tom Robinson; one of the tracks on this side is a very early version of "Glad to be Gay," which was overhauled and became a hit for Robinson a couple years later as "Sing If You're Glad to Be Gay," recorded with the Tom Robinson Band. The B side is two tracks attributed to the Bradford Gay Liberation Front, including "Stand

Together," a song by Neil Greig which was rerecorded in 1979 by Greig, Robinson, and Jill Posener as a benefit for London Gay Pride.

Children of the Revolution
UK

A third-wave punk label based in Bristol, Children of the Revolution released a little over thirty records between 1984 and 1987. Most of the initial dozen records were solidly anarcho-punk, including 7″s by Potential Threat and Political Asylum (the Scottish punk band featuring Ramsey Kannan, who would go on to found both AK Press and PM Press), a 12″ by AOA, an LP by Chaos UK, and *The Lives and Times of the Apostles* LP by the experimental post-punk anarchist group The Apostles.

Chile-Kommittén
Sweden

Also known as the Svenski Chilekommittén, this broadly anti-imperialist solidarity organization existed for twenty years, from 1971–91, and released a small handful of albums, most featuring Jan Hammarlund, a singer and songwriter who translated a number of songs by Violeta Parra and other Chilean folk artists into Swedish. The committee also worked with Chilean musicians in exile in Sweden, such as Francisco Roca, and put out a Swedish/Finnish pressing of Venezuelan nueva canción singer Alí Primera's LP *Canción para los Valientes* (Song for the Brave). The LP was co-released with the organization's Finnish counterpart, Soumi-Chile-Seura (Finnish-Chile-Club), under the title *En Solidaridad con la Resistancia Chilena contra el Facismo*. Some of the organization's releases were pressed and distributed by fellow left label MNW.

Chile Solidarität

Chile Solidarität
West Germany

Released at least two LPs of politicized nueva canción chilena, one each by Violeta Parra and Victor Jara. The records were put out in the sixties, long before Pinochet's coup in Chile, so the organization must have been working in support of the broad Chilean Left, likely as part of building the Popular Unity movement which would elect Salvador Allende in 1970.

CHILI AKTIE

Chili Aktie
Netherlands

Solidarity organization that released a 7″ in 1975 in support of Chileans fighting against the Pinochet dictatorship. The record features the Kollektief Internationale Nieuwe Scene, a Belgian Brechtian political theater and music troupe similar to Dario Fo's La Commune in Italy.

Chimurenga Music
Zimbabwe

"Chimurenga" is a Shona word that translates to "revolutionary struggle" and was the name given to the armed struggle against Rhodesia that led to the independence of Zimbabwe in 1979. It is also associated with a form of music that developed out of the struggle, which mixes traditional African instrumentation with electric guitar. The foremost proponent of chimurenga

music is Thomas Mapfumo, and he took on the word for his personal record label. From 1981 through the late nineties, Mapfumo released roughly two dozen records under the name Chimurenga Music.

Chol Soo Lee Defense Committee

Chol Soo Lee Defense Committee
USA

A California-based activist group formed to defend Chol Soo Lee, a Korean immigrant wrongfully convicted of a 1973 murder. The group released a 7″ record in 1978 called "The Ballad of Chol Soo Lee," which featured musicians from the Asian-American jazz outfit Yokohama, California. Lee eventually won his freedom in 1983.

Cigarrón
Venezuela

A South American nueva canción label from the seventies and eighties, its output is dominated by Venezuelan singer Alí Primera. It also released Uruguayan singer Ali-Ko, and a collection of pro-Chilean Left nueva canción chilena titled *Cantos de la Resistencia Chilena.*

Circolo Ottobre
Italy

A cultural project connected to the Italian ultraleft group Lotta Continua. The latter ran a newspaper and record label (both called "Lotta Continua"), releasing a series of 7″ singles. Similarly, Circolo Ottobre was conceived of as a "social club," with a network of social centers across Northern Italy. The group also created an eponymous magazine focused on criticism (with a strong emphasis on design), a screenprint poster workshop, and a small record label. It released about a half dozen LPs, including an album by Pino Masi (who recorded most of Lotta Continua's 7"s) and one by Collettivo Victor Jara, an Italian political folk group named after the martyred Chilean songwriter. In addition, some of the Masi 7"s released on the Lotta Continua label were also put out by Circulo Ottobre with the same cover designs, just different label logos printed on them. I suspect these records were released simultaneously in both the *Lotta Continua* newspaper and the *Circolo Ottobre* magazine.

CirCus
UK

An ad hoc label set up by the socialist big band The Happy End to release their first album, *There's Nothing Quite Like Money*. The LP is a giant mash-up of Brechtian cabaret, Maoist anthems, Cuban trova, and songs from the English Revolution. The band went on to release two additional LPs on the broad-based UK indie label Cooking Vinyl.

Clarté
International

Clarté (Clarity) was an international communist youth group originally founded in 1925 in France, with chapters eventually spreading across Scandinavia. Multiple local chapters have released records, including the French (a 1961 10" of unattributed songs in solidarity with the Spanish resistance to Franco) and the Swedish (a 1963 10" of songs by Chicho Sánchez Ferlosio, also in solidarity with the Spanish resistance to Franco, and published under the auspices of the Swedish *Clarté* magazine).

Clarté ML
Sweden

A front organization of the KFML(r), or Communist League Marxist-Leninist (revolutionary), a hardline antireformist Maoist group that released a single 7" in 1972 by the progg group Knutna Nävar. The label is directly connected to the publishing outfit Ungkommunistens Förlag, which also released a Knutna Nävar record, and was connected to the KFML(r).

Le CLEF
France

From 1974 through the mid-eighties, this organization produced around twenty-five LPs under the series name "archives sonores de la littérature noire" (sound archives of Black literature). Each album features interviews and readings with and by a different Francophone African authors, including Camara Laye, Sembène Ousmane, Ferdinand Oyono, and Léopold Senghor.

Clergy and Laymen Concerned
USA

Label for Clergy and Laymen Concerned About Vietnam (CLAC), an antiwar organization founded in 1965 by Daniel Berrigan, Rev. Richard Neuhaus, and Rabbi Abraham Joshua Heschel. Martin Luther King, Jr. was the national cochairman of the group. In 1971, it released a recording of antiwar speeches and radio spots, *American Report/Help Unsell the War*, which was distributed for free to radio stations. The first part of the title refers to the weekly publication of CLAC, the second part to a broader public relations project against the Vietnam War called "The Campaign to Unsell the War."

CLOUDS RECORDS

Clouds Records
USA

This is the name used by political folk singers Steve and Peter Jones to release their self-titled 1985 LP. The album features songs about the United Farm Workers' Gallo Wine boycott, young men facing going to war, George Bush, civil disobedience, and abolition.

Club Sandino
UK

The label name used by the British Nicaragua Solidarity Committee for their 1987 release of an LP by the Nicaraguan band Zinica, who play a unique mix of calypso, salsa, and nueva canción. The name Club Sandino is taken from the political dance events the Solidarity Committee held in London throughout the eighties.

C. MINER RECORDS

C. Miner Records
UK

This label put out one 7″ in 1984, "Get Off Your Knees (Unity)" b/w "Propaganda" by Charlie Livingstone. It came in a plain white sleeve, so the only information is on the record labels, which don't say much except the words "They Shall Not Starve" in small letters on the B side. This was a slogan popularized during the 1984–85 miners' strike in the UK. Considering this, and also the date, the label name (likely short for "Coal Miner"), and the lyrics to these two working-class-focused folk/country songs, it's fair to say

this is a labor solidarity record. Livingstone doesn't appear to have recorded any other releases.

CMS
USA

A spoken word and poetry label which was not particularly ideological, but in the late sixties and early seventies put out albums of speeches by Mao, Ho Chi Minh's *Prison Diary*, Ghandi's *Man on Trial*, and an A. J. P. Taylor lecture on the Soviet Revolution of 1917. The label also specialized in sound recordings related to Black America, including two separate James Baldwin recordings, a William Melvin Kelley LP, and an album of excerpts from *The Life and Times of Frederick Douglas*. The name "CMS" started out in the fifties as an acronym derived from Chesterfield Music Shops, which originally began in the forties as distributors of classical music. By the mid-sixties, the full name had been dropped in favor of the acronym.

édité par le comité national de soutien à la lutte de libération des peuples des colonies portugaises (C.N.S.L.C.P.)

CNSLCP
France

Le Comité National de Soutien à la Lutte de Libération des Peuples des Colonies Portugaises (CNSLCP, or the National Support Committee for the Liberation Struggle of the People of the Portuguese Colonies) released a single long-playing 7″ in the seventies titled *Chants des peuples des regions libérées* (Songs of the peoples of the liberated regions). It featured songs attributed to liberation movements of the former Portuguese colonies in Africa—the People's Movement for the Liberation of Angola (MPLA), the Mozambique Liberation Front (FRELIMO), and the African Party for the Independence of Guinea and Cape Verde (PAIGC)—but no specific musicians are identified.

CNT Productions
UK

Named after the Spanish anarchist union (Confederación Nacional del Trabajo, or National Worker's Confederation), CNT was a Leeds-based punk and new wave label that was ideological in intent, although the politics of some of its output was not entirely clear. Records by Dutch anarchists The Ex and punk/dance band Redskins announced their positions, but those by goth progenitors Sisters of Mercy and experimental new wave act The Three Johns were a little more obscure. The label released about twenty records between 1981 and 1984, when it folded. A 1985 compilation of CNT-released songs—*They Shall Not Pass*—was put out by another Leeds label, Abstract Sounds, and that record is dedicated to the then-striking British miners.

Cobiana
Guinea-Bissau

Label for the band Super Mama Djombo, named after the spirit that fighters from the PAIGC (Partido Africano da Independência da Guiné e Cabo Verde, or African Party for the Independence of Guinea and Cape Verde) would pray to for protection in Guinea-Bissau's struggle for independence from Portugal. The label (and band) released a half dozen highly politicized LPs, including an epic concept LP dedicated to anticolonial thinker and guerrilla leader Amílcar Cabral. Since Guinea-Bissau did not have a record pressing plant in the seventies, most of the Cobiana releases were pressed in the Eastern Bloc, and some of the later records even carry Melodiya logos and a "Made in the USSR" tag on the sleeves.

Colecção Revolta
France

The personal label of Portuguese folk musician Tino Flores. The four or so records (all 7"s) Flores put out under this banner were all released in the early seventies in France, where he was in exile from the totalitarian Portuguese regime. On the surface, the records look and sound like the kind of political folk and fado that flooded Portugal after the Carnation Revolution, but they actually all predate it.

Collective Chaos
USA

A short-lived political punk label from Chicago, started by James Mumm, co-founder of the long-running anarchist space the A-Zone and eventual key organizer for People's Action Institute. The label released two 7"s in 1993, one by Chicago's Prophets of Rage (featuring *Punk Planet* founder Dan Sinker) and the other by Minneapolis noise-punks Dogfight (with cover art by prolific *Profane Existence* artist Donovan).

Collector Records
USA

The label founded in the early seventies to release records by Joe Glazer, folk singer and popular bard of US labor unions. It put out about three dozen records over twenty years, half of them Glazer LPs (including *Songs of the Wobblies*, *Down in a Coal Mine*, and *Jellybean Blues: Songs of Reagonomics*). The other releases include Louis Killen's *Gallant Lads Are We: Songs of the British Industrial Revolution* and Peyton Hopkins's *Let the Teachers Tell the Story*.

COLLETTIVO TEATRALE DI PARMA

Collettivo Teatrale di Parma
Italy

A political theater group, it released two records: an undated (but likely around 1969–70) LP documenting a performance about a 1920 factory occupation, titled *Le Canzoni de la Grande Paura*, and later re-pressed by I Dischi del Sole; and then a 1971 double 7″ recording of *Occhio Operai* (Worker's Eye), a performance written by Mario Di Stefano.

C. T. LA COMUNE

Collettivo Teatrale la Comune
Italy

One of the labels run by Dario Fo and his theater troupe La Comune. In addition to a dozen or so Fo records, they also put out a single by Fo's partner, Franca Rame (a significant actress, playwright, feminist, and activist in her own right), documents of La Comune's performances, and an Italian pressing of a Karaxu LP (also released in France on Expression Spontanée and in West Germany on Trikont—a good example of the interconnectedness of European radical labels in the seventies).

Comitato per i Soccorsi Civili e Umanitari al Popolo Greco
Italy

A solidarity organization (Committee for Civil and Humanitarian Assistance to the Greek People) that released a Mikis Theodorakis 7″ titled *Il Grido della Grecia Antifascista* (The Cry of Antifascist Greece) in 1967. The record itself is a combination of music and speeches, pressed by Dario Fo's label NR Produzioni.

Comitato Vietnam-Milano
Italy

A political solidarity organization which became involved in music (and possibly got its name) by curating a 12″ mini-album of covers of US and UK folk songs against the Vietnam War for Record Film Productions, and then went on to release two albums under its own name, both of nueva canción chilena musicians—Victor Jara and Quilapayún.

C.A.M.

Comité Anti-Militariste
France

A radical antimilitarist organization active in the seventies, Comité Anti-Militariste (also known by its acronym, CAM) released one 7″ as an insert in a 1973 issue of its magazine *Lutte Anti-Militariste* in 1973. The record is a much-sought-after two-song single of political free jazz/prog by Mouvement Anarcho Héroïque des Joyeux Utopistes Nébuleux (Anarcho-Heroic Movement of Joyful Nebulous Utopians), a fictitious name for the influential French psych group Maajun/Mahjun.

Comite Promotor de Investigaciones del Desarrollo Rural
Mexico

Not a label but an organization that released an LP of Emiliano Zapata–themed corridos by the political psych/prog/folk group Tribu, with guest vocals by Pilar Pellicer, in honor of the Fifth World Congress for Rural Sociology in 1980.

Comité Québec-Chili
Québec

A solidarity organization set up in the wake of Chile's 1973 coup, Comité Québec-Chili (CQC) was a collaboration between labor unions and radicalized Chileans who had fled to Québec. CQC mobilized the Québécois Left against Pinochet in the form of boycotts and support for political events, including North American production and distribution of a Karaxu LP (which itself was in support of the left Chilean political party MIR) originally pressed by Expression Spontanée in France.

Comité Révolutionnaire d'Agitation Culturelle
France

The Comité Révolutionnaire d'Agitation Culturelle (CRAC) was a political grouping from the liberated Sorbonne in May '68. It released five issues of a magazine called *CRAC*, and also two 7"s by chansonnier Evariste. The first is titled *La Révolution* and was put out in '68 on the heels of the revolt. The second, *Reviens Dany, Reviens* (Come Back Dany, Come Back), was put out in 1970; the title is a reference to May '68 student leader Daniel Cohn-Bendit. In '68, Evariste was under contract with the label Disc'Az, and it would not release his *La Révolution* 7", which is why he turned to CRAC to do it. The covers of the records were drawn by Georges Wolinski, a cartoonist who was killed in the attack on the French satirical magazine *Charlie Hebdo* in 2015.

Comité Solidarité Salvador
Vlaams El Salvador Komitee
El Salvador Komitee Nederland

Comité Solidarité Salvador
Belgium

A Belgian solidarity organization that released a 1980s benefit LP by the Salvadoran folk group Yolocamba I-Ta titled *Canta su solidaridad con el pueblo de El Salvador* (Sing your solidarity with the people of El Salvador). The record was released in association with two other Benelux organizations, Vlaams El Salvador Komitee and El Salvador Komitee Nederland. Yolocamba I-Ta was directly connected to the then-guerrilla group the FMLN (Frente Farabundo Martí para la Liberación Nacional, or Farabundo Martí National Liberation Front), an El Salvador–based leftist organization.

Commision "Popularisation" des Travailleurs LIP Besançon-Palente
France

This is the name used on a 7" released in 1973 in support of striking workers at the LIP watch factory in France. The record was pressed by the Commission "Popularisation" des Travailleurs LIP Besançon-Palente (Popularization Commission of LIP Workers–Besançon-Palente is the location of the factory), and is a combination speeches, meetings, and two short songs (attributed simply to "Claire") with lyrics culled from a recording of the general assembly of the workers held on June 18, 1973. The record was produced in support of the workers, not simply because they went on strike, but because they occupied their factory and began running it themselves, without the managers or owners. The oversized triple gatefold sleeve contains information about the LIP struggle, a series of humorous cartoons, quotes from public figures in support of the workers, and song lyrics.

COMMITTED ARTISTS RECORDS

Committed Artists
South Africa

Committed Artists was a project run by Mbongeni Ngema, the South African playwright, composer, and director who created *Sarafina!*, the hit musical about students in the 1976 Soweto Uprising that was eventually adapted into a Hollywood film starring Whoopi Goldberg. It appears that the name "Committed Artists" was primarily used for a production company, but at least one LP was put out under the moniker, the soundtrack to the 1990 play *Township Fever*. The actual vinyl pressing was done by Gallo, one of South Africa's largest record labels.

Committees for the Defense of the Revolution
Cuba

In Cuba, the Committees for the Defense of the Revolution (CDR) are the neighborhood revolutionary groups that, depending on your political position towards the Cuban regime, either enact community control, or enforce Cuban state policy. A small number of records were released under the CDR name in the sixties, mostly field recordings of speeches by Che, or songs celebrating the Cuban Revolution. CDR's vinyl was pressed by EGREM, the Cuban state record company.

Disque édité par les communistes de la Radio et de la Télévision

Les Communistes de la Radio et de la Télévision
France

An ad hoc group that worked together to produce the 1975 LP *La lutte du peuple entier jusqu'à la victoire/Hommage du monde entier á la mutte du peuple vietnamien* (The struggle of the whole nation to victory/Tribute from the whole world to the Vietnamese people's struggle), a interesting audio document containing pieces of Ho Chi Minh speeches, field recordings from anti-Vietnam War protests, and Joan Baez songs. The record was released and sold at the Fête de l'Humanité in 1975 (*L'Humanite* is a French Communist daily newspaper). It's possible that the group that produced this LP was connected to the more formal UNI/CI/TE label.

Confederação Geral dos Trabalhadores Portugueses-Intersindical
Portugal

Often referred to by its acronym, the CGTP is the largest labor union in Portugal. It was organized underground by workers in 1970, and formally launched in 1974 after the Carnation Revolution in Portugal. Although it is not directly affiliated, it has historically had connections with the Portuguese Communist Party, with many of its workers also being party members. In the wake of the revolution, multiple renditions of the union's them song, "Hino da Intersindical" (Interunion Anthem), were recorded. One by Pedro Osório was released by Guilda da Música. Another by an unnamed artist was pressed by Diapasão (with a Luis Cilia track on the B side). A rendition by the Grupo Coral dos Operários Mineiros de Aljustrel was released on their 1975 self-titled LP on Orfeo. In 1986, the union released its own double LP celebrating the hundred-year anniversary of May Day.

FEDERATION NATIONALE DES TRAVAILLEURS DU SOUS-SOL (CGT)

Confédération Générale du Travail
France

The Confédération Générale du Travail (CGT) is one of France's largest confederation of unions. In the seventies and eighties, various member unions released records under the CGT name, including the Fédération Nationale des Travailleurs du Sous-Sol, which put out an LP of mining songs in 1980, and the Fédération Textile, which released a 7" by political chansonnier Francesca Solleville.

Confederation of Iranian Students (National Union)
West Germany

An international organization made up of politicized groups of anti-Shah Iranian students studying abroad in the sixties and seventies. The West German chapters (both the Frankfurt and Munich groups) produced records of male choral groups singing anti-imperialist anthems. These were likely intended for distribution beyond Germany as they contain information in Persian, English, French, and German.

CONTEXT MUSIC

Context Music
USA

The label name used on *Regeneration Report*, a 1981 LP by Sedition Ensemble. The record and the band are an explicitly political free jazz/funk/salsa mash-up from New York City, featuring Melvin Gibbs (who played bass with a diverse array of musicians, from Vernon Reid to Rollins Band) and Bern Nix (who played guitar with Ornette Coleman for over a decade).

Corpus Christi
UK

Corpus Christi was founded by members of Crass Records and John Loder from Southern Studios in 1982. It quickly became the home of many anarcho-punk bands in the early

eighties, including Conflict, Icons of Filth, and Rudimentary Peni. Many of the bands on Corpus Christi had released a record on Crass, but were encouraged to move to Corpus Christi so they could have more autonomy and learn how to press records themselves, with Loder's support. It ran from 1982 to 1989 and released sixteen records. Some of the bands actually did spin off and start their own labels with the knowledge gained from Crass and Corpus Christi, including Conflict (Morterhate Records), Rudimentary Peni (Outer Himalayan Records), and UK Decay (UK Decay Records).

THE COUNCIL FOR
UNITED CIVIL RIGHTS LEADERSHIP

The Council for United Civil Rights Leadership
USA

The Council was formed in 1963 as a coordinating and fundraising body for the Civil Rights Movement, encompassing multiple groups such as the Southern Christian Leadership Conference, the Student Nonviolent Coordinating Committee, the Congress of Racial Equality, and the National Association for the Advancement of Colored People. One of its earliest actions was the organizing of the August 1963 March on Washington, and later that year it released an LP documenting the event titled *We Shall Overcome! (The March on Washington)*. The same recording was released simultaneously under the same name, but with different cover designs, by both the Broadside and Folkways labels—I can only assume that each of these was intended for different audiences.

CounterAct

CounterAct
UK

A political theater troupe active in Britain in the seventies. In 1976 they toured a production called *The Cuts Show*, and in 1977 released an LP of the same name documenting the performance. *The Cuts Show* was part of a broader anticuts/antiausterity movement in the UK. According to the insert in the record,

CounterAct defined themselves as "a group of socialists working with a wide variety of media. We offer workshops in silk-screen, video, street theater, and AgitProp drama, lay-out and design, kids' plays, inflatables and the use of games. We perform where there is an audience, and we work with students, trade unionists, women's groups and community groups active in the fight for socialism."

CPM
West Germany

A small prog rock label which called itself "the progressive artist's cooperative record production." It put out only three albums, one by didactically political krautrock band Checkpoint Charlie, the first LP by Missus Beastly in 1970—who would go on to put out the political psych/jazz classic *Spaceguerilla* in '78—and an avant-garde jazz album by Limbus 3.

Cramps
Italy

Founded in 1973, this label was part of the Italian rock explosion of the seventies. Home to political prog bands like Area, the label also released a range of experimental classical, jazz, and rock, including records by avant-garde stalwarts John Cage and Gruppo di Improvvisazione Nuova Consonanza. In addition, Cramps released LPs by feminist folk groups and early Italian punk bands. Its logo, featuring a cartoon Frankenstein, exhibits a strong pop and comic sensibility, often missing amongst the Italian political music scene of the sixties and seventies.

Crass
UK

Crass Records was founded in 1978–79 by the punk band and media project of the same name. Like the band's music and aesthetic, the label was intended to promote anarchism and the do-it-yourself ethos. After the band's initial 12″ on Small Wonder Records was censored, they set up the label as a way to have more control over their output—the first release was a 7″ of the censored song, "Reality Asylum" (originally simply titled "Asylum"). Although the majority of the label's catalog consists of Crass recordings and members' side projects, it also released a number of singles and albums by fellow political punk bands (Flux of Pink Indians, Poison Girls, Zounds). Usually after an initial release, Crass encouraged the band to take the knowledge gained through putting out that record to either start their own label, or to sign to another where they could maintain as much control as possible. Some of these bands (Conflict, Rudimentary Peni) ended up releasing their music through the Crass-founded sublabel Corpus Christi.

Cravos de Abril
Portugal

A private press label named after the April 1974 Carnation Revolution, Cravos de Abril released two 7″s by fado singer Ana Pinto.

Crazy Planet Productions
USA

Crazy Planet is the label and band name of Vic and Rob Sadot, singer-songwriters from Newark, Delaware. They released a 7″ and an LP of political folk-rock that sound like soundtracks to late eighties despair, with songs about nuclear disaster, apartheid, police harassment, yuppies, TV evangelists, and social alienation.

Credo
USA

I've found little information about this short-lived spoken word label launched in 1962 in order to release an LP of an interview between James Baldwin and Studs Terkel (titled *Black Man in America*). Over the next decade it also released LPs by Buckminster Fuller and Sylvia Plath, and it appears to have closed up shop towards the end of the seventies after putting out about a half dozen records.

CRUCIAL RESPONSE RECORDS

Crucial Response
Germany

One of the longest-running, and most politicized, of the European straightedge hardcore labels. Founded by Peter Hoeren in 1989 (after he shuttered his first label, Anti-Schelski Records), it was home to more socially engaged straight-edge bands, such as Brotherhood, Think Twice, and most relevant here, the communist youth-crew band Man Lifting Banner.

CS-LD-PD
Italy

This label name is a long acronym for the Comitato per il Salario al Lavoro Domestico di Padova, or Wages for Housework Committee of Padova. The organization had its own musical group and recorded two LPs. The first one, *Canti di Donne in Lotta* (Songs of Women in Struggle), was initially self-released, and was then re-pressed in 1975 by I Dischi dello Zodiaco. The second was released directly by I Dischi dello Zodiaco. Wages for Housework–Padova was only one of many feminist groups in Italy in the seventies that had musical acts and released records.

CSM
Italy

CSM was a small record label connected to the Centro Studi per il Medio Oriente based in Rome. In the eighties it released a handful of records by Palestinian composer Youssef Khasho (who was also the technical and musical adviser of the center), performed by the Symphony Orchestra of Naples and the Rome Opera Theater Orchestra. Most of Khasho's work, if not directly focused on Palestinian liberation, features strong pan-Arab revolutionary themes.

Cuba Records
Finland

A Finnish label that ran from the mid- to late seventies entirely dedicated to rereleasing records from Cuba. Of the eight or so records released, the majority are politicized trova and Cuban jazz, with re-pressings of Sara González, Carlos Puebla, Silvio Rodríguez, and Grupo Irakere. Like Eteenpäin!, Cuba Records was produced and distributed by the larger Love Records.

Cutting Records
UK

Cutting Records was the label name used to release the 1979 LP *I Like Me Like This* by the Gay Sweatshop Women's Company, a late seventies lesbian rock group from London.

Cutty Wren Records
USA

The name used to release Jacqueline Sharpe's (aka Jacqueline Steiner) 1966 pop-folk LP *No More War*. Sharpe was active in both the folk scene (recording an LP with Pete Seeger under the name Jackie Berman) and a broad range of social justice organizations. The label also released a Béla Bartók commemorative record in 1970. "Cutty Wren" is the name of a popular British folk song, sometimes sourced back to the 1381 Peasant's Revolt.

CW Records
USA

An ad hoc label based in the "Peace Pentagon"–339 Lafayette St.–in New York City. The building at this address, known as the AJ Muste Building, was for years the Manhattan headquarters of a broad range of leftist organizations, from the War Resisters League to the Workers Solidarity Alliance to Paper Tiger Television. I believe CW was Charlie King's label, and only released one LP, his 1976 political folk record *Old Dreams. . .and New Nightmares*. King was a regular in the East Coast political activist and folk music scenes of the seventies and eighties, writing songs for a number of struggles as they unfolded, including tracks like "Acres of Clams" written for the Clamshell Alliance campaign against the Seabrook Nuclear Power Plant in New Hampshire. He went on to help found the polit-folk band Bright Morning Star, and their own label, Rainbow Snake Records.

Danmarks Lærerforening
Denmark

The Danish Teacher's Union, which documented its hundredth anniversary by releasing a live LP of a 1974 concert celebrating the union.

DARE TO STRUGGLE
RECORDS

Dare to Struggle
USA

An ad hoc label that released a 7″ by Kathy Kahn and Danny McMahan in support of the 1977 Coors Brewery strike.

David Volksmund Produktion
West Germany

The label set up in 1971 by Rio Reiser to release records by his band Ton Steine Scherben, the archetypal political krautrock band. "David Volksmund" isn't a person's name, but a combination of "the underdog" (David of David and Goliath fame) and "the people's voice" (literally, Volksmund). The logo featuring a slingshot compounds the meaning, but also references the popularity of the weapon in the German antiparliamentary and autonomous left scenes.

December 7
Sweden

A protest, not really a label. December 7 is the name that rock/blues musician Thomas Zidén used to release his 7" in support of a mass-based Swedish environmental mobilization on that day in 1991.

DEFENCE AND AID FUND

Defence and Aid Fund
Netherlands

A solidarity organization focused on southern Africa (likely a Dutch offshoot of the International Defence and Aid Fund based in London) that released an early and eclectic anti-apartheid 10" record in 1966. Songs include Dutch covers of Depression-era songs ("Brother Can You Spare a Dime"), gospel ("We Shall Overcome"), as well as experimental classical music and big band jazz.

Del-Aware
USA

Del-Aware was an ad hoc label and activist group that released a single agitprop 7" in 1983. The record is by a group calling themselves The USA Band ("USA" here stands for "Unami Sunburst Assortment," with Unami being the language of the Indigenous Lenape people who lived in southern Pennsylvania and northern Delaware in the late seventeenth and early eighteenth centuries). In the early eighties, there was a plan to build a pump that would pull out two hundred million gallons of water a day from the Delaware River and reroute it so that it could be used to cool a nuclear power plant. The record (which doesn't have a pictorial sleeve) features two songs, "Peepers vs. Pumpers" b/w "The River's Song," with the words "Dump the Pump" written on the labels on both sides.

Delta
France/Greece

Delta was founded in 1971 in Paris by producer Demosthene Vergis. It put out a wide array of records by Mikis Theodorakis, as well as other left-leaning éntekhno musicians like Petros Pandis. Delta also had some form of production and distribution relationship with the small Italian label Manifesto.

Delta Records
USA

A vanity label for singer-songwriter Gary Punch,

who used it to release his 1979 7" "Goodbye T.M.I. (The Ballad of Three Mile Island)" under the name Gary & The Outriders. The song is a folk/doo-wop ode to the closing of the Three Mile Island nuclear power plant after March 28, 1979, the date of a catastrophic accident there, the largest ever in the United States. The song is sung from the perspective of a local resident living in the shadow of the plant.

Delyse
Wales

A protofeminist label, not necessarily in output but in organization. Delyse was the first record label owned and run by a woman (Isabella Wallich) and the first to employ a female producer. In addition, nationalist sympathies led to the release of a number of records of Welsh mining songs and union choirs.

Demos
Denmark

Originally set up in 1969 by the Danish Anti-Vietnam War Committee, Demos was a publisher, bookshop, and record label. Demos was unique not only because it evolved out of direct social-movement work, but because it was cooperatively and collectively run. It was organized with a general assembly of shareholders, and each shareholder had a single vote, regardless of the amount of their capital investment. One of the main groups involved with Demos was Røde Mor (Red Mother), a communist band and print collective that released six records on the label. Demos actively released music from 1970–78, with a list heavy on Danish political folk and rock,

along with kids' songs and documents of leftist theater performances. It also released the first LP of music from Greenland (Sume's *Sumit*), the first record in Denmark celebrating homosexuality (Bent Jacobsen's *Bøsse*), and three compilation albums of feminist songs. The label split in 1976, with key acts like Røde Mor leaving Demos. In addition to its own list, Demos worked with Love Records, SAM-Distribution, and Plateselskapet Mai to produce and distribute DICAP releases in Scandinavia. In 1979, Demos dissolved as a record label and became the Demos Association, a socialist political group that maintains a storefront and offices where the label used to be housed.

Derry Records
Northern Ireland

Founded in 1972, Derry released a dozen albums of pro-Republican Celtic folk music during its decade-long run. Some of these records were distributed by Trikont in West Germany.

Deutsche Kommunistische Partei
West Germany

The German Communist Party was originally founded in 1918, banned by the Nazis, revived in West Germany after the war as the unacknowledged representative of the East German Communist Party in the West, but then banned again in 1956 because of its ties to the East. In 1968 it was revived, although still secretly funded and ideologically driven by the GDR. The party released a series of records in the seventies and early eighties, under its own name (most often its acronym, DKP) and on sublabels such as Marx-Disc.

VEB DEUTSCHE SCHALLPLATTEN BERLIN DDR

Deutsche Schallplatten Berlin
GDR

The umbrella state record label of East Germany. Most records were released on sublabels such as AMIGA, Aurora, and ETERNA.

Deviant Wreckords
UK

This ad hoc label was used to release a single 7″ in 1979, a benefit for that year's London Pride events. The record was put together by Tom Robinson, Noel Greig, and Jill Poser (who was in the musical theater group Gay Sweatshop, but is much better known for her work doing feminist and lesbian advertisement takeovers, and for her books about them, *Spray It Loud* and *Louder than Words*).

DIAP
Costa Rica

Modeled after Chile's DICAP, the Discoteca del Arte Popular released a couple of LPs in the late seventies by Nicaraguan folk singer Luis Enrique Mejía Godoy. These militantly pro-Sandinista records were likely smuggled into Nicaragua in the throes of revolution.

Diapasão
Portugal

Medium-sized folk and fado label that released about one hundred records primarily ranfrom 1976 through the mid-eighties. It released records by many of the artists that became the musical voice of the Carnation Revolution in Portugal, including José Afonso, José Barata Moura, José Mario Branco, Luis Cilia, and José Jorge Letria. It also released albums by Angolan musician Ruy Mingas and Mozambiquen musician Virgílio Massingue.

DICAP
Chile/France/Spain

In 1970, Discoteca del Cantar Popular (DICAP) was the new name given to Jota Jota, the label started in 1967 by the Communist Youth of Chile. The label was committed to releasing mostly Chilean music from the nueva canción tradition, although it also pressed records by Blops, a Chilean psychedelic rock band, and Cuban musicians Carlos Puebla and Grupo de Experimentación Sonora del ICAIC (Instituto Cubano del Arte e Industria Cinematográficos). Although small, independent, and far-left-leaning, DICAP put out some of the most important Chilean music of the early seventies and controlled about a third of the country's record market. In 1970–73, the label had subsidiaries in both Peru and Uruguay that released DICAP records locally with unique catalog numbers and often alternative artwork. It is unclear how much autonomy these foreign offices had. With the fascist coup in Chile in 1973, the label was raided, many of its master recordings were destroyed, and it was forced into exile, initially in France, and then Spain. Although the label successfully released and licensed Chilean music for another decade across Europe and the Americas, its records were censored at home by the Chilean dictatorship. DICAP-licensed series—dedicated to the release of nueva canción chilena—existed in many countries, including France (on the sublabel Canto Libre) and the Netherlands (on the sublabel Vrije Muziek). In addition, larger labels such as I Dischi dello Zodiaco/Albatros (Italy), Discos Pueblo (Mexico), Movieplay (Spain), AMIGA (GDR), and Pläne (West Germany) released many, if not most, DICAP records in their respective locales.

Dickworz Bladde
West Germany

Founded in 1977, this label from the Rhine/Main area of Germany released politicized folk-rock and blues-rock, often in the Hessian dialect, including a number of records in support of organizing efforts against the construction of an airport runway at Startbahn West near Frankfurt, Germany.

Dihavina
Vietnam

The state-controlled record label of Vietnam, Dihavina was founded in North Vietnam in the early sixties and still exists today. Early records—most composed of martial music supporting the Vietminh against the French and the US—were pressed in the Eastern Bloc, while later records and CDs were made at pressing plants that had been in South Vietnam.

Dikanza
Angola

A label that briefly existed in the early seventies, putting out seven 7"s in a couple years, just prior to decolonization. The name is taken from a wooden musical instrument made of bamboo, across which you scrape a drumstick to make sound. The records are Angolan folk with a social and pro-independence focus, as heard in songs such as "Louvor aos herois" (Praise to heroes) and "Avante camaradas" (Forward comrades).

Direct Hit Records
USA

The name used for a self-released 7" by the band Prairie Fire in 1979. Here the band not only sheds their previous label name (One Spark Records), but also their folk side, attempting a more straightforward rock approach to match their ultraleft lyrics. See also One Spark Records.

Disaster Electronics
Netherlands

Gramschap was a small Dutch anarchist publisher that released a series of fifty zines/pamphlets from the late seventies through 1986, most including a vinyl record (almost entirely 7"s) with the label name Disaster Electronics. Most are politicized punk or art-rock, including releases by The Ex. While technically the proper label is Disaster Electronics, some of the actual records simply list "Gramschap."

I Dischi dello Zodiaco
Italy

A sublabel of the larger and broader Vedette Records, I Dischi dello Zodiaco (Discs of the Zodiac) was focused on international folk music. In many ways, the closest comparisons would be Folkways in the US and Chant du Monde in France (and many of its releases are actually licensed from these labels). In just shy of twenty years (1969–86), Zodiaco released over one hundred albums and singles, with a primary focus on left-leaning Italian folk (both historical and contemporary), Latin American nueva canción (particularly from Chile, but also Mexico, Venezuela, and Uruguay), as well as left, militant, feminist, and working-class-centric folk from Spain, Greece, Cuba, Vietnam, Brazil, Angola, and the US.

I Dischi del Sole
Italy

With a name that translates to "Discs of the Sun," this label was founded in Milan in 1962, a collaboration between ethnomusicologist Roberto Leydi and members of the popular Italian band Cantacronache (including Fausto Amodei and Michele L. Straniero). The goal of the label was to unearth and reanimate the radical folk traditions of Italy, including the history of partisan, worker, anarchist, socialist, communist, and prisoner's songs. Rather than turn to pop music for signs of revolt, the Dischi del Sole group felt that the seeds of Italian radicalism were rooted in people's

existing traditions, not in the importing of foreign aesthetics of rebellion. By the late sixties the label also began releasing new songs, often music being written as part of, or in response to, the growing rebellion within Italian society. It also released a set of singles of speeches from figures such as Che Guevara and Ho Chi Minh, as well as a series of more experimental music. The label released a small number of records by non-Italians, including Judith Reyes (Mexico), Barbara Dane (US, and founder of Paredon Records), and an album of US blues songs.

Dischord
USA

Washington, DC punk label founded in 1982 by Ian MacKaye and Jeff Nelson, then of the Teen Idles, but soon to both be in the genre-defining hardcore band Minor Threat (with MacKaye going on to form Fugazi). Dischord is known for both its dogged commitment to independence—setting caps on the prices of its records, eschewing most merchandising—and its allegiance to the DC scene, where it would help many local rock bands release a record, giving it a half number within its catalog. If the label liked a band and felt it was a good fit, it would bring them on to the main roster.

Discófilo
Portugal

A small label that seems to have only existed for a couple years in the mid-seventies, releasing about twenty records. It was cofounded by the singer Tonicha, her husband João Viegas (an ethnomusicologist), and José Carlos Pereira Ary dos Santos (a singer-songwriter and dedicated communist). The majority of the records the label released were fado and folk recordings inspired by the Carnation Revolution in Portugal, with Tonicha as the core artist. Tonicha, who began her career in the sixties and early seventies as a pop singer, became extremely successful with a turn to reinterpreting Portuguese folk music in the seventies, and worked with Ary dos Santos to record some of the most popular songs of the Revolution.

Disco Libre
Puerto Rico

Putting out just shy of twenty LPs between the late sixties and mid-seventies, Disco Libre was based in San Juan and was the record label of the Puerto Rican Socialist Party. The label was home to militant folk/nueva trova musician Roy Brown, and also released records by Cuban trova artists Silvio Rodríguez and Pablo Milanés. Disco Libre records are recognizable by their powerful and savvy cover design, often merging photography with flat fields of bright color.

Discos America
Venezuela

A small "Latin" label that is included here because it released the first three LPs by influential and political nueva canción and trova singer Soledad Bravo.

Discos Coquí
USA

A Puerto Rican–focused, New York City–based spoken word label from the early seventies founded by Pepe Sánchez. It released an LP version of Pedro Albizo Campos's final speech in 1950, simultaneously released in Puerto Rico by Disco Libre, and later repackaged and released by Paredon Records.

Discos Lara-Yarí
USA

New York City–based label of Roy Brown, a folk singer and activist for Puerto Rican independence. He released his records on the label from 1979 onward, and rereleased his earlier records (originally pressed in Puerto Rico on Disco Libre).

Discos NCL
Mexico

A label focused on nueva canción and nueva trova. From 1974–91 it released about fifty records, most by musicians from Mexico, Cuba, and Chile. One of the label's most interesting groups was La Nopalera, who mixed a nueva canción core with jazz, salsa, bossa nova, and rock music.

Discos Pueblos
Mexico

Founded by the group Los Folkloristas in 1973, for its first decade this label focused almost exclusively on socially conscious folk music from Latin America, being the Mexican outlet of many of the usual suspects (Inti-Illimani, Victor Jara, Pablo Milanes, Isabel and Angel Parra, Silvio Rodríguez, Daniel Viglietti). In addition, it released a number of records by Mexican musicians and songwriters, including Amparo Ochoa. The early releases on the label are noteworthy for having triple gatefold covers and being heavily (and beautifully) illustrated, many with graphics from movement artist Rini Templeton.

Discos Sanjuancito
USA

The record label of the Esneider, the singer of the New York City–based (although he is originally from Colombia) Latinx punk band Huasipungo. An informal project, Discos Sanjuancito released three Huasipungo 7"s (one a split with Los Crudos and the label Lengua Armada), and a handful of CDs by the band and by other Latin American punk bands. The label name is written as "Discos Sanjuanito" on some releases.

DISCOS VIPAR

Discos Vipar
Mexico

An ad hoc label created to release an album of songs by Angel Parra recorded live in Mexico City in 1975. The album was rereleased a year later by Discos NCL.

Discoteca Polo Norte
Angola

An Angolan folk label with an anticolonial focus, undated but likely from the seventies. A couple of the records are produced by Portuguese accordionist Helder Reis, who also played on a number of pro-Carnation Revolution records in Portugal. For some reason, the various logos on the 7"s I have say "Polar" instead of the actual full name.

Discovale
France

A folk label that put out about forty records between 1976 and 1982. It doesn't appear to have a clear ideological alignment, but did release a significant amount of vinyl with political intent, including an LP of revolutionary Algerian songs, a record of songs from the Solidarity movement in Poland, and a lot of regional folk music from Corsica, Provence, and Alsace-Lorraine.

DISJUNCTA
RECORD

Disjuncta Records
France

Founded in 1972 by experimental musician Richard Pinhas. It released about a dozen records in the mid-seventies. The label is an interesting example of the cross section of the political conception of freedom and the musical one, with releases of both extreme experimentation and extreme political content. Pinhas's band Heldon contained both elements, mixing electronic noise and solidarity with armed struggle, as illustrated by a 1975 7" released in support of the Red Army Faction.

Dislaohaksat
Laos

The record-production side of the publisher Neo Lao Haksaet—propaganda arm of the Pathet Lao, the communist party that took power in Laos in 1975. I own, and have only ever seen, one record produced, a 7" titled *The Champa Flower*, featuring a mix of folk and military songs.

Disques Alvarès
France

A chanson-focused project, Alvarès released a number of left-leaning chanson, folk, and nueva canción records, including Francesca Solleville's first directly political LP (her self-titled album from 1969, featuring songs about the 1968 Olympics in Mexico City, the Vietnam War, and US imperialism), recordings from the Chinese Cultural Revolution, and an Inti-Illimani LP.

Disques Cyclope
France

Label used to release Benito Merlino's chanson concept LP *La Banda del Matese*, the songs based on the April 1877 anarchist insurrection in Matese, Italy carried out by Errico Malatesta and

the Italian section of the International Worker's Association (AIT). The label has a logo and an address, so it looks like it was set up to continue putting out records, but this is the only LP I can find evidence of it releasing.

Disques Droug
Brittany

Droug translates as "anger" and is a small label founded by Evgen Kirjuhel to promote "chanson bretonne," music sung in the Breton language and/or rooted in the cultural traditions of Brittany. Kirjuhel, a singer-songwriter himself, was a participant in the events of May '68, and this, along with the label's focus on regional linguistic folk music, engenders a platform supporting working people, feminism, and international solidarity, as can be seen in the label's dozen or so releases. Most of its 7" output came in beautifully produced, duotone-printed, multi-gatefold covers that unfold into large 21" × 21" plus (+) signs. Some releases state that Disques Droug is the label of the "Atelier du C.C.D.C.P." but I haven't been able to source what the C.C.D.C.P. is.

Disques Espérance
France

Founded around 1970, with a focus on music from Africa and the African diaspora. In addition to putting out Miriam Makeba, Bob Marley, and Ali Farka Touré, it released a number of key records by the political Moroccan chaabi/gnawa groups Nass El Ghiwane and Jil Jilala.

Les Disques ICEM-CEL
France

ICEM is the acronym for Institut Cooperatif de l'Ecole Moderne (Cooperative Institute of the Modern School), and CEL for La Coopérative de l'Enseignement Laïque (Secular Education Cooperative). Both grew out of the international Modern School movement, and this is their collective sound recording project. Most of their two dozen or so releases are field recordings, some of music, others of pedagogy or speeches. Of particular interest here is an LP of recordings from a 1973 strike at the LIP watch factory and a 7" documenting the response of eight- and nine-year-old students to their experiences during the May '68 revolt (and how it related to their schooling), and a series of recordings about alternative pedagogy.

Disques Pavé
France

This label released the 7" "Vive les Étudiants! (Chanson Enragée)" by Simon Saguey. The song is inspired by the events in France in May '68, and might have even been released towards the tail end of the upheaval (the record is undated). The record has the catalog number of "no. 200," but I haven't been able to find any information about a "no. 100" or any other records on this label. The record was coproduced by a small French/Swiss left-Zionist label called Productios Nili.

Disques Perspective (ASBL)
Belgium

A short-lived mid-seventies label that was founded to release an album of Léo Collard's speech *Socialisme: Perspective 75*. Collard was a leader of the Belgian Socialist Party. An additional LP of Cuban music (*Cuba Chante et Rit*) was also released, but neither record is dated. It is possible that this is an evolution of the earlier Belgische Socialistische Partij label.

Disques Sol 7
Québec

This label, founded by Stéphane Venne, seems to have been primarily a platform for the Québécois singer-songwriter Emmanuëlle, but sometime in the mid-seventies it put out an LP titled *Chansons et Musique de la Résistance Chilienne*, which features Inti-Illimani, Angel and Isabel Parra, Quilapayún, Illapu, and a speech by Salvador Allende. Although much on the label is not explicitly political, its release of this LP speaks to the broad support amongst many elements within the music industry for the exiled folk musicians of Chile, as well as the popular resistance to the military dictatorship.

Disque Terra Nostra
Catalonia

A pro–Catalan independence label that released fourteen records between 1977 and 1991, including a half dozen LPs in the series "Cançons Populars Catalanes/Chansons Populaires Catalanes."

District 65 DWA

Distributive Workers of America
USA

A union with a long radical history, New York City's DWA released a single LP, *Dr. Martin Luther King, Jr. Speaks to District 65 DWA.* Undated, but likely released after King's death in 1968 or 1969, the back cover states: "District 65 Declares Martin Luther King's Birthday Jan. 15, a Paid Union Holiday," presaging the movement to turn King's birthday into a federal holiday, a struggle championed by musicians Stevie Wonder and Gil Scott-Heron, and eventually won in 1983.

DMO
France

DMO was a sixties/early seventies religious label that was connected in some way with the Jeunesse Ouvrière Chrétienne (JOC) movement, releasing at least three records in support of the Christian labor union. For more information, see JOC-JOCF.

DNG
Italy

An Italian label that evolved out of Italia Canta in 1963. It had a strong connection to the Cantacronache group and the Gruppo del Nuovo Canzoniere Italiano, as well as a clear Marxist/

leftist bent. DNG was owned and run by CEDI (Compagnia Editrice e Discografica Internazionale), an Italian music publisher based in Torino.

Dolphin
Ireland

A Dublin-based label featuring a broad array of Irish and Celtic folk music, including a number pro-Republican groups who supported freedom for Northern Ireland. One Dublin City Ramblers LP I have is titled *Irish Republican Jail Songs*, while The Wolfe Tones put out LPs with the titles *'Till Ireland A Nation*, *Rifles of the IRA*, and *Up the Rebels!*

DOM
France

This label released global folk music, including a French pressings of the Albatros Records subseries "Cile Canta e Lotta" (Chile Sings and Struggles), featuring Victor Jara, the Parras, and Inti-Illimani. It also released an album of songs from the Mexican Revolution by a group called Los Ninos, and an LP of Armenian songs by Rouben Yerevantsi. In the mid-seventies DOM took over distribution of Expression Spontanée, and by the early eighties it had subsumed the leftist label, placing stickers over the Expression Spontanée logo on the record covers, and even pressing some records slated as Spontanée releases as DOM records.

La Do Si Discos
Portugal

Cape Verde– and Guinea-Bissau–focused label

that released a stack of postindependence records by politicized groups África Tentação, N'Kassa Cobra, and Kolá.

DT64 Polit-Song
GDR

DT64 Polit-Song was a 7″ singles series coproduced by the AMIGA and ETERNA labels. DT64, the namesake of the series, was a youth-driven radio show in East Germany which actually had its own label, but these records (by Victor Jara, Quilapayún, Jahrgang '49, José Afonso, and others) were instead released on either AMIGA or ETERNA. Regardless, all the records carried the same "Polit-Song" logo. After the fall of the Berlin Wall, German punks released a benefit 7″ in hopes of keeping DT64 going as a youth-run radio station, but it was eventually closed in 1993.

Dubious Records
USA

Dubious is the record label of Bill Oliver, a Texas-based war veteran and folk singer. Throughout the seventies and eighties he toured with his friend Glen Waldeck as "environmental troubadours," playing eco-focused folk-rock across the US. In 1976, Dubious Records released a 7″ of two of his songs, "Fourth of July in Chu-Lai" b/w ""Little Rocks and Big Holes (In the Road)." The label's motto was "Dubious Records Speak for Themselves."

Earthworks
UK

Earthworks started in 1981 as a "world music" subsidiary of Virgin Records, and was then sold to Stern's Africa in 1992. With a focus on southern Africa in the eighties and early nineties, it was unavoidable that a significant portion of the label's output would be political. It released over a dozen albums of South African township jive, and almost as many of chimurenga music from Zimbabwe. In addition, Earthworks released Youssou N'Dour's *Nelson Mandela* LP and a great compilation called *Rai Rebels*.

East/West World Records
USA

An early eighties folk and pop label focused on Asian-American artists, started by Japanese-American saxophonist Alan Furutani. It was short-lived and only released two LPs. The first was a 1982 split album by Chris Iijima and Charlie Chin that was a follow-up to their trailblazing 1973 LP *A Grain of Sand* (on Paredon Records). The second, released a year later, was by the Asian-American pop-jazz ensemble Visions, featuring and produced by Furutani.

EDIÇÃO DA COMISSÃO ORGANIZADORA DAS COMEMORAÇÕES DO 25 DE ABRIL, DIA DA LIBERDADE

Edição da Comissão Organizadora das Comemorações do 25 de Abril, Dia da Liberdade
Portugal

A committee dedicated to the memory of the Carnation Revolution in Portugal, it released a 7″

by Pedro Osório on the five-year anniversary of the revolution. The record contained Osório's rendition of "Grândola, Vila Morena," José Afonso's song used by the revolting military officers as the cue to begin their leftist coup in 1974.

EDIÇÃO FORA DO COMÉRICO
OFERTA DOS COMUNISTAS BRASILEIROS
A SEUS AMIGOS

Edição Fora do Comércio Oferta dos Comunistas Brasileiros a Seu Amigos
UK/France/Italy

Although I've found little about this label that is definitive, it appears that Tit is the name used by a group of Brazilian communists exiled in Europe to release a series of records of Brazilian dance music in the seventies. Ostensibly to celebrate the International Year of the Woman in 1975, the first record—*A Mulher Na Musica Popular Brasileira* (The woman in Brazilian popular music)—is a mixed bag of songs by women and about women, including tracks by well-known artists such as Chico Barque and Caetano Veloso. It was produced in the UK. Then in 1977 a second album, titled *Musica Popular Brasileira*, was released in France. Another LP titled *Canzoni e Danze Popolari 2 (Il Mondo Urbano)* was released in Italy, and a cassette of songs also came out in France. The label name, which roughly translates to "An Offer of the Brazilian Communists to Our Friends," is a mystery, as no such organization actually existed. But the name might have been a legal work-around to avoid copyright concerns, offering up the records as a "gift," as each states something to the effect of "*Disco fora do comércio*" (Record not for commercial trade).

EDIÇÃO
Instituto Caboverdeano
de solidariedade

Edição Instituto Caboverdeano de Solidariedade
Netherlands

A Dutch solidarity organization that released two records, an LP by Cape Verdean singer Zézé with musical backing by Paulino Vieira, and a 7″ by Os Kings, pressed for June 1, International Day of the Child, featuring a song titled "Flor di nos revolução" (Flower of our revolution).

Ediciones América Hoy
Uruguay

An early seventies nueva canción label that released around three dozen records. The focus was on militant recordings from Chile and Cuba, with records by Che Guevara, Nicolás Guillen, Carlos Puebla, Inti-Illimani, and the Parras. The label also put out music by political Uruguayan musicians such as Héctor Numa Moraes and Yamandú Palacios.

Edições Avante
Portugal

A label connected to the Portuguese Communist Party. It released albums of songs and speeches in honor of multiple party congresses in the seventies, elaborately packaged in boxes and accompanied by books and posters.

Editions Borgson
Benin

Borgson was a seventies label that released about a dozen records, most of them by the groups Orchestre Super Borgou de Parakou and Tout-Puissant Poly-Rythmo de Cotonou, both rhumba/Afrobeat big bands with deep nationalist sympathies. Songs released on the label include "Non à l'Exploitation de l'Homme par l'Homme" (No Exploitation of Man by Man) and "Hommages aux Martyrs de 16 Janvier 1977" (Homage to the Martyrs of January 16, 1977)—the latter a tribute to those who thwarted a 1977 coup attempt in Benin, led by foreign mercenaries against the Marxist-Leninist military.

Editions Musicales du Grand Soir
France

An ad hoc label name used to release a 1974 compilation LP titled *Pour en Finir avec le Travail: Chansons du prolétariat pévolutionnaire Vol. 1* (To the End of Work: Songs of the revolutionary proletariat). The album is a collection of situationist-tinged chanson, with songs penned by Guy Debord, Raoul Vaneigem, and Alice Becker-Ho. Becker-Ho's song "Chanson du CMDO" (Conseil pour le Maintien des Occupations, or Council for Maintaining the Occupations) is an ode to the May '68 strike committee that held the strong council-communist line of maintaining the general strike, as opposed to negotiating with the state. The "Vol. 1" in the title implies other volumes, but I don't believe they were ever released.

Editions Syliphone Conakry
Guinea

The national label of Guinea, set up in 1967 by then-president Sékou Touré. The label was a nationalist project developed out of the broader movement for African independence, and unlike a lot of African labels focused on popular music, it featured a broad selection of folk, jazz, choral, military music, and even ballet. In contrast to a number of former British colonies (such as Nigeria, Ghana, and Kenya), Guinea and many other former French colonies never had pressing plants, so the records were actually created in France and imported for domestic distribution.

Editori Riuniti
Italy

Editori Riuniti was a publishing house associated with the Italian Communist Party (PCI) and based in Rome. In the sixties, it released a series of flexi discs, including poetry from Turkish communist author Nâzim Hikmet and a field recording from the massacre at Reggio Emilia on July 7, 1960, when five workers and PCI members were killed by the police during a labor protest. In the seventies and eighties the label released a handful of vinyl 7"s, including a celebration of Lenin and speeches by PCI leadership. These records were sometimes packaged with annual "almanacs" of the Communist Party.

Edizione Corsica
France

This label only lasted about two years, from 1983–85, but in that short time it released a dozen politicized experimental music releases, including an LP of Palestinian songs by Tunisian singer Mohammad Bhar, an LP featuring the Intercommunal Free Dance Music Orchestra, and a couple cassette-only releases of Albanian songs/chants. It also pressed a couple of albums focused on the musical traditions of the Morvan region in Burgundy. I believe Edizione Corsica was—at least in part—organized by Jean-Pierre Graziani, who had previously founded Disques Vendémiaire.

Edizioni Circolo Culturale Popolare Massa
Italy

The label of an Italian anarchist organization that released a single LP, Collettivo del Contropotere's

L'Estate dei Poveri: dalla realtà di classe al progetto libertario (Counterpower Collective's The Estate of the Poor: from class reality to the libertarian project) in 1976. Funds raised were used to support Radio Popolare Massa.

Vento Rosso

Edizioni del Vento Rosso
Italy

The label of the folk band Il Canzoniere Nazionale del Vento Rosso (The National Song of the Red Wind), which released a small clutch of records in the early seventies. The one I have, *Han Gridato Scioperiamo* (They Shouted Let's Strike), has a bilingual cover (Italian and German) and was co-released with Neue Welt.

Edizioni di Cultura Popolare
Italy

A Milan-based free jazz and improvisation label that existed for a couple years in the mid-seventies, it veered into more directly political territory with a handful of releases, including a polit-folk LP by Cooperativa La Taba, an improv record about the environment by Quartetto di Guido Mazzon, a Palestinian solidarity album of spoken word and jazz improv by Gaetano Liguori and Giulio Stocchi, and the Italian edition of Frederic Rzewski's *The People United Will Never Be Defeated!* It is also likely that after its initial handful of releases, ECP was produced and distributed by Vedette, as all the records carry VPA catalog numbers (just like the releases of Vedette's other sublabels—Albatros, I Dischi dello Zodiaco, and Way Out).

Edizioni Lotta Poetica
Italy

This label, with a name that roughly translates to "Poetic Struggle Editions," released about two dozen vinyl LPs between the mid-seventies and mid-eighties. All were part of a series called "Radiotaxi," and feature avant-garde sound poetry and experimental audio. Founded by Italian poet Sarenco, the label released records from an impressive list of poets and performers, including albums by both the Guerrilla Art Action Group and anarchist-pacifist poet Jackson Mac Low. Other artists include Julien Blaine, Henry Chopin, Paul De Vree, and Hermann Nitsch.

Edizioni Movimento Studentesco
Italy

A label that evolved out of the far left, extraparliamentary student movement in Milan, it released about a half dozen records in the early seventies. Many of these listed the Movimento Studentesco Milanese as the musicians, but the songs were actually performed and recorded by Stormy Six. Solidarity with Palestine is a sustained refrain in both the songs and the artwork on the records.

EGREM
Cuba

Empresa de Grabaciones y Ediciones Musicales (EGREM, or Company of Recordings and Musical Editions) was founded in 1964 as the state-run record label of Cuba, superseding Imprenta Nacional de Cuba (National Press of Cuba). EGREM maintained a monopoly over the production and distribution of Cuban music for more than twenty years. It was the parent entity for all Cuban labels, including Areito and Casa de Las Américas.

Eigelstein
West Germany

A Cologne-based project that evolved out of the Neue Welt label. While Neue Welt was focused on highly political international folk, this label branched out into krautrock, prog, new wave, and punk. Many releases were political, but much of the politics were less didactic and more personal, especially after the early eighties.

EKO
Sweden

A very small progg label which likely only released three 7″s, one an explicitly antinuclear record by Torvmossegossarana—1979's *Atomkraft? Nej Tack* (Nuclear Power? No Thanks).

ENAFEC
Algeria/France

The Entreprise Nationale des Fournitures Educatives et Culturelles (ENAFEC, or National Enterprise of Educational and Cultural Supplies) was a Algerian cultural organization that also produced vinyl LPs. One of its major projects was a three-record box set by Palestinian folk musician Marcel Khalifé celebrating the thirty-year anniversary of the founding of the Algerian National Liberation Front on November 1, 1954.

ENIGRAC
Nicaragua

Similar to EGREM in Cuba, Empresa Nicaragüense de Grabaciones Culturales (ENIGRAC, Nicaraguan Company of Cultural Recordings) was the state-controlled record label set up in 1980 by the Sandinistas in the wake of the Nicaraguan Revolution. Although other labels existed in Nicaragua (see Ocarina), I believe that—at least in the eighties—ENIGRAC produced all of the records coming out of the country, even if it didn't directly release them.

EN LUTTE!

En Lutte
Québec

A Montreal-based label that released the 1973 LP *Chants Revolutionnaires du Canada et du Monde 1*. Contrary to the number in this title, I don't believe any further volumes were ever released.

ESP-Disk
USA

Seminal New York City–based experimental music label that released a slew of socially conscious and sonically challenging recordings. These included jazz musicians such as Revolutionary Ensemble, Sun Ra, and Marzette Watts ("Backdrop for Urban Revolution"); proto-punk anarcho-noise-folk band The Fugs; a spoken word album by Timothy Leary; a vinyl LP edition of the underground newspaper *The East Village Other*; and an album of civil rights songs called *Movement Soul*.

Eteenpäin!
Finland

An explicitly leftist label, Eteenpäin! (Forward!)
ran from 1970–77, and released thirty LPs.
Like similar labels in others countries—such
as Paredon (US) and Expression Spontanée
(France)—Eteenpäin!'s focus was not just on
the radical within domestic music, but also
the songs of liberation movements spanning
Angola to Cuba, Chile to Korea, Armenia
to South Africa. It is unclear if this label is
related to—or inspired by—the one of the same
name started in 1966 by Finnish experimental
musician and provocateur M. A. Numminen and
ethnomusicologist Pekka Gronow. Eteenpäin!
was produced and distributed by the larger
independent label Love Records.

ETERNA
GDR

Like its sister project AMIGA, ETERNA was
a sublabel of the East German state record
company Deutsche Schallplatten Berlin. Its main
output was classical, but in the sixties it began
releasing communist and antifascist anthems (i.e.,
"L'Internationale," Soviet marching songs, chants
from the Spanish Civil War, etc.). By the late
sixties a steady stream of folk music was pressed,
including nueva canción, younger GDR polit-folk
bands, and records documenting the Eastern Bloc's
annual Festival des Politischen Liedes (Festival
of Political Song), which featured tracks by
communist groups from across Eastern, Western,
and Northern Europe, as well as a lot of groups
from the Americas. In the seventies the label
released a couple series of political 7"s, including
DT64 Polit-Song (a sublabel shared with AMIGA;
see DT64 for more information) and a set of
recordings under the "Solidarity Mit Chile" moniker.

Ethiopian Tourist Organization
Ethiopia

One of the stranger entries in this book, the
Ethiopian Tourist Organization pressed a 7"
(produced in Kenya) titled *Revolution Song* in
honor of the 1974 Ethiopian Revolution. Although
undated, it was most likely produced in the
late seventies in celebration of the Derg (the
military junta that governed Ethiopia at the time)
and of Mengistu Haile Mariam, who would rule
Ethiopia as the head of the Communist state
from 1975–91. He was the architect of the "Red
Terror," Stalin-like purges of those he saw as
enemies or even potential enemies. The writing
credit to the music on one of the songs on the
7" is attributed to Mariam.

Ewuro Productions
Nigeria

Ewuro is the ad hoc label name used to release
Unlimited Liability Company in 1983, a critique of
postindependence corporate cronyism in Nigeria
disguised as a highlife LP. The lyrics were written
by Wole Soyinka, and the music by Tunji Oyelana
& The Benders, a popular Nigerian highlife band
that mostly recorded for EMI. Ewuro means
"bitter leaf" in Yuroba.

Ex Records
Netherlands

The Ex is a Dutch political punk and experimental
music outfit that emerged out of the Amsterdam

anarchist and squatting scene in the late seventies. Although they used several label names on their early records (such as More Dirt Per Minute, FAI, and Eh Records), most were self-released and carried Ex Records catalog numbers even if they weren't explicitly marked as "Ex Records." In many ways the label was in keeping with a broad tendency among anarcho-DIY bands to self-release albums, but unlike Crass Records or Chumbawamba's Agit-Prop, Ex Records has only ever released records by The Ex and by the direct side projects of the band members.

Expression Spontanée
France

A direct product of the student and worker revolt across France in May '68, Expression Spontanée was founded by Jean Bériac to release songs inspired by the protests. Seven-inch records by Dominique Grange and a group called Les Barricadiers were released as the uprising was ebbing in June '68. Expression Spontanée quickly became an explicitly radical left label with a catalog diverse in geography and musical style. It ran from 1968 to roughly 1981. Although there are over eight hundred labels in this book, only a handful really have such a broad, explicitly internationalist, and left-wing focus (Paredon, Eteenpäin!, and Trikont being some of the others). Expression Spontanée put out around seventy-five albums and singles, comprising regional European folk, nueva canción (including multiple from Chile), songs from Palestine, records documenting political struggle (May '68, a 1975 French telecom strike), kids' music, feminist songs, and more. In the seventies, Expression Spontanée was distributing (and possibly even producing) Trikont and I Dischi del Sole albums in France. In the early eighties, as the label was ending, it was taken over by its distributor, DOM, leading to a messy overlap of the two labels on some releases. For instance, Rosalie Dubois's *Chants de Révoltes et de Liberté* (undated) has the Expression Spontanée logo on its cover and a label-specific catalog number of ES-67, but the vinyl labels feature the DOM logo and list DOM

as the sole label. On other records, "Expression Spontanée" is stickered over on the covers, with DOM listed as the producer and distributor.

Extraplatte
Austria

Long-running Vienna-based label that began with a folk focus in 1978, but quickly expanded to rock, jazz, and experimental music. In its thirty-five-year run (it went bankrupt in 2013) it released close to one thousand records, but it was only in the first couple years that there was any real attention to politics. The first two dozen releases saw a compilation LP dedicated to fighting nuclear power (*Künstler Gegen Zwenendorf*–Artists Against the Zwenendorf Nuclear Power Plant), multiple records by the political folk-rock acts Auflauf and Walter Mossman, and a coproduced (with the West German Eigelstein label) compilation against the right-leaning *Bild* tabloid newspaper.

Falkenscheiben
West Germany

A folk-rock label from Bonn that released three LPs, featuring then-popular political "*songgruppes*," which mixed folk, schlager, and cabaret music. Falkenscheiben, which translates to "Falcon Discs," is the record label of Falken Rote and the Sozialistische Jugend Deutschlands (Socialist Youth of Germany).

Fédération Espagnole des Déportés et Internés Politiques
France

The Fédération Espagnole des Déportés et Internés Politiques (FEDIP, or Spanish Federation of Deportees and Political Prisoners) was a Spanish political organization in exile in France. It released a single 7"–folk songs by Juan Vilato and Ricardo Garriga pressed in the mid-sixties, drawing attention to the seriousness of the plight of post–Civil War Spanish deportees and exiles by comparing their fate to those who were held in the Nazi-run French concentration camp Mauthausen.

Fédération Nationale des Déportés et Internés Résistants et Patriotes
France

The Fédération Nationale des Déportés et Internés Résistants et Patriotes (FNDIRP, or the National Federation of Deported and Imprisoned Resistance Fighters and Patriots) was founded by political concentration-camp survivors in France right after the Nazi defeat. FNDIRP was dedicated to maintaining the memory of those who died in the camps, and to researching Nazi war crimes. It released a 7" recording of Chorales de la Federation Musicale de Paris titled *Le Chant des Partisans* in the sixties (produced and distributed by Le Chant du Monde), and also sponsored a seventies or eighties (the record is undated) release by Jean-Pierre Rosney titled *Poésie de la Résistance et de la Déportation* (on the Voxigrave label).

The Fellowship of Reconciliation
USA

The Fellowship of Reconciliation is one of the oldest interfaith peace and justice groups in the world, and began in the US fighting for conscientious objectors during World War I. It was involved in the anti-Vietnam war movement, and in the late sixties released two spoken word LPs, *Poets for Peace* (under the label name The Spoken Arts of the Fellowship of Reconciliation) and *Cry of Vietnam* (under the label name The Compassionate Arts of the Fellowship of Reconciliation). *Cry of Vietnam* features a very young Thích Nhất Hạnh.

Femme Records
USA

This label released a single LP, the early seventies feminist folk collection *Reviving a Dream: Songs for Women's Liberation* by Ruth Batchelor and Voices of Liberation. Batchelor had been a pop musician who released a couple singles, but also wrote songs for a number of film soundtracks and early R&B musicians like Ben E. King and Elvis. In the seventies she took a sharp turn towards women's liberation, putting out this LP, as well as a couple singles, such as 1974's "Barefoot and Pregnant" b/w "Stand and Be Counted" on Pye Records.

Final Call Records
USA

The Final Call is the newspaper of the Nation of Islam (NOI), and it is also one of many names the organization used when it pressed vinyl records. Sometimes it is written as F/C

Records, and other NOI labels include A Moslem Sings, AVC Records, Black Family Records, Muhammad's Mosque of Islam, Salaam Records, and 7 Speeches. The vast majority of NOI records are either music or speeches by Louis Farrakhan (as Louis X, and before that as a calypso crooner called The Charmer).

Finnadar Records
USA

Experimental and contemporary classical label run by Turkish composer and magnetic tape musician İlhan Mimaroğlu. Beyond the politicized nature of free experimentation, the label also released records by Frederic Rzewski and John Cage, as well as Fred Houn's *Bamboo That Snaps Back*, a Marxist jazz epic about Asian-American history.

Fire on the Mountain
USA

An ad hoc label that released a single LP in 1984 titled *Out of the Darkness*. It's an antinuclear compilation featuring Holly Near, Pete Seeger, Sweet Honey in the Rock, and more. The record was an explicit attempt to use song to support the broader antinuclear movement, and inexpensive copies of the record were offered to like-minded organizations to sell for their own financial benefit.

First Amendment
RECORDS

First Amendment Records
USA

One-shot label that posthumously released a speech by Malcolm X in Detroit titled *Ballots*

or Bullets. The sleeve claims that all proceeds would be paid to Betty Shabazz, Malcolm's widow. This is one of a half dozen seemingly fly-by-night operations that pressed Malcolm X records soon after his death when he was at the height of his popularity.

Flat Earth Collective
UK

A long-running anarcho-punk label that began in 1986 as a collective of members of two of the bands on the label's roster (Generic and One by One). The initial release was Generic's . . . *For a Free and Liberated South Africa* 7", and later records include Disaffect's *An Injury to One Is an Injury to All* 7" and the UK edition of Los Crudos' LP *Canciones Para Liberar Nuestras Fronteras*.

FLM
Belgium

The full name of this label is Fonds Leo Magits (Leo Magits Fund), although that never shows up on the actual records. FLM was a Dutch-Belgian label that put out two records: the first, released in 1978, was a 7" with a rendition of "De Internationale"; the second, released in 1982, was a compilation LP titled *Boos Blijven* (Stay Angry), with a wide range of bands, styles, and political subjects (including songs about nuclear war, antifascism, solidarity, and more). The same compilation was also released in the Netherlands on VARAgram. The content of the two records and the red rose in the label's logo likely means that FLM was ideologically democratic socialist.

FLVM
France

FLVM stands for "Faites le Vous-Même," or "Do It Yourself," and this was not a label so much as an organization that helped musicians self-produce their records. Founded by the large independent label Gratte-Ciel, it operated almost like a cooperative buyer's club, where FLVM negotiated for large groups of independent artists in order to get good prices on mastering and pressing records at the major manufacturing plants. It is included here because of its mutual aid structure, not the politics of any of the 150 plus records it helped produce from roughly 1978 to 1988.

Flying Dutchman
US

A jazz label founded by producer Bob Thiele and most active from 1969–83. Best known within political circles as Gil Scott-Heron's label, it also released spoken word albums by Angela Davis and H. Rap Brown, as well as threewo Rosko-narrated/Pete Hamill audio documentaries—one on the Mỹ Lai Massacre in Vietnam, one on the shooting of student protesters at Kent State University in Ohio, and one on People's Park in Berkeley.

Flying Fish
USA

A Chicago-based blues, country, and folk label, the vast majority of its output is not directly political, but it did release socially conscious albums by Sweet Honey in the Rock and Si Kahn, and a compilation documenting the Great Hudson River Revival, a concert supporting the Hudson River Sloop Clearwater, an environmental project founded by Pete Seeger.

Folkebevægelsen Mod EF
Denmark

Ad hoc label name (which translates as "People's Movement Against the EF") used in 1972 to release a split 7″ by Louis Miehe-Renard and Den Røde Lue in opposition to Denmark joining the Europæiske Fællesskab (or European Community), a precursor to the European Union.

Folk Freak
West Germany

A broadly left-leaning folk label from Lower Saxony. It ran from 1977 through the end of the eighties, releasing roughly fifty records, including a number dedicated to peace and environmental issues. The logo also clearly references the popular European representation of the anarchist as a black-clad, hat-wearing mischief maker, although here the bomb has been replaced with a banjo.

Folk Internazionale
Italy

A series of the Italian label Cetra. In the mid-seventies Cetra released about twenty international folk albums under this moniker, including LPs by Americanta and Amerindios de Chile from Latin America, and two fabulous LPs from Lusophone Africa—*Canti Rivoluzionari dell' Angola* and *Canti Rivoluzionari del Mozambico*. Most of the albums feature impressive cover illustrations by Beppe Madaudo.

Folksång
Sweden

Folksång started out as the house label for the Marxist theater/folk/progg group Fria Proteatern in 1971, but went on to also release records by Mikis Theodorakis and an orchestra from Pol Pot's Cambodia.

Folkways
USA

The largest—and likely most influential—label in this publication, Folkways released over twenty thousand titles from 1949 until founder Moses Asch's death in 1987. It was home to not only music, but field recordings, spoken word, and even sound effects. Folkways put out much of the left wing of the US folk scene (Woody Guthrie, Cisco Houston, Peggy Seeger, Pete Seeger), and a wide swath of musicians connected to international political struggles—

particularly in Africa, with records from Algeria, Angola, South Africa, and the Sudan.

Forlaget Tiden
Denmark

A political folk and rock label connected to the Danish Communist Party (DKP) which ran for a decade, 1973–82. It released a range of music, from political theater groups, an anti-NATO 7" by rock group Den Røde Lue (who also released records on Demos), and an album of revolutionary songs by the DKU, the youth wing of the DKP.

FORWARD SOUNDS INTERNATIONAL LTD
Forward Sounds International
UK

A London-based eighties label that was home to polit-folk singer-songwriter Rory McLeod and experimental rap/electro group Akimbo. It also released the 1985 pro-miners' strike benefit LP *Dig This: A Tribute To The Great Strike*, featuring Chumbawamba, The Ex, Poison Girls, The Mekons, and more. Four of the six releases on the label feature covers designed by anarchist artist Clifford Harper.

Fotón
Mexico

Discos Fotón was one of multiple Mexican licensors of DICAP LPs, releasing a dozen Chilean albums from the mid-seventies through the mid-eighties. These include records by Victor Jara, Inti-Illimani, and the Parras. It also released nueva canción and nueva trova albums by Alfredo

Zitarrosa (Uruguay), Vicente Felíu (Cuba), Magaly Tars (Cuba), and Los Olimareños (Uruguay). The label only released a couple of Mexican artists, including blues guitarist Javier Batiz.

France Amérique Latine
France

As the name implies, this is a French solidarity organization that released albums of folk music from Latin American countries it supported. The one I have is by the Salvadoran group Banda Tepeuani, a Latin fusion band that supported both the armed FMLN (Farabundo Martí National Liberation Front) and its aboveground political organization the FDR (Democratic Revolutionary Front).

Frauenbuchveetrieb
West Germany

A women's book distributor that also helped release and distribute a handful of German lesbian rock and folk records in the late seventies and early eighties by Die Bonner Blaustrümpfe, Carolina Brauckmann, and Lysistrara.

Frauen Offensive
West Germany

The label of the all-women's rock and pop music collective Flying Lesbians. The group, made up of seven women, played together from 1974–77, and released a single self-titled LP in 1975. Although

the seven women were named as performers on the album, they listed the songwriter as "Emily Pankhurst," a pseudonym that expressed the collectivity that went into the writing (Pankhurst was an early twentieth-century British suffragette). They were born out of the first Berlin Women's Festival in 1974, and continued to almost exclusively play all-women's events and venues. Unlike much of the feminist movement, which gravitated towards folk music, they performed a diverse and aggressive mix of pop, rock, and jazz.

Fredsång
Sweden

Fredsång, or "Peace Song," was the label of the Swedish Peace Committee (Svenska Fredskommittén). It released a single 7″ in 1982: "I mänsklighetens namn: Fred" b/w "Våra krafter" ("In the name of humanity: Peace" b/w "Our forces") by progg act Röda Kapellet. The lefty label and recording studio Nacksving helped Fredsång to produce the vinyl.

Freie Deutsche Jugend Westberlins
West Germany

A political party, Freie Deutsche Jugend Westberlins (FDJW) was the West Berlin chapter of the Free German Youth (FDJ). It's all a bit of acronym soup, but the FDJ was the youth wing of the Socialist Unity Party (SED), which was a West Berlin front for the East German Communist Party, which was legally banned in the West. (The SED played a role in Berlin very similar to the one played by the DKP in the rest of West Germany.) Anyway, the FDJW celebrated its thirtieth anniversary in 1977 by pressing a split 7″ by Gruppe Vorwärts and Linkerton, two lefty krautrock/folk acts.

FRELIMO
Mozambique

FRELIMO is the popularly used acronym for the Frente de Libertação de Moçambique (Mozambique Liberation Front), the political and military organization that liberated the country from Portuguese colonialism. Once decolonization began, FRELIMO became the ruling political party of the country, originally with a Marxist orientation, but now it hews to a more tame version of democratic socialism. FRELIMO took over and used the Portuguese record-pressing plant in Mozambique, Somodiscos, but didn't create a state label as happened in other Communist countries such as Cuba and Nicaragua. Instead, it released a number of records under combinations of its own moniker, such as the pressing plant name (Somodiscos), the state radio station Radio Moçambique, and the popular music label Ngoma (which might have had state sponsorship but was not a state-controlled label in the way that EGREM functioned in Cuba or Zhongguo Changpian in China).

Fretilin/Comité 20 de Novembro
East Timor/Portugal

This is one of the names that records were released under by the Frente Revolucionária de Timor-Leste Independente, the armed group that fought for Timorese independence, first from Portugal, and then Indonesia. See also Vento de Leste, which I believe is the label name the same group used for the records that were pressed and released in Portugal.

Friends of Bogle Records
UK

Friends of Bogle is the sound-recording wing of the Bogle L'Overture book publishing company, a London-based Afro-Caribbean book publisher that put out books by Walter Rodney and Linton Kwesi Johnson. The label only released a single LP, a compilation of Afro-British-Caribbean poetry titled *Come From That Window Child*. The politicized reggae label People Unite provided technical support for the album.

Friends Records
Canada

Friends was a short lived (1979–82) Vancouver-based punk label that released records by both D.O.A. (see their own label Sudden Death Records) and The Subhumans (the Canadian band, not the UK one). The Subhumans bass player Gerry Hannah, aka Gerry Useless, was also a member of the antiauthoritarian armed struggle group Direct Action, and spent time in prison for his involvement in a series of early eighties actions against nuclear installations, private military companies, and pornographic bookstores.

Frihets Förlag
Sweden

Frihets Förlag (Freedom Publishing) was the publishing wing of the Sveriges Socialdemokratiska Ungdomsförbund (SSU, or Swedish Social Democratic Youth Federation). It released a series of compilation polit-folk records in the seventies, including a variety of groups (Röda Röster, Trots Allt, Tobasco) singing about Vietnam, Chile, and workers' rights.

Front Page Entertainment
USA

Front Page is the label/moniker used by KRS-One on his later releases, starting with *Return of the Boom Bap* in 1993 (although it was produced and distributed by Jive Records). The first vinyl release on Front Page that was not co-released with a major label was KRS-One and Channel Live's 1995 12" *Free Mumia*.

FSLN
Nicaragua

The Frente Sandinista de Liberación Nacional (FSLN) is the group that led the Nicaraguan Revolution, but was also the moniker used for one of the early postrevolutionary LPs released in the country in 1979. The label name appears only on the Nicaraguan pressing of the Mejía Godoy brothers' album *Guitarra Armada* (which was also released in the US on Rounder, in Mexico on Pentagrama, and in Cuba on Areito).

FSM Records
USA

The record label of the Berkeley Free Speech

Movement, which released an LP and a 7" in the mid-sixties. The LP was a mix of songs and field recordings from the protests, while the 7" is titled *Free Speech Carols* and is a recording of eleven Free Speech Movement–themed a cappella reworkings of Christmas carols. A twenty-year-anniversary pressing was made of the 7" in 1984, with a redesigned cover. Another audio document of field recordings from Free Speech Movement rallies and speeches was released in 1964 by KPFA, the local Pacifica radio station in Berkeley.

Full Circle Productions
USA

The label used to release Floyd Westerman's 1984 LP *The Land Is Your Mother*. Westerman is a political Dakota folk/country singer who released two LPs on independent country label Perception in 1969 and '70. Later in the seventies he found new popularity in Germany and had these albums reissued by Trikont. Trikont also released a German edition of *The Land Is Your Mother*.

FUSE MUSIC

FUSE Music
USA

A project organized by Mike Rawson and Rob Rosenthal that released a compilation LP against austerity in 1984 titled *Reaganomics Blues*. The players are regulars from the US political folk scene, including Barbara Dane, Joe Glazer, Si Kahn, and Holly Near. Many of the songs on the album had previously been released on records put out by Folkways, Paredon, and Redwood Records. Both Rawson and Rosenthal had also been involved in the 1983 Folkways LP *We Won't Move: Songs of the Tenants' Movement*. *Reaganomics Blues* and *Seattle 1919* are in many ways follow-ups to that project.

Fuse Records
UK

Fuse was founded in 1975 to release records by leftist English songwriters and folk singers Leon Rosselson and Roy Bailey. I'm unsure of either musician's direct involvement in the workings of the label, but one or both of them were part of all three dozen records it released.

Gala Gala
Angola

A small Angolan record label that released a series of 7″ singles and a couple LPs in the seventies. Like Movimento and Merengue, a number of these were national independence and anticolonial themed; artists included David Zé and Taborda Guedes. One unique aspect of Gala Gala is that a number of the records state that they were manufactured in Mozambique, which is not common for Angolan music.

General Federation of Iraqi Women
Iraq

A political organization that released at least one record, a 1980 LP of songs by the choral group La Troupe Ghali. The Federation was founded in 1969 by the ruling Ba'ath Party, and largely orchestrated by the regime from above. But in 1975 it merged with the Iraqi Women's League—a communist organization—and carved out a small amount of autonomy.

GEORG-BÜCHNER-EDITION

Georg-Büchner-Edition
West Germany

The label name used to press a 1978 collection by political folk musicians and song groups from the city of Darmstadt titled *Osttangenten Blues*. . . . The record was released in protest of the building of East Tangent ring road, a four-lane highway that faced major protests between the seventies and early 2000s, and wasn't completed until 2006. The label is named after Georg Büchner, a nineteenth-century German romantic and naturalist playwright whose work humanized and showed deep compassion for the oppressed.

Geste Paysanne UPCP
France

Geste Paysanne means "Farmer's Gesture," and the UPCP is the Union pour la Culture Populaire en Poitou-Charentes-Vendée, founded in 1968 to "defend and promote" the history and folk culture of the southwestern region of France, which has its own unique languages/dialects (including Occitan, Poitevin, and Saintongeais) and rural economic systems. Geste Paysanne released over sixty records between 1972 and the early nineties.

GOLDEN TRIANGLE RECORDS

Golden Triangle Records
USA

The label alias used to release Larry Saunder's ("The Prophet of Soul") song "Free Angela" in 1971, as well as a compilation LP of the same name pulling together soul, funk, and R&B songs in support of the National Committee to Free Angela Davis. The records were organized and produced by Alexander Randolph, who also ran the Sound of Soul label from the same Manhattan office.

Gong
Spain

Also known as Serie Gong, this sublabel of the larger Movieplay was founded in 1974 by Gonzalo Garciapelayo as a Spanish outlet for Latin American music (and Spanish prog rock). In its early days it was home to many nueva canción and nueva trova artists—the first release was Victor Jara, followed by a steady stream of other DICAP albums.

Gougnaf Mouvement
France

An eighties French punk label founded by Rico Maldoror (aka Hector Chabada, aka Thierry Pujol), Gougnaf came from an anticorporate and class-struggle position, releasing records by political punk bands Parabellum (whom Maldoror managed) and Les Thugs, as well as 12″s from London communist oi band Red London, and East Bay Ray, the guitarist from the Dead Kennedys.

Great Leap
USA

An ad hoc label name used by Joanne Nobuko Miyamoto (one of the three musicians who recorded the seminal Asian-American folk LP *Grain of Sand* on Paredon Records) for her 1983 solo LP *Best of Both Worlds*.

G Records International
Philippines

The record label of Filipino protest folk singer Freddie Aguilar. After a couple albums on major labels in 1979–80, he became increasingly marginalized because of his outspoken political views, and was eventually banned from mass media in the Philippines by the Ferdinand Marcos dictatorship. He had also been releasing his music on politicized local labels such as Ugat Tunog Ng Lahi and G Records. G released a half dozen records by Aguilar, including the song he is best known for—his version of the traditional Tagalog protest song "Bayan Ko" (My Country), which became the theme song of the movement against the Marcos regime.

Greenbelt Records
UK

An ad hoc label created to release politicized Christian folk singer-songwriter Garth Hewitt's anti-apartheid 12″ *Litany for Africa* in 1986. The label is connected to the festival of the same name, founded in 1974 in the UK as a large-scale faith-based social justice arts event.

Greenpeace Records ApS
Denmark/International

The label of the international environmental organization. It was initially set up in Denmark (thus the ApS, which is Danish for "Ltd.") and released two folk and pop records in 1983. In 1985, the organization worked with EMI to release a major benefit album in the UK featuring major-label pop and new wave acts like Tears for Fears, Peter Gabriel, and Depeche Mode, but maintained the "Greenpeace Records ApS" label. A follow-up double LP compilation, *Rainbow Warriors/Breakthrough* (featuring a who's who of mid-eighties pop music, with Aswad, The Eurythmics, the Grateful Dead, Lou Reed, R.E.M., Sade, Talking Heads, and U2), was released by Geffen/RCA in 1988, with the Greenpeace label dropped. As a small piece of Cold War trivia, the record was simultaneously released in the Soviet Union by Melodiya, and became extremely popular. The hefty booklet that came with the album was a major entry point for Eastern European youth into both Western pop culture and Western environmental activism.

Gridalo Forte Records
Italy

Started in the early nineties, Gridalo Forte was a street punk, oi, and ska label that released music by bands with a working-class and internationalist focus. It put out albums by Basque rockers Kortatu and their follow-up band, Negu Gorriak; Italian punks Banda Bassoti; and Sardinian oi band Kenze Neke, whose LP *Naralu! De Uve Sese* features a cover with an array of European subaltern flags: Basque Country, Corsica, Northern Ireland, and Sardinia.

Gross National Products
South Africa

The house label, or imprint, of the South African punk/noise band Kalahari Surfers. The Surfers were a highly politicized, loosely organized group of musicians orbiting around Warrick Sony, Shifty Studios, and its label, Shifty Records. Largely anonymous for political reasons, the Kalahari Surfers put out about a dozen records of anti-apartheid experimental art noise with almost as many labels (including the aforementioned Shifty, as well as Recommended Records and RēR Megacorp), but many of them also listed Gross National Products as a co-label.

Groucho Marxist Record Co:Operative
UK

This situationist-inspired, Scottish punk label released four 7″s between 1979 and 1981, each one labeled Communique 1, 2, 3, and 4 as catalog numbers. The first record is called *Spectacular Commodity!*, and the second *Ha! Ha! Funny Polis*, with four tracks mocking law and order. None of the bands on these 7″s ever recorded for any other label, and although most of the bands are from Scotland, the address used on the records is a postbox for Rock Against Racism in London.

GR Records
USA

This label appears to have only released a single LP, *The Second American Revolution: His Way or His Way*. Undated but likely released in the mid-sixties, the album is an interesting document of its moment, taking for granted the coming of a new US revolution, the question being whose ideas would shape it, Martin Luther King, Jr. or Malcolm X. The record features a speech from the former on one side and a speech from the latter on the other.

Guilda da Música
Portugal

One of a series of Portuguese labels that were largely nonpolitical until the Carnation Revolution—after which they pressed a solid chunk of political folk and rock (~1975–79). The label released a series of 7″ singles (by the likes of Luis Cilia, Carlos Cavalheiro, José Mário Branco, Baraka Moura, and José Jorge Letria, and José Barata Moura) with titles like "Pino da Reforma Agrária" (Hymn of Agrarian Reform) and "Apelo às Mulheres na Revolução: No Ano Internacional da Mulher" (Call to Women in Revolution: In the International Year of Women). They also put out a series of revolutionary field recordings, including speeches by Samora Machel, the leader of Mozambique's FRELIMO (Mozambique Liberation Front), and a collection of street recordings from April 25, 1974, the day of the Portuguese Revolution.

Guimbarda
Spain

A folk label which ran from the mid-seventies to 1985. It distributed and re-pressed records from other international folk labels such as Paredon, Rounder, DICAP, and Disco Libre, as well as releasing some unique political LPs of its own, including *¡Polisario Vencerá!*, a double album of great sahrawi music performed by the Martir el Uali Mustafa Sayed Grupo Nacional de Cantos y Danzas Populares, the song and dance troupe of the Polisario Front.

GYN Records
USA

A Boston-based label created to produce at least two undated (but likely mid-seventies) feminist LPs by the Arlington Street Church Women's Caucus, *Honor Thy Womanself* and *Leave the Bread A-Burning*. The Arlington Street Church Women's Caucus was a feminist folk group that developed out of a Boston-area Unitarian Universalist church. *Honor Thy Womanself* was re-pressed later by Rounder Records with additional liner notes, lyrics, and photographs (also undated, but the catalog number most likely places the release between 1973 and 1975).

Healing Earth Productions
USA

Released a single 7″, a commemorative record to accompany the 1983 Christopher Street West–Los Angeles Parade, a precursor to the contemporary LA Pride Parade. The record features two "theme songs" for the parade, 1982's "A New Gay Dawning" by LeRoy Dysart, Larry Kephart, and Donna J. Wade, and 1983's "Sharing the Magic" by Joanna Cazden and Lorin Sklamberg.

Hermonikher
USA

Label used to release a one-off 1985 LP by Candace Anderson titled *A Sampler of Michigan Women*. The record is a folk concept album, with each song telling the story of a woman from Michigan (e.g., "Sojourner Truth" and "Mary Wallace").

Herri Gogoa
Basque Country

A small folk label and recording outfit that began putting out music in the Basque language in 1968, when Spain was still under Franco's rule and music not sung in Castilian was sometimes banned, and always looked down on. In 1980 it also co-released a double LP—with fellow Basque labels Tic-Tac and IZ—of Basque antinuclear songs.

Hexensaite
West Germany

A label created to release the 1979 album *Witch is Witch* by the lesbian folk duo of the same name. "Hexensaite" means "witch's string" in German.

HHH Productions
UK

HHH is short for "Heads Held High," an ad hoc musical theater group formed to support Jarrow 86, a huge march of the unemployed that was carried out in 1986 on the fifty-year anniversary of the 1936 Jarrow March, when two hundred unemployed men marched for a month from Jarrow to London. Along with the theatre group, other acts involved included Billy Bragg, The Mekons, and Tom Robinson.

hide

Hide
Canada

Hide was the label of the Toronto-based queer, feminist, punk/art-rock band Fifth Column (along with fellow traveler Candy Parker). Begun as a zine in the very early eighties, each of the five issues featured an audio cassette of music and sound art. It pressed two pieces of vinyl, both LPs by Fifth Column: *To Sir With Hate* in 1986 and *All-Time Queen of the World* in 1990. Fifth Column were pioneers of what was to become "queercore," fiercely independent and politically astute, with songs focused on gay and lesbian history and identity.

High Hopes Media
USA

High Hopes was the label of The Crustaceans, a Seattle-based pop cabaret band founded in 1977 and active into the mid-eighties. They were active in the antiwar and antinuclear movements, and released a single 7″ in 1983—"Dear Ronnie." The record cover, a faux letter to Ronald Reagan featuring an affixed stamp and cancellation mark, was designed by Art Chantry.

Hilltown Records
USA

The name of the label references the hilltowns of Western Massachusetts, nestled between the Green and Hoosac mountain ranges, and specifically Holyoke, Hadley, and Amherst—a cluster of towns with long ties to social justice movements that have become home to robust lesbian communities since the seventies. Hilltown released at least a couple LPs in the mid-eighties, one by lesbian singer-songwriter Catherine D'Amato and another by lifelong peace activist, minister, and folk singer Andrea Ayvazian.

Hippycore
USA

Hippycore was a small Arizona hardcore punk label that released six 7"s between 1988 and 1990. Two of the records were benefit compilations: *Metal Gives Us A Headache*, with proceeds supporting animal rights, and *Earth Rapers and Hell Raisers*, a double 7" in support of the Earth Liberation Front. Hippycore also published the influential vegan cookbook *Soy Not Oi!* In 1990. Key Hippycore member Joel Olson went on to become an editor of the seminal anarchist punk newspaper (and record label) *Profane Existence*, join the Love and Rage Anarchist Federation, and eventually help found Bring the Ruckus, a radical political organization focused on race as the key to unlocking radical social change in U.S. society.

HKA Productions
Hong Kong

This is the label used to release a 1989 Tiananmen Square commemorative LP called 血染的風采 (紀念歌集), which roughly translating to "Bloodstained glory (Memorial songbook)." The record sleeve and notes are entirely in Chinese, but the album appears to be both in censure of the Chinese government for the violence at Tiananmen, but also in support of the *ideals* of Chinese Communism, with renditions of both "L'Internationale" and classic Chinese Communist songs included. The musicians on the

record are largely from Taiwan and Hong Kong, but some of the lyrics were written by mainland Chinese authors. The cover features an image of the Goddess of Democracy, a thirty-foot-high statue of a woman carrying a torch constructed by students of the Central Academy of Fine Arts as part of the protests at Tiananmen Square. It became a popular representation of the revolt, with replicas created in solidarity across the globe.

Hot Wire
USA

Hot Wire, subtitled "The Journal of Women's Music and Culture," released thirty issues between November 1984 and September 1994. Most of the issues featured a flexi disc (or what they called a "soundsheet") stapled to the back cover, each one double-sided and holding recordings by at least two female musicians or bands. Not all the music was political, but a significant amount of it was explicitly feminist, with a lot of queer content.

IDAF Records
UK

The International Defence and Aid Fund was an organization founded in 1956 to support and fund those facing trial in South Africa for organizing against apartheid. Eventually the group was banned in South Africa and moved to London, where they became part of the broader solidarity movement for independence in southern Africa. They had a rigorous publishing schedule of books and pamphlets, and in 1984 they launched a record label, pressing *Namibia Will Be Free* by Onyeka (The Torch), the cultural group of SWAPO. As far as I know, this was the only album the label ever released, but see also Defence and Aid Fund. A song from the LP was re-released in 1985 as the B-side to Robert Wyatt and the SWAPO Singers' "Winds of Change" single on Rough Trade.

ifk
West Germany

A small political label organized by the Initiative Fortschrittlicher Kulturschaffender (Initiative of the Progressive Cultural Worker, usually stylized as "ifk" in all lowercase), which was founded in 1976 by musicians, theater people, designers, and filmmakers connected to the political krautrock bands Oktober and Schmetterlinge. Interested in delving deeper into political organizing, ifk initially focused on antinuclear work, and collaborated with the label Verlag Arbeiterkampf to release the 1977 compilation *Wehrt Euch!* (Defend Yourselves!). ifk then started its own label to release its next project, the 1978 the compilation *Keiner oder Alle* (All or None), a broad collection of krautrock, polit-folk, and political theater songs about diverse issues including the antinuclear movement, prisons, and police repression.

İmece Plâkları
Turkey

The label of Ruhi Su, a left-wing Turkish folk singer and saz player. Su joined the Turkish Communist Party in the 1940s, and in 1952 was imprisoned for five years for being a Communist, effectively ending his career as an opera singer. Upon his release he travelled the Anatolian peninsula playing traditional Anatolian folk music in a Western format, effectively creating a new Turkish song style. While he often avoided directly ideological themes, he sung in direct support of the oppressed. In the sixties he joined the Turkish Workers' Party (which, like the Turkish Communist Party—with which it eventually merged in 1987—has been banned multiple times in Turkey).

Imedyazen
France

The record label of the Algerian protest band Imaziɣhen Imula. The band, made up of Berber activists and led by Ferhat Imaziɣhen Imula (aka Ferhat Mehenni), played protest songs in the Kabyle style.

Im-Hotep Records
USA

A Harlem-based, Black nationalist record label that released five records in 1973 and '74. Three of these are by jazz drummer Roy Brooks and his group The Artistic Truth, including the LPs *Ethnic Expressions* and *Black Survival: "The Sahal Concert" at Town Hall*—a benefit concert to battle drought in the Sahel region of Africa. One of the other records is a spoken word LP titled An Historical Narrative: The Black Bill of Rights, written and recorded by Robert Harris and Gus Williams, disciples of Marcus Garvey.

Imparja Records
Australia

An Indigenous Australian label that released two LPs by the band Coloured Stone, and a cassette by Ilkari Maru. It was connected to CAAMA (the Central Australian Aboriginal Media Association), the organization that released the majority of Aboriginal music in the eighties and nineties, although entirely on cassette and CD.

Imprenta Naciõñal de Cuba
Cuba

This was the first attempt by revolutionary Cuba to nationalize the music industry. The label ran from 1961–64, until it was retired and replaced by EGREM.

Indian Records
USA

After its initial release in 1964 (*12 Northern Cheyenne War Dance Songs*), Indian Records went on to produce and release 106 field recordings of Native American music, chants, and songs from across North America.

INALD
Angola

INALD stands for the Instituto Nacional do Livro e do Disco. The label roughly ran throughout the eighties and released a range of Angolan music, including a number of albums of kids' songs informed by Angolan folk traditions, and an undated compilation album (likely from the early eighties) titled *1º Festival Nacional de Trabalhadores* (1st National Workers' Festival).

Indisha
Honduras

This label released a 1986 LP of politicized corridos titled *Luz y Fuerza* (Light and Power) by the musical group of the Sindicato de Trabajadores de la Empresa Nacional de Energía Eléctrica Honduras (Union of Workers of the Honduran National Electric Company). The record includes songs such as "Honduras Tierra de Paz" (Honduras, Land of Peace) and "El Mundo Gira al Reves" (The World Turned Upside Down). Formed in 1981 as the musical wing of the union, the group's focus was touring the country to build class consciousness through song. I don't believe the Indisha label was related directly to the band, and might have just been a general-purpose label in Honduras, but I have yet to find any other records it released.

Index Records
USA

Index was the label of working-class lesbian and feminist singer-songwriter Ila Meyer. She used this label name (taken from the town in which she lived, Index, Washington) to release her 1981 folk LP, *The Woman That I Am*. Meyer also set up her own publishing company, called Womansong.

Initiative für Demokratie und Umweltschutz
West Germany

This is the name used to release a late seventies

7″ by a group calling themselves Bunte Liste/ Wehrt Euch (Colorful List/Resist). There is scant information on the record and sleeve, but I believe this is connected to the small Lower Saxony political party Wählern/Wählerinnen Initiative für Demokratie und Umweltschutz (Voters' Initiative for Democracy and Environmental Protection), which in 1980 merged with the a number of like-minded groups to form Die Grünen (The Green Party).

Initiativgruppe KKW-Nein!
West Germany

An action group that organized against both a lead plant in Marckolsheim and a nuclear power plant in Wyhl, both in the Baden-Alsatian area on the German border with France. The group released a 7″ of polit-folk by Walter Mossman in support of their actions, which was packaged in an oversized gatefold sleeve that folded out into a infosheet about the struggle. The record features no label name beyond the political group, but was distributed by Trikont.

INSTITUTE OF POSITIVE EDUCATION

Institute of Positive Education
USA

The Institute was a Black nationalist educational organization set up in 1969 by Haki R. Madhubuti, his wife Safisha Madhubuti, and others in Chicago in the seventies (and still exists on Chicago's South Side). It released a single LP, Madhubuti and the Afrikan Liberation Art Ensemble's jazz/poetry album *Rise Vision Comin* in 1976 (co-released with a DC-based sister project called Nation House).

Instituto Cubano de Amistad con los Pueblos
Cuba

The Instituto Cubano de Amistad con los Pueblos (Cuban Institute of Friendship with the People, sometimes referred to as ICAP) is a Havana-based, internationalist cultural and political organization. It's propaganda wing released a couple LPs of Castro speeches in the 1960s, and then another half dozen records of Cuban musicians for international distribution in the seventies and eighties. ICAP functioned as one of a series of sublabels of the Cuban state label EGREM.

EDIÇÃO DO
INSTITUTO NACIONAL DO LIVRO E DO DISCO

Instituto Nacional do Livro e do Disco
Mozambique

Not to be confused with its Angolan counterpart INALD, this Instituto Nacional do Livro e do Disco usually had its name written out, and released and/or distributed a handful of LPs after the Mozambican Revolution, including a 1983 LP narrating the rise and triumph of the Frente de Libertação de Moçambique (FRELIMO, or Mozambique Liberation Front) against the Portuguese colonizers titled *FRELIMO: Libertad e Revolução*.

International Physicians for the Prevention of Nuclear War
International

This Nobel Peace Prize–winning organization, which represents doctors and health workers from sixty-three countries, released a 1986 LP of classical music with a pretty straightforward descriptive title:

Swedish Physicians in Concert for the Prevention of Nuclear War. The album features songs written by Bach and Handel, as well as a couple Black gospel tunes. In addition, the record comes with a booklet that gives background on the organization and on the concert of which this is a recording.

International Union of Students
Czechoslovakia

The IUS was founded in 1946 as an umbrella organization for university student organizations from over one hundred nations across the globe. Although it claimed nonpartisanship, it functioned as a Communist entity, if not a total puppet of the Comintern. Its record label released two LPs in the seventies, both titled *Songs of Struggle and Protest*. While one is a collection of international protest songs, the other is a Chile solidarity record, one side all Victor Jara, the other mostly Quilapayún, with additional songs by the Parras and Inti-Illimani.

Intersound
Sweden

A small Swedish folk label whose inaugural release in 1969 was an LP of Joe Hill tunes sung by socialist singer-songwriter Finn Zetterholm. Another record dedicated to Hill would be released the following year, and for the next decade the label put out about three dozen recordings, many by the stable of lefty Swedish folk musicians who also recorded for Amalthea, Silence, and YTF.

IRA Records
Greece

The label of composer and musician George Georgiades, which released a half dozen records in the mid-seventies, including two highly politicized concept albums in 1976, one concerned with international solidarity, the other a document of a Greek National Theater production about the military junta titled Να Μη Ξαναματώση (Do Not Go Back).

IRT
Chile

The state radio and television company in Chile, which has released music and field recordings on vinyl on and off since the early seventies. It was particularly active from 1971–73 under the Popular Unity (UP) government, releasing a number of pop records, but also a series of documentary LPs celebrating the work of the UP in Chile, a political spoken word record by a group calling themselves Los Tupamaros, and a number of nueva canción LPs by Amerindios. The politics disappeared after the coup on '73.

Italia Canta
Italy

Italia Canta was the original home of the Cantacronache, a group of left-wing musicians who unearthed and politicized Italian folk songs as a tool for struggle. The label was founded in 1956 and ran until 1963, when the name was changed to DNG. On top of about fifteen albums of Italian political folk, it also released records documenting revolutionary music in Angola, Cuba, and the Soviet Union.

IUSY
Austria

The International Union of Socialist Youth is a consortium of social-democratic and labor-union youth organizations from around the world. It is part of the Socialist International (of which the Democratic Socialists of America is also a member). In the seventies, it released a compilation LP titled *Songs of Struggle and Solidarity*, with fifteen songs from political folk groups connected to the tendency from across the globe.

IZ Disketxea
Basque Country

Folk and rock label founded in 1975 and dedicated to the release of music in the Basque language, including protest records by Imanol, Gontzal Mendibil, and a compilation of antinuclear songs (co-released with Herri Gogoa and Tic-Tac).

Jabula
UK

The label of the band Jabula, made up of South African musicians in exile in the UK. The label put out four LPs, a couple of which were original, and a couple re-pressings of earlier albums released on larger labels. The group also licensed its music to left-leaning labels in Germany (Pläne), Sweden (A Disc), and the Netherlands (VARAgram). Much of Jabula's music was a response to, and commentary on, apartheid and the struggle for African liberation.

Jår'galæd'dji
Norway

Jår'galæd'dji was a music and book publisher founded by Odd Ivar and Aage Solbakk in 1974. It was the largest and most significant Sami publisher in the seventies and eighties, and the early LPs it released were pressed and distributed by leftist label Plateselskapet Mai. The Sami people are Indigenous to the northern parts of Finland, Sweden, and Norway and a small part of Russia, and speak a family of languages also known as Sami.

JCOA Records
USA

The record label of the Jazz Composer's Orchestra Association, Inc., JCOA was explicitly nonprofit, and began releasing records in 1968. It pressed nine unique records, many with multiple re-presses featuring alternative cover art and reworked song listings. The label and organization were founded by Carla Bley and Michael Mantler, and the label's records reflect their belief in jazz rooted in social engagement. The Jazz Composer's Orchestra, at different times, has included Anthony Braxton, Don Cherry, Pharoah Sanders, Clifford Thorton, and over two dozen others.

Jeunesse de Front de Libération Nationale
Algeria

The youth wing of the FLN, or National Liberation Front, which successfully fought the French in what has come to be known as the Algerian War, and forced the colonial power to sign a ceasefire in 1962 and initiate full independence. Although autocratic after coming to power, the FLN has remained part of the Socialist International, and the youth wing has tended to be further left-leaning than the parent party. The Jeunesse de Front de Libération Nationale (JFLN) released a couple of undated records, seemingly from the sixties, which feature a mix of speeches (some by charismatic freedom fighter and first president of Algeria Ahmed Ben Bella) and Kabyle music.

Jihad Productions
USA

Jihad Productions is the name of both a book publishing house and a short-lived record label based in Newark, New Jersey and run by militant Black poet Amiri Baraka né LeRoi Jones. The label only released a handful of albums, including a 1965 Sonny Murray LP, and two 1968 LPs by Jones, one a musical with the Sun Ra Arkestra doing the music—*A Black Mass*—and the other by his group The Jihad—*Black and Beautiful. . .Soul and Madness*.

JMPLA
Angola

The youth wing of the political party MPLA (Movimento Popular de Libertação de Angola, or People's Movement for the Liberation of Angola), which freed Angola from Portuguese colonialism in 1975. The group worked with the Dutch solidarity group Angola Comité to release an LP titled *A Vitória é Certa* (Victory is Certain) by Agrupamento Kissanguela, a musical group that strongly supported the Angolan Revolution.

Jobs for a Change
UK

Jobs for a Change was a series of music festivals organized by the Greater London Council (GLC) starting in June of 1984. The concerts were free, and intended as a protest against unemployment under the Thatcher government, but also in support of the miners' strike and against Thatcher's plans to defund the GLC. Community groups tabled at the events, small agitprop theater was performed, and huge rosters of politicized bands played, including Aswad, Billy Bragg, The Communards, The Flying Pickets, Thomas Mapfumo, The Pogues, and Redskins. A free flexi disc was produced in support of the campaign, featuring a song by The Flying Pickets.

JOC-JOCF
France

JOC is the record label of the *jocistes*, members of the Jeunesse Ouvrière Chrétienne (Christian

Youth Workers), a Catholic union movement founded in Belgium in 1925, with its core constituents being young working-class people. JOCF is the women's wing of the organization. It spread internationally, but its core has always been Francophone. Relatively collective and collaborative, its founders were part of the resistance to the Nazis, and it took an even further turn to the left in 1969, embracing class struggle in the wake of the protests and revolutionary movements of 1968. The French wing put out a handful of 7″s in the seventies, one a document of protest songs from the apprentice movement, another a document of the group's fiftieth anniversary.

John Paul Records
USA

This appears to be an ad hoc label used to release Paul August's 1982 7″, "Mindworker" b/w "We Teach the Children." Both songs are about the struggles of being a teacher. "Mindworker" is a synth new wave jam, and "We Teach the Children" is a light prog rock rendition of the theme song of the National Education Association.

De Jongleurs
Belgium

The label of the political theater group Kollektief Internationale Nieuwe Scene, later known more simply as Internationale Nieuwe Scene. Influenced by both Dario Fo and Bertolt Brecht, they used music and theater to address political issues from a revolutionary perspective. The label, whose name translates to "The Jugglers," released at least two vinyl LPs in the eighties. The group had self-released a number

of records in the seventies and early eighties, but don't appear to have started using the name "De Jongleurs" until 1984.

Jota Jota
Chile

The record label of the Juventudes Comunistas Chilenas (Communist Youth of Chile, or JJCC), with the name derived from the group's nickname, "La Jota." From 1968 to 1970 it released about ten records of nueva canción chilena before changing names to "DICAP." Although it only released records by musicians from Chile, the label's internationalism was apparent in the choice of its initial release, Quilapayún's *Por Viet-nam*.

Jumbo
UK

A label dedicated exclusively to releasing material related to pirate and offshore radio. It released double LP collections documenting Radio Caroline and Radio Nordsee, and the record I have is a nice double 7″ collection of radio jingles from one hundred offshore stations.

June Appal
USA

The record label started by Appalshop in 1974. Appalshop is an organization dedicated to the folk and cultural traditions of Appalachia. It is also the home to the Mountain Musicians Cooperative, which released the 1975 benefit LP *Brown Lung Cotton Mill Blues*, as well as a dozen additional country and folk LPs addressing Appalachian social struggles, particularly around mining.

Jungsozialisten in der SPD
West Germany

The youth wing of the Social Democratic Party of Germany. Beginning in 1969, the Jungsozialisten (Jusos) swung to the far left of the larger party, proclaiming an explicitly feminist, socialist, and internationalist position. In 1972, it helped organize a demonstration against a proposed chemical plant in Rheinberg for environmental reasons, and released a 7″ of two songs that the folk-rock group Kattong performed at the protest.

Ka KKW-Records
Austria

An ad hoc label used to release the 1977 antinuclear benefit LP *1. Österr. Anti-Atomkraftwerksplatte*, a collection of folk songs assembled by the Anti-AKW group, an antinuclear activist organization.

Kalakuta Records
Nigeria

The label on which Afrobeat superstar Fela Kuti released his albums in Nigeria from 1976–92. It

was during this period when Fela was the most vocal in his criticism of the government. He seceded from the country to set up the "Kalakuta Republic" and was brutally beaten and imprisoned for his music and activism. The strident politics can be seen in the album titles: *Authority Stealing*, *Coffin for Head of State*, *International Thief Thief*. Most of these records are now extremely rare, and have been re-pressed by multiple labels, including Barclay, Stern's Africa, and most recently Knitting Factory Records.

Kāllan
Sweden

Similar to EKO, another small progg label, Kāllan released three to four records in the late seventies, including one that is explicitly antinuclear.

Kansankulttuuri Oy
Finland

Originally founded in 1940 as a publishing house for Soviet literature in Finland, the label (its name translates to "People's Culture") began pressing records in 1969. Early records are either workers' songs or folk songs from across the USSR, and within a couple years all of the records were pressed by Melodiya in the Soviet Union. Although owned privately, it is clear that the label was used primarily to extend Soviet ideology into Finland and to create another market for Soviet recordings. The "Oy" at the end of the name simply means "Ltd." in Finnish.

KARAXÚ

Karaxu
France

Karaxu was a crew of young Chilean musicians in exile in France after the 1973 coup in Chile. They supported the MIR (a pro-armed struggle Marxist group) and used nueva canción chilena as a vehicle to spread their politics. They released records on Arbeiterkampf, Expression Spontanée, R-Edition, and Trikont, as well as pressing a Swedish edition of their first LP—named *Rebellisk Musik* here—under their own Karaxu name in 1975.

Karibe
Barbados

Karibe released a 1981 12″ by soca performer Flying Turkey celebrating the Marxist revolution in Grenada in 1979. "Innocent Blood" and "Freedom Day" are both tracks that explicitly support revolution and the working class of this small Caribbean nation.

KGM Records
South Africa

The label of South Africa musician Blondie Makhene. Makhene had a successful career as a Afro-synth/disco star in the eighties, and in the early nineties formed the group Amaqabane (the Xhosa word for fellowship), which played a socially conscious African funk. Their second LP was released on KGM in 1991, and features a number of pro-African National Congress songs, including "Woza ANC" (Come to the ANC) and

"Joyin' Umkhonto We Sizwe" (Umkhonto We Sizwe was the armed wing of the ANC).

King Kong Records
Netherlands

Rotterdam-based label run by the Rondos, who along with The Ex were one of the most influential Dutch political punk bands. The label only put out a handful of releases, including records by Rondos, Railbirds, and Tändstickorshocks. If The Ex were the anarchists of the scene, Rondos were the communists (including reclaiming as their logo the red triangle that the Nazis used to mark communists in the death camps).

Kill Rock Stars
USA

A broad-spectrum independent music label from Olympia, WA, Kill Rock Stars is important here for being the label of Riot Grrrl progenitors Bikini Kill, as well as other feminist acts Bratmobile, Mecca Normal, and Penny Arcade.

Le Kiosque d'Orphée
France

Founded in the fifties, Le Kiosque d'Orphée was as much a facilitator of independent releases as a label in its own right. While it did release records under its own name, it also helped manufacture and distribute a wide range of self-organized releases by political groupings, experimental musicians, independent chanson singers, and more. I've got a number of the records it helped produce, including antinuclear polka, communist folk from Comoros, and student protest chanson.

KKLA
Netherlands

With a focus exclusively on Latin America, KKLA released about twenty-five albums from the late seventies to the late eighties. Most of the music was connected to political struggles in Nicaragua (the Mejía Godoy brothers), El Salvador (Cutumay Camones), Guatemala (Kin-Lalat), and Uruguay (Numa Moraes). KKLA records were also released in other countries by Discos Pueblos, Ocarina, Paredon, Pläne, and others. KKLA is an acronym for "Kultuur Kollektief Latijns Amerika," but the half dozen records I have refer to it by its acronym.

Kofia
Sweden

The label of the band of the same name, a Swedish Palestine-solidarity troupe founded by Palestinian singer George Totari and populated by a large, evolving group of Swedish musicians. Although put out under its own name, Kofia's three records (released between 1976 and 1984) were produced and distributed by Plattlangarna.

KomistA
Germany

KomistA began in the late eighties as an

experimental cassette label, then in 1991 began releasing vinyl, including a 7″ compilation of anarchist punk and noise bands (titled *Six Ways...*, with a back cover stating "Documents of Music and Change #1"). It also released a 7″ recording of a John Cage composition, and a double 7″ of Washington, DC political punk band Soul Side recorded live in Germany in 1989.

Komitee für Frieden und Abrüstung und Zusammenarbeit
West Germany

A peace organization (whose name translates to "Committee for Peace and Disarmament and Cooperation") that released a seventies LP of live antinuclear folk music by activist and singer-songwriter Fasia Jansen, titled *"Los kommt mit": Ostermarsch-Lieder an der Abschussramp* ("Come with me": Easter March Songs at the Launch Pad).

Kommunistisk Ungdom
Sweden

Label of the Swedish Communist Youth Organization, which released a 7″ in 1983 by polit-folk singer Pierre Ström (who has also recorded with the labels Intersound and YTF). Members of the group Röda Kapellet were also part of the organization, even though they released their music through other labels (Arbeitarkultur, Avanti, and Fredsång).

Komotion International
USA

Komotion was a club, recording studio, art

gallery, and cassette magazine based in San Francisco and cofounded by Mat Callahan, who had been half of the communist folk act Prairie Fire. Although not a label per se, Komotion was at the center of the Bay Area political music scene in the late eighties, helping spawn groups such as The Disposable Heroes of Hiphoprisy and Pansy Division.

Konkurrel
Netherlands

Began in the mid-eighties as a home for politicized and experimental punk, including the Dog Faced Hermans, De Kift, and Social Unrest. They also released a series of benefit LPs for active political struggles, two for the anti-apartheid movement in South Africa and one in support of the first Intifada in Palestine. It was a sublabel of the larger, and less focused, Konkurrent.

Korean Gramophone Company (조선레코드)
North Korea

North Korea, or the Democratic People's Republic of Korea, set up the Korean Gramophone Company soon after the Korean War ended in the mid-fifties, initially pressing 78 rpm shellac records. Between the sixties and the nineties, it released a couple hundred vinyl records, often 10″s, a format also popular with the Chinese state label, Zhongguo Changpian. The content of the records is also similar to China, with equal parts martial music, revolutionary opera, and the words of the Benevolent and Great Leader Kim Il Sung.

KPFA
USA

Based in Berkeley, California, KPFA is the flagship station of the Pacifica Radio Network, a left alternative to National Public Radio in the US. The station has produced a number of albums. The first was a folk, speech, and poetry compilation in 1961 that featured a Pete Seeger song and Rev. Ralph Abernathy discussing the Civil Rights Movement. The station followed this with a 1964 LP of field recordings from the Free Speech Movement, titled *Is Freedom Academic?* It then went on to release a small series of folk and poetry records, mostly recorded at the station.

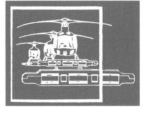

Kronchtadt Tapes
France

Political punk/noise/dub label set up in 1982 by Laurent Malfois, initially to release his band Kommando Holger Meins (named after a military unit of the Red Army Faction that carried out an attack on the West German embassy in Sweden in 1975, which itself was named after one of the original RAF members who died on hunger strike in a German prison in '74). Primarily a cassette label, only a half dozen of its twenty or so releases were on vinyl, including the 1985 compilation of political punk *Les héros du peuple sont immortels* (The heroes of the people are immortal), co-released with like-minded punk label Gougnaf Mouvement.

Ladyslipper
USA

Ladyslipper was launched as a record label in the early eighties to release records by feminist and lesbian classical and jazz musicians such as Debbie Fier, Sue Fink, and Kay Gardner. It quickly expanded to include folk and rock musicians, and began distributing other feminist and lesbian releases, especially those that were on smaller labels or self-released (including Women's Wax Works and Ani DiFranco's initial self-produced cassette album in 1990). In addition, it distributed international feminist music in the US, importing women's music from across Europe, including albums on Demos, Hexensaite, and more.

Landelijk Vietnamkomitee
Netherlands

Landelijk Vietnamkomitee (Rural Vietnam Committee) was a Dutch solidarity organization that released a single LP in 1972, an experimental jazz record composed by Konrad Boehmer. Released as *Voor de overwinning van de vietnamese revolutie* (For the victory of the Vietnamese revolution) in the Netherlands, a German edition was also released by a group called the Nationales Vietnamkomitee under the title *Alles für den Sieg des Kämpfenden Vietnamesischen Volkes!* (Everything for the Victory of the Fighting Vietnamese People!)

Larrikin Records
Australia

The Australian Folkways, or maybe more appropriately the Australian Rounder, Larrikin was founded by Warren Fahey in 1974 as an extension of his Folkways Music store. The label quickly became one of the largest independent folk and country outfits in Australia, and released a number of highly politicized groups (such as Redgum and Black Diamond Corner) and compilation albums (*On the Steps of the Dole Office Door* and *Rebel Chorus: A Concert of Contemporary Political Song*). Larrikin was also one of the first labels to release records by Aboriginal musicians.

Lengua Armada Discos
USA

Founded in Chicago by Los Crudos vocalist Martin Sorrondeguy, Lengua Armada has released about eighty records since 1993. Initially focused on Spanish-language hardcore, this was one of the first labels to give voice to the growing Chicanx, Latinx, and Latin American punk scene in the US. The label's range spread to political punk from Chicago and then even more broadly, but the focus has consistently been on bands with political and internationalist intentions.

Leona Records Corporation
USA

A small and local Corpus Christi, Texas label that released a number of important Chicano records in the late seventies, including Little Joe y La Familia's *La Voz de Aztlan* and Big Lu Valeny's *El Corazon de la Nacion*.

Lesbian Feminist Liberation
USA

A New York City–based political grouping involved in the release and distribution of *A Few Loving Women*, a 1973 lesbian folk LP featuring a consortium of lesbian musicians, including Lee Crespi, Jeriann Hilderly (also known as Jeritree), Roberta Kosse, Margaret Sloan, Mary Solberg, and Lucy and Martha Wilde.

Liberation Music
USA

This was the name used by Sid Brown to release the initial eponymous 10" EP by his Peace, Bread & Land Band. In the mid-sixties, Brown had been in the Detroit folk rock band the Spike-Drivers, then moved to Berkeley, enrolled in the Ali Akbar College of Music, and the Eastern-influenced psychedelic sound of Peace, Bread & Land was formed. The highly politicized 10" features a Ho Chi Minh song set to music and covers of two songs written by Black Panther Party leader Elaine Brown.

LIBERATION

Liberation Records
UK

The label used to release recordings from the Dialectics of Liberation Congress in London in July 1967. Recordings include Allen Ginsberg, Paul

Goodman, Stokely Carmichael, Herbert Marcuse, and more. Almost all the records feature identical covers, with a grid of photographs of the Congress speakers printed in magenta/purple and a list of twenty-three LP releases on the back—the specific record is only noted on the vinyl labels themselves. Not all twenty-three records were released; only about eighteen saw the light of day before the project ran out of steam.

Liberation Support Movement
Canada

LSM was a North American solidarity organization which existed from 1968 to 1982. Marxist and anti-imperialist, it primarily sought to build support within the US and Canada for African liberation movements. LSM built direct connections with representatives of movements from Angola, Mozambique, Namibia, South Africa, Zimbabwe, and more. With its own printshop and an ambitious political program, LSM published dozens of pamphlets, newsletters, posters, buttons, and records. It put out one LP on its own, *Africa in Revolutionary Music* (undated), and then had its field recordings used for an album of Angolan songs on Paredon, as well as in tracks on a Charlie Haden LP.

Liga de Unidade e Acção Revolucionária
Portugal

A Portuguese far-left political party that was founded in exile in the sixties. The Liga de Unidade e Acção Revolucionária (LUAR, or League of Unity and Revolutionary Action) existed as an armed underground group until the Carnation Revolution in Portugal, when it emerged and became one of dozens of new political parties. Like many parties in postrevolution Portugal, LUAR released a record— one 7″ by José Afonso, with "Viva o Poder Popular" (Long Live the People's Power) on the A side, and his rendition of the traditional folk song "Foi na Cidade do Sado" on the B side.

Ligue Suisse pour la Protection de la Nature
Switzerland

The Swiss League for the Protection of Nature released a single 7″ in 1970, titled *SOS Nature*, that featured four tracks of environmental-themed Swiss chanson.

Lilla Raven Records
Sweden

The label name used to put out a 1980 LP of the Energioperan, or Energy Opera, which featured a twenty-three-piece orchestra and forty-eight-person choir performing fifteen songs about and against nuclear power in Sweden.

Lima Bean Records
USA

A Washington, DC label created to release music by lesbian-feminist country music singer-

songwriter Willie Tyson. It released 1974's *Full Court* LP, 1979's *Willie Tyson*, and a 7″ version of "You'd Look Swell In Nothing." Tyson also released an LP on Urana Records.

Lince Producciones
Argentina

A label which ran from the late sixties into the seventies. It put out around two dozen records of nueva canción, nueva trova, speeches, and poetry, all focused on Latin American and Spanish politics, from left and populist positions, including lots of Chileans such as Rolando Alarcón, Quilapayún, and the Parras, as well as Che speeches and songs from the Spanish Civil War.

Linea Rossa
Italy

A singles-only sublabel of I Dischi del Sole, from 1967 to 1974 the project released about two dozen 7″s. I'm not 100 percent sure what distinguishes these releases from the parent label's list—many appear very directly anarchist and communist, but not all of them. It released two separate 7″s with songs about murdered anarchist Giuseppe Pinelli, as well as a 7″ dedicated to the release of Giovanni Marini, a young anarchist poet imprisoned in the early seventies for killing a fascist student in a street fight. In 1970, the label also released a jukebox version of one of its singles, implying a significant level of popularity among young people.

Lion's Roar Records
USA

The label of singer-songwriter/activist Lenny Anderson, which he used to release his eighties LPs *A Song Would Be Better* and *Hot Off the Press*. Lenny is best described by the text on the back cover of *Hot Off the Press*: "Sixteen years ago I bought my Gibson Hummingbird and started picking and singing a bunch of Dylan and Guthrie tunes. About the same time I began running an offset press for the Draft Resistance, printing flyers and pamphlets. I've been juggling music and printing ever since."

Live Oak Records
USA

An ad hoc label used to release Bill Oliver's 1982 *Texas Oasis: Environmental Songs for Texas and the World*, an album-length country music ode to the natural world in Texas. The record was produced and distributed by the Lone Star Sierra Club with support from dozens of additional Texas-based environmental organizations. (Not to be confused with the *other* Live Oak Records from Texas, a born-again Christian label.)

Local 1199 Drug and Hospital Union
USA

Originally a base for unionized drugstore workers, Local 1199 was a far-left New York City–based union that began heavily organizing Black and Puerto Rican hospital workers in the sixties. It released an LP of excerpts of a speech Martin Luther King, Jr. gave at the union on March 10, 1968, less than a month before his murder. The album, called simply *At Local 1199*, includes King discussing and praising the union directly. By the eighties, 1199 had spread across more than a half dozen states and began to splinter from its base in the Retail, Wholesale, and Department Store Union (RWDSU), with most districts eventually joining the Service Employees International Union in the eighties, becoming 1199SEIU. *See also* Bread and Roses.

LONGO MAÏ

Longo Maï
Switzerland

A Swiss label run by political folk musician Willi Stelzhammer. It only put out a handful of records in the seventies, including a sprawling double album of antifascist songs called just that, *Antifaschistische Lieder*. Stelzhammer was part of a group of antiauthoritarian students from Switzerland who bought a parcel of land in the Alps in 1973 to set up an anticapitalist commune and farming coop, also called Longo Maï.

Longview Records
USA

Longview was Roy Berkeley's label once he moved up to Shaftsbury, Vermont in the early seventies. He used the name to release his 1979 LP of labor and Depression-era songs, *Songs of the FDR Years*. Berkeley was mainly a folk singer, but he also had a brief career in rockabilly, and also performed as a bluegrass guitarist in the Old Reliable String Band with Tom Paxton. In his early years, Berkeley had been a Trotskyist, but in the nineties he swung to the right, joining the NRA and becoming a local deputy sheriff.

Loony Tunes
UK

Loony Tunes was started in 1986 as the label for the anarcho-punk bank Active Minds. The initial dozen records also included a number of compilations, the *Destroy Fascism!* 7″ by Antidote (a supergroup of sorts mixing members of Chumbawamba and The Ex), and UK anarcho-punk bands Alternative Attack, Atavistic, and Generic. The label has been doggedly committed to releasing only vinyl, still presses records, and has released fifty-two in its thirty-two-year run.

Lotta Continua
Italy

Lotta Continua was an extraparliamentary far-left group active in Italy from the late sixties into the late seventies. While it was important as an organization, it was most known for its newspaper, which from 1972–74 was a daily. Between 1969–1974, the organization released a series of about fifteen 7″ singles, most of them by Pino Masi, a political folk singer from the Gruppo del Canzoniere Pisano. Many of the records seem as if they were theme songs for Lotta Continua political campaigns, such as "Prendiamoci la Città" (Take Over the City) and "L'Anno del Fucile" (Year of the Gun). At least some of the records were released as supplements to—and distributed in—the newspaper. Also connected to the label Circulo Ottobre.

Love Records
Finland

Love was one of the largest independent labels

in Finland. Founded in 1966 by musicians Otto Donner and Christian Schwindt and producer and critic Atte Bloom, it ran for fourteen years and released over seven hundred vinyl records. It manufactured and distributed both Cuba and Eteepain!, a couple of much smaller political labels, but also has some political output in its own right. In the sixties and early seventies it pressed records in solidarity with Vietnam and Latin America, by the political community theater troupe KOM-Teatteri, and by the Marxist folk group Agit-Prop.

Love Conquers All
UK

An interesting subproject of small UK disco label TMT. It appears as if it put out one record, a 7″ with a deep funk track titled "Thank You, We Love You" by The Power of Love, mixed with speech elements from Nelson Mandela and Oliver Tambo of the African National Congress. The record is undated, but likely from the early nineties and timed to coincide with Mandela's release from prison.

Macondo
Uruguay

A small independent label which ran roughly from 1968–79. It had a broad output of Latin American music, including politicized psychedelic folk, blues, rock bands El Sindykato and Montevideo Blues, the Chilean folk singer Rolando Alarcón, a poetry 7″ by Pablo Neruda, as well as a number of cumbia acts. The name is most likely taken from the fictional town in Gabriel Garcia Márquez's novel *One Hundred Years of Solitude*, first published in 1967.

Manchester Greenham Common Women's Support Group
UK

Solidarity organization that released a 7″ of feminist folk in 1983 to support women protesting nuclear weapons at the Greenham Common military base.

MANIFEST

Manifest
Sweden

Rock/folk label that released a little over three dozen records between 1975 and 1985. Early records had a political slant, with a focus on progg as well as historically Nordic folk music. Produced and distributed by the larger label MNW.

MANIFESTO

Manifesto
Greece/Italy

A joint Greek and Italian project, Manifesto released a small number of records in the late seventies, which appear to have been pressed in Italy with the intent of distributing them in Greece. Releases include an album of international revolutionary songs (*Chants de la Revolution des Peuples*, featuring a picture of Che on the cover), a field recording of the antifascist uprising at the Athens Polytechnic in 1973 when Greece was still ruled by a right-wing military junta, as well as a couple records of Greek protest music.

il manifesto

Il Manifesto
Italy

Small label run by the lefty newspaper of the same name. Almost the entire catalog was released only on CD, but its inaugural record was a Palestinian solidarity 7″ by an ad hoc group calling itself Coro Al Aqsa. This record accompanied issue 298 of the paper.

Marx-Disc
West Germany

This was a one-off label of the Deutsche Kommunistische Partei used to release a gimmick 7″ flexi disc by the fictitious rap group Kohl and the Gang. The record mocks then-chancellor Helmut Kohl for playing games while people are out of work and without prospects. The flexi is housed in a surprisingly hip-looking record sleeve for such a traditional Communist party, with a cover that states: "Dancing is good, says Marx. 'Man must force these petrified relationships to dance by giving them their own tune.'"

Mary Records, Inc.
USA

The label of Mary Lou Williams (born Mary Elfreda Winn). Williams used the label to release four albums and a number of 7″ singles from 1964–75. Williams is notable as one of the few women involved in the post-bop jazz scene, and while she is relatively unknown outside of jazz circles, the male musicians she wrote and arranged for, as well as played with, are household names: Duke Ellington, Charlie Parker, Miles Davis, Thelonious Monk, Dizzie Gillespie, and more. A pianist, she wrote and performed jazz that was more religious than overtly political, but she did release (on Mary Records) the 1970 LP *Music For Peace*.

Mascarones
Mexico

There appear to be two labels called Mascarones from Mexico in the 1970s, and it is quite difficult to separate them. One was a Mexico City-based theatre group who released a combination of music and theatre performance recordings and at different points collaborated with El Teatro Campesino. The other was a record label, book publisher, and project of the Centro Cultural Mascarones de Cuernavaca, a social center in Morelos, Mexico. The Centro was driven by the ideas of Mexican revolutionary Emiliano Zapata and the spirit of broader Latin American radicalism embodied by both Che Guevara (with his image used as a logo—actually Che was used by both Mascarones!), and Salvador Allende and his Unida Popular party in Chile.

Medisch Komitee Angola
Netherlands

Technically not a label, this was one of the organizations that helped produce a series of seventies Dutch solidarity records with southern Africa. It was connected to the Anti-Apartheids Beweging Nederland, and when not used as a label name, it is often listed as one of the

beneficiaries of the proceeds of record sales of Dutch southern African solidarity releases.

Melodiya (Мелодия)
USSR

The state label founded in 1964, which functionally monopolized the record industry in the Soviet Union. In its thirty years as the exclusive Soviet label, it released over twenty thousand recordings. The vast majority are not of interest here, but in that ocean there is a pool of insurgent political releases, including nueva canción and anti-imperialist folk from Latin America and Africa—from Victor Jara to Amandla, the cultural group of the African National Congress.

Menyah
USA

This label put out only one record, a 1976 recording of El Teatro Campesino performing songs of the United Farm Workers titled *¡Huelga en General!*

Merengue
Angola

Merengue was produced and distributed by the larger Angolan CDA label. The group Conjunto Merengue was the label's house band, and they are the lead or backing group on more than half of the label's seventy-five or so 7"s released in the mid- to late seventies. While much of the catalog is not expressly political, the excitement of Angola's liberation from Portugal can be felt in the records, especially in songs supporting the MPLA (People's Movement for the Liberation of Angola), women's liberation, vigilance for the revolution, and more.

Metro-Som
Portugal

Founded in 1974 by folk/prog musician Branco de Oliveira around the same time as the Carnation Revolution in Portugal. Several of the early releases were products of the revolution, from Arlindo de Carvalho's *Canções para a Liberdade* LP to a number of 7"s by Coro Nacional on behalf of the MFA (Movement of the Armed Forces, the left-wing generals who led the coup that launched the revolution).

Michga
USA

Focused on music from Haiti, this small label released a number of records by musicians critical of the Duvalier dictatorship, including Les Freres Parent, a group featuring Jean Jacques Parent, once an opposition figure, now a Haitian senator. Their 1986 record *Operation Dechoukaj* (Operation uprising) celebrates the general strike in February of that year against the Duvalier regime.

Michigan Interchurch Committee on Central American Human Rights
USA

This Detroit-based interfaith activist group released a single 7" in 1982, featuring two original folk songs dedicated to El Salvador and Nicaragua. The musicians are all amateurs, with careers as social workers, educators, and religious workers.

Milkyway
Netherlands

A label run by the Melkweg Club in Amsterdam. In the late seventies and early eighties it released about a dozen records documenting performances at the club, including an album from the 1979 Vrouwenfestival (Women's Fest), a series of *Africa Roots* compilations pulling together songs from highlife, soukous, and Zulu jive acts, and a double LP of political poetry with tracks by Ed Sanders (of the Fugs), Linton Kwesi Johnson, and Diane di Prima.

Miner Hits Records
UK

This is an ad hoc label name used to produce a 1984 7" by the Kellingley Colliery Band, recorded

and released in remembrance of Joe Green,
a North Yorkshire miner killed while picketing
during the miners' strike that year.

Ministry of Power
UK

Ministry of Power (MOP) was the label of the
London noise and industrial band Test Dept.
Although they usually had production and
distribution deals with other independent labels
(such as Invisible, Jungle, and Some Bizzare),
the band used this label name on most of
their releases in the eighties and early nineties,
starting with 1985's *Shoulder to Shoulder*, an LP
recorded with the South Wales Striking Miners
Choir and in support of the UK miners' strike.
Test Dept. was one of the more consistently left
of the eighties British industrial bands, recording
songs with amazing titles such as "Long Live
British Democracy Which Flourishes and Is
Constantly Perfected Under the Immaculate
Guidance of the Great, Honourable, Generous
and Correct Margaret Hilda Thatcher. She Is the
Blue Sky in the Hearts of All Nations. Our People
Pay Homage and Bow in Deep Respect and
Gratitude to Her. The Milk of Human Kindness."
(from their *A Good Night Out* LP, with the catalog
number "MOP 3").

Minos
Greece

Founded in 1960, Minos was the first label in
Greece to release rebetiko music. Rebetiko has
multiple origin points, but is basically working-
class Greek folk music that developed in poor
urban neighborhoods in the fifties and sixties.
It is a Greek parallel to nueva canción in Latin

America. Named after its founder, rebetiko
composer Minos Matsas, the label released
records by Panos Tzavelas, Manos Hatzidakis,
and Mikis Theodorakis. In 1991 it was purchased
by EMI and became a broad-based pop label
with no political sympathies.

MISEREOR

Misereor
West Germany

A small German religious label from the late
seventies and early eighties that grew out of a
recording studio of the same name, and released
politicized folk music in the tradition of liberation
theology. I have one album—a collection of songs
from Soweto titled *How Long Must We Suffer?*—
and have found listings for a half dozen more,
mostly music from the Americas (nueva canción,
Brazilian MPB, Haitian music) and a 7″ of music
from the Philippines.

MMM Records
Netherlands

The label name used to the release the satirical
punk LP *Miljoenen Magen* by Verz Ed. He was part
of the punk scene from Wormer in the northern
Netherlands, and connected to the band The Ex.
This record was released along with an issue of the
anarchist magazine *Gramschap* and is a co-release
with the magazine's label, Disaster Electronics.

MNW
Sweden

Musiknätet Waxholm (almost always written
simply as MNW) was a large independent label

founded in 1969 that was eventually swallowed up by Universal Music. In its early days it released some important Scandinavian polit-folk and polit-rock, including the Marxist-inspired groups Södra Bergens Balalaikor, NJA-Gruppen, Fickteatern, Røde Mor, and the far-left Chilean exile Francisco Roca. MNW was also a major distributor of smaller Swedish independent labels.

Boston Mobilization For Survival

Mobilization for Survival
USA

Mobilization for Survival (MFS, or popularly known as The Mobe) was founded in 1977 as a coalition of groups and individuals organizing against nuclear power and weapons. It was broadly antimilitarist, and in the early eighties worked closely with groups organizing against US intervention in Central America. In 1981, the Boston chapter, in association with the Boston branch of Committee in Solidarity with the People of El Salvador (CISPES), released a 7″ titled *For El Salvador*. The A side is a track called "No More Vietnams" by Boston political folk stalwart Fred Small, and the B side is "Tarde Obrera" by the pan–Latin American immigrant group Ñancahuazú, with additional musicians from the Puerto Rican group Cimarrón. Sales of the record helped fund both organizations. The record sleeve is very nicely designed and was produced by Brushfire Graphics, one of whose members was Keith McHenry, who also founded Food Not Bombs.

Moker
Netherlands

An ad hoc label name (which translates to "Sledgehammer" and is also a play on "Mokum," local slang for Amsterdam) used for a single 7″ released in Amsterdam sometime in the seventies. The record is a collaboration between

squatters and long-time residents in the working-class Jordaan district, fighting together against displacement generally, and more specifically the building of a subway, which tore through part of the district.

MUSIC OF THE WORLD

Monitor
USA

Monitor was founded in 1956 by Michael Stillman and Rose Rubin to, in part, provide the US access to music from Eastern Europe. This quickly expanded to music from all over the globe. In terms of politics, Monitor's big contribution was putting out Victor Jara and Inti-Illimani records for a US audience, as well as other politicized folk such as the songs of the Brazilian protest singer Zelia Barbosa.

More Record Company
USA

In 1968, More released a recording of an Eldridge Cleaver speech given at Syracuse University (creatively titled *Eldridge Cleaver Recorded at Syracuse*), then reissued it in 1970 under the catchier name *Soul on Wax* (riffing off the title of his best-selling book, *Soul on Ice*).

Mortarhate
UK

Mortarhate is the label started by the anarcho-punk band Conflict in 1983 after leaving the

Crass-sponsored Corpus Christi label. Its initial activity was from '83–95, and in addition to a couple dozen Conflict records, it also released vinyl from Icons of Filth, The Apostles, Hagar the Womb, and a handful of other bands, most from the second wave of anarcho-punk groups from the late seventies/early eighties. In addition, a number of compilations were released, including one in support of the Animal Liberation Front. The label still exists, largely to release Conflict records.

Movimento
Angola

The most overtly political of the small Angolan labels putting records out in the years right after liberation from Portugal. Like Merengue, this was a singles-only label, with production and distribution handled by the larger CDA Records. Movimento released less than a dozen 7″s, but some of them are amazing documents of anticolonial music, including David Zé's song "O Guerrilheiro" and Maiuka's "Viva Cabral."

Movimento Democrático de Mulheres
Portugal

The Movimento Democrático de Mulheres (MDM) is a Portuguese feminist organization that was founded in 1968 to promote the rights of women. After the 1974 Carnation Revolution in Portugal, MDM took on a larger role in society, fighting for maternity leave, affordable child care, equal pay, and access to abortion. In 1975, MDM released a 7″ by political folk musician José Barata Moura (with the record produced and distributed

by Guilda da Música) with the songs "Apelo às Mulheres na Revolução" (Appeal to Women in Revolution) b/w "No Ano Internacional da Mulher" (In the International Year of the Woman).

MOVIMENTO FEMMINISTA ROMANO

Movimento Femminista Romano
Italy

A seventies feminist collective from Rome that released two LPs. *Canti Delle Donne in Lotta* by Fufi Sonnino and Yuki Maraini was released by the collective in 1976 and then re-pressed by I Dischi dello Zodiaco later that year. Sonnino then released an album of profeminist and lesbian folk songs (*. . .Ma. . .Un Giorno Di Luna Ancor Piena. . .*) under the MFR imprint in 1980.

MPLA/DIP
Angola

A very small Angolan label that appears to be connected to the MPLA (Movimento Popular de Libertação de Angola, or People's Movement for the Liberation of Angola), the political group that freed the country from Portuguese rule. It released a couple 7″s and an LP right around the time of Angolan independence in 1974. Although there is no clear and consistent label logo on the records, there is always a version of an interlocking V and C. At first glance this is very similar to the logo of Portuguese production and distribution company Valentim de Carvalho, so I suspect that the latter actually produced and distributed the records. But at the same time, it also might just be a coincidence, and the V and C could actually represent the MPLA slogan "A Vitória é Certa!" (Victory is Certain!).

al-Mu'assasa al-Fanniya al-Ālamīya
Lebanon

A Lebanese label (whose name roughly translates to "International Technical Foundation") that released a number of records during the Lebanese Civil War in support of Palestine, internationalism, and the armed left political parties.

Muhammad's Mosque of Islam
USA

This Chicago-based label was one of many run by the Nation of Islam, but Muhammad's Mosque of Islam was specifically used to release a series of religious sermons in the sixties by the group's leader, Elijah Muhammad.

Mundo Novo
Portugal

A label from the late seventies, with a focus on Portuguese folk acts inspired by Latin American nueva canción, including Brigada Victor Jara and Grupo Trovante.

Musangola
Angola

A small Angolan 7″ label that put out between half a dozen and a dozen records in the mid-seventies. Most are Angolan merengue, with themes related to anticolonialism and Angolan independence. The politics are strengthened by striking cover designs featuring protest scenes montaged with placards and banners listing the musicians and song titles ("Independência," "Neto").

Music for H-Block
Ireland

A project launched in 1978 by Irish musicians to use their cultural sway to support the hunger strikers in Northern Ireland. An LP and a 7″ were released, including music by Francie Brolly, Mick Hanly (Moving Hearts), Matt Molloy (The Chieftains), and Christy Moore. All of the royalties from the project went to the Relatives Action Committee, an organization of family members of Republican POWs set up in 1976, which took a leading role in supporting the hunger strikes used by POWs to both highlight their abject living conditions and as a political tool in the struggle for Northern Ireland's independence.

Music Is Life
Jamaica

The label name used to release the 1985

benefit 12″ *Land of Africa*. A reggae *We Are the World*, the single was used to raise money for the victims of the Ethiopian famine. A number of reggae heavyweights played on the song, including David Hinds (Steel Pulse), Gregory Isaacs, and Mutabaruka.

Musikant
West Germany

This medium-sized independent German rock label presents an interesting case for assessing what is "political." While the label doesn't appear to have any specific ideological leanings, the vast majority of its catalog does. It was the original home of BAP, a wildly successful German rock band that sings in Kölsch, a dialect from Cologne, as well as social-democratic singer-songwriter Klaus Lage and the left-wing Dutch polit-folk act Bots. Musikant also released records by Wolf Biermann, artist Joseph Beuys, and krautrock group Schroeder Roadshow.

MUSIK·PRES

Musikpres
Denmark

Musikpres was a Copenhagen-based label that released a small but eclectic list of local projects, including a compilation LP in celebration of the community-based political space Folkets Hus (People's House), a 7″ by the neighborhood activist group Nørrebro Beboeraktion, and an LP of Brecht/Eisler songs by Husets Teater.

A MUSLIM SINGS

A Muslim Sings
USA

For a short time, this was the record label of the

Nation of Islam. In the late fifties/early sixties it produced a series of calypso 7″ singles by Minister Louis Farrakhan, then known as Louis X—including the song "A White Man's Heaven Is a Black Man's Hell." *See also* Salaam Records.

Nabate
Belgium

Third-wave anarchist punk label founded by Al Plastic and Manu, both members of the band Unhinged. It released about two dozen records between 1987 and 2000, including material from The Ex, Hiatus, Los Crudos, and One by One. An important part of the post-Crass anarchist DIY punk scene in Europe.

Nacksving
Sweden

Another political progg label, releasing records by Swedish polit-folk/progg standby's Nationalteatern and Text & Musik, and a 7″ of US singer-songwriter Jim Page's "Song for Leonard Peltier."

Nadiya
UK

Label run by Hilton Fyle, a musician, radio host of the BBC's *Network Africa*, and originally from Sierra Leone. The label focused on Fyle's electro-tinged funk, but also released an LP of anti-apartheid songs from South Africa and a speech by Bishop Desmond Tutu.

NARREN

Narren
Sweden

Narren was a Swedish political theater troupe, similar to Dario Fo's Collettivo Teatrale La Comune in Italy. They self-released a number of records under their own name, including an LP with Chilean exile Francisco Roca, and a 7″ with Dario Fo and La Comune.

Nationale Koordination der AKW-Gegner
Switzerland

This coalition of Swiss organizations opposed to nuclear power (also known as Nationale Koordination der Schweizer Atomkraftgegner) released a single record in 1979, a 7″ titled *Atom-Alarm* by the ad hoc group D'Gift-Lobby, featuring Daniela and P. J. Wassermann, a husband-and-wife team who went on to form the synth-pop bands Matterhorn and Schaltkreis Wassermann, as well as the trance act Eternal Bliss.

Nationales Vietnamkomitee
West Germany

A Vietnam solidarity organization that released *Alles für den Sieg des Kämpfenden Vietnamesischen Volkes!* (Everything for the Victory of the Fighting Vietnamese People!), a German edition of an experimental jazz record composed by Konrad Boehmer. The original Dutch version was released in 1972 by Landelijk Vietnamkomitee.

Neg FX
France

A small political punk label from Grenoble, France that released a half dozen records in the mid-eighties. Two of its bands were Power Age, one of the first punk bands from South Africa, and Rattus, a Finnish band obsessed with the dangers of nuclear war.

Neue Welt Schallplatten
West Germany

Started out in the mid-seventies releasing records directly connected to political struggles—songs from the PAIGC, or African Party for the Independence of Guinea and Cape Verde; antinuclear songs; a 7″ demanding freedom for Red Army Faction prisoner Horst Mahler. The label folded in 1978 or '79 after putting out about a dozen records. Some portion of the label administrative crew went on to found Eigelstein Musikproduktion in 1979.

New Army Records
UK

New Army was the name used by the anarcho-punk band Conflict to release benefit records. In 1986, Conflict used the label to release a live album, *Only Stupid Bastards Support EMI*, used to raise funds for the Riot Defence Fund. The name of both the label and the record are a reference to fellow punk band New Model Army, who signed to EMI in 1985 (which was very

controversial in political punk circles because
EMI also manufactured guided missiles). The
back of the record claims it is the second LP
released on New Army, but I have yet to find the
first or any subsequent records.

New Clear Records
USA

A private-press, California-based folk label, the
majority of its releases are by singer-songwriter
Mark Levy, and all half dozen records have heavy
antinuclear and pro-environmental themes. The
label's initial release was a 7″ by Rick Kirby and
The Vigilantes featuring the songs "Radiation
Nation on a 3 Mile Isle" and "Overexposed."

New Dawn Production Company (NDPC)
Libya/Malta

A Libyan propaganda label that released a half
dozen or more LPs of Maltese synth-pop and
light disco dedicated to Pan-Arabism, Muammar
Gaddafi and his *Green Book*, and a free Palestine.
These are extremely interesting records as they
don't conform to any of the usual markers of
political music. The NDPC has some connection
to the Voice of Friendship and Solidarity, another
Libyan propaganda label with a very similar
recorded output.

New Morning Records
USA

New Morning was a New York City–based label
that released *City Dreams*, a 1977 LP by working-
class, left-wing singer-songwriter Michael Glick.
The LP contained his own compositions as well
as protest songs by José Afonso, Ewan MacColl,
and Pablo Milanes.

New Vista Arts
USA

This label released a single vinyl record: an early
eighties protest 7″ by Naomi Cohen performing
"Hell No, We Won't Go" and "Saigon Waitress"–
two songs written by Phil Wilayto. This pair also
released a couple albums on cassette under the
name New Vista Arts, *Songs of Struggle* (1982)
and *Songs of Struggle II* (1983), both of which
came with significant booklets including Cohen's
liner notes and Wilayto's musical scores. Both were
also affiliated with the Workers World Party.

New Wave Records
France

A punk label started in 1983 (by Patrice Lamare
and Aline Richard) with a number of explicitly
left-wing bands on its roster, including Agent
86, Kronstadt, Revolucion X, and Verdun. It also
focused on releasing Eastern European bands,

including Abaddon (Poland) and a comp 7″ of Hungarian bands (*Vilag Lazadoi Harcra Fel*).

Nexus Records
USA

An Olympia, Washington–based folk label active in the eighties. It released a half dozen albums of explicitly feminist folk, including records by Motherlode and the Righteous Mothers. The label also released the first LP by Geoffrey Morgan, one of the first explicitly feminist male folk singers; he sung about men's emotional lives, male violence against women, and sexual abuse.

N'Gola
Angola

A pre-independence Angolan label produced and distributed by the Portuguese label Valentim de Carvalho (which had a pressing plant in Angola). Although much of the music released was not explicitly political, by 1973 many musicians on the roster had strong ties to the independence movement, including Teta Lando, Carlos Lamartine, and Sofia Rosa. Rosa was eventually assassinated by right-wing forces because of his political affinities.

Ngoma
Mozambique

While Angola had a plethora of small labels releasing pro-independence music in the seventies (MPLA, CDA, Movimento, Merengue, etc.), such labels were much more sparse in Mozambique. Ngoma was one that was launched in the late seventies, releasing more than three dozen records over the following decade, including an album of a cappella songs by the FRELIMO (Mozambique Liberation Front) choral group; politicized LPs by Conjunto 1° de Maio and Awendila, Wili, & Aníbal; and a couple albums by South African singer Miriam Makeba. It also pressed a documentary history of FRELIMO (with the Instituto Nacional do Livro e do Disco) and an album of the speeches given by both sides at the 1974 Lusaka Accords, where the conditions of Mozambique's decolonization were set (coproduced with Rádio Moçambique).

Nicole Going to Africa
Jamaica

Nicole Records was an eighties reggae label that pressed its records in Jamaica but distributed them through New York City's massive independent reggae label VP Records. Most of Nicole's thirty-odd records are by Carlene Davis. At a time when many socially conscious musicians were singing about Nelson Mandela, in 1986 Davis released a 7″ of her song "Winnie Mandela," a tribute to Mandela's wife, who had become a leader of the ANC in her own right. The song became a hit in Jamaica, and in 1987, under the label name Nicole Going to Africa, she released a 12″ version, backed with a dub remix called "Nelson Mandela Chant." This record is the only one that features this variation on the label's name.

Nikos Productions
Greece

Small label that released a series of political LPs in the seventies, including a collection of Greek partisan songs and a folk record by Alexandros Panagoulis, a leading activist against the military junta. In 1968, Panagoulis attempted to assassinate the head of the junta, Georgios Papadopoulos.

Nimbus West
USA

Started in 1979 in Los Angeles, Nimbus West became the main outlet for Afrocentric jazz pioneers Horace Tapscott and the Pan-Afrikan Peoples Arkestra, acts that were attempting to organize themselves and their music along Pan-African and Black nationalist political lines. Some records list the label as Nimbus Recordings, Ltd. See also Union of God's Musicians and Artists Ascension.

Nô Canta Nô Liberdadi
Guinea-Bissau

The label of the Conselho Nacional de Cultura of Guinea-Bissau. It released one LP in 1974 right after independence, a great collection of songs under the title *Uma Cartucheira Cheia de Canções* (A Bullet Cartridge of Songs).

Noise Against Repression
Germany

The ad hoc label used to release the 1991

double LP of the same name, featuring an international collection of political punk bands including Active Minds (UK), The Ex (Netherlands), and Verdun (France). The project was spawned as a solidarity action in support of Red Army Faction hunger strikers but evolved to become about political repression more broadly. Along with information about the bands, the double LP included a hefty newspaper about solitary confinement, political prisoners, and the repression of political ideas.

Nonantzin Recordings
USA

An ad hoc Sacramento-based label created to release a 1985 LP of social commentary–based corrido and ranchera music titled *Chicano Music All Day* by Trio Casindio and the Royal Chicano Air Force. The Royal Chicano Air Force is better known for its graphic wing, which was one of the primary producers of Chicano political posters in the seventies and eighties.

Non Serviam Productions
USA

This was the label of the eighties antiauthoritarian Detroit-based jazz/punk/funk band The Layabouts. The band was associated with the anarchist newspaper *Fifth Estate*, and also released their own publication, *Urbane Gorilla*, which they included in their record sleeves.

Noona Music
Canada

Personal label of David Campbell, a folk singer originally from Guyana and of Arawak ancestry, who settled in Vancouver. His songs focus on Indigenous life, and speak to the history of many tribes whose land is now considered "Canada." Campbell recorded a handful of records on major labels in the sixties and early seventies, then in 1974 he began releasing a string of records on Noona in concert with Toronto's Development Education Center, with production by Columbia Records' Special Products wing.

Nô Pintcha
Guinea-Bissau

Nô Pintcha is a postindependence newspaper in Guinea-Bissau produced by the government's Comissariado de Estado de Informação e Turismo. In 1974 it released a single LP, consisting of the national anthem of the República da Guiné-Bissau and a recording of the last public speech by the country's leading anticolonial revolutionary, Amílcar Cabral—his 1973 "Message for a New Year."

Nørrebro Beboeraktion
Denmark

A political group organized by the community of Nørrebro in Copenhagen. Nørrebro is the long-standing home of a large lefty community supported by multiple grassroots institutions,

including the Folk Haus. Nørrebro Beboeraktion (Nørrebro Resident Action) had a house folk band, Nørrebro's Beboeraktions Akkustiske Musikgruppe (NAM), which self-released a 7″ in 1977 under the Nørrebro Beboeraktion label, with songs about housing activism and antidevelopment. The band released another 7″ with Demos, and one with Musikpres.

NOURPHONE

Nourphone
France

A mysterious label which appears to have only released a single 7″, *La Poésie de la Résistance Palestinienne* by Abed Azrié, likely sometime in the late sixties (the record is undated). Azrié, a Syrian composer who has long lived in France, has a long discography but his first LP, *Le Chant Nouveau des Poètes Arabes*, was released as part of the "Nouveau Chansonnier International" series by Le Chant du Monde in 1972.

Le Nouveau Chansonnier International
France

Loosely translating as "New International Singer-Songwriter," this political project of parent label Le Chant du Monde was a collection of records by socially engaged artists who were reinventing folk music around the world. Highlights include José Afonso (Portugal), Zelia Barbosa (Brazil), Mikis Theodorakis (Greece), Marcel Khalifé (Palestine), and Imanol (Basque).

Le Nouveau Clarté
France

A socialist label (whose name translates to "New Clarity") from the sixties that released at least a couple 7"s—one by Mikis Theodorakis (*Dans la Clandestinité: Chante la Lutte du People Grec Contra la Fascisme*) and another—*Poèmes et Chants Viet Nam*—read and sung by actor Laurent Terzieff.

NR Produzioni
Italy

An early label name used by Dario Fo, Franca Rame, and the Collettivo Teatrale La Comune to release a 7" (*Settimo: Ruba un Po' Meno*) in 1964. The record was rereleased later that year by I Dischi del Sole.

NTYE
Gabon/France

The record label of Gabonese poet, singer, and guitar player Pierre Akendengue, known for his songs infused with Pan-African politics (i.e., "Salut aux Combattants de la Liberté" and "Afrika Salalo," songs about the murders of African revolutionaries such as Lumumba and Cabral, and the wait for true African liberation). Although NTYE appears to be an acronym, I'm unsure what it stands for, and it doesn't appear to be spelled out on any of the records. At different points Akendengue also used the label name NTCHE, which shares both the logo (a tall drum on a triangle) and the unarticulated acronym.

Nuestro Canto
Peru

It has been tricky to track down background

information on this small Peruvian label focused on nueva canción. I believe Nuestro Canto is the public-facing name for the parent label EPOCAP. EPOCAP in turn appears to have evolved sometime in the eighties out of the Peruvian wing of the DICAP label. Nuestro Canto put out at least a half dozen records as part of its "Our Song" series, which began with the Peruvian nueva canción act Tiempo Nuevo, and included an Inti-Illimani LP and an album by Vientes del Pueblo.

Nueva Trova
International

Not so much a record label as a logo created by Areito to put on all its nueva trova releases. This logo was then used as a nueva trova sublabel graphic for multiple European record houses, including Gong (Spain) and I Dischi dello Zodiaco (Italy).

Nueva Voz Latino Americana
Mexico

This label released somewhere between a dozen and two dozen records in the seventies and eighties. Most are by political folk/nueva canción/corrido singer José de Molina. It appears that the label released all of de Molina's albums except one, which was released on the left-wing German label Neue Welt.

Un Nuevo Amanecer del 30 de Agosto
Puerto Rico

Un Nuevo Amanecer del 30 de Agosto was a political organization created to support the Puerto Rican *independista* militants arrested on August 30, 1985 for participating in the 1983 attack on a Wells Fargo bank in Hartford, Connecticut. All were part of the armed group Los Macheteros, and claimed political-prisoner status in the US. The support organization released a compilation album of Puerto Rican trova, folk, and salsa titled *A Traves de las Rejas* (Through the Bars). It is undated, but most likely from soon after the arrests.

Nuevo Arte
Puerto Rico

The record label of Puerto Rican *jibaro* and folk performer Andrés Jiménez, which he used to release a half dozen albums of his versions of other people's music, mixing nueva canción and various Latin music styles. His records were also released by Disco Libre and Paredon.

N'Zaji
Angola

A very small Angolan label from the seventies. I have one 7″, political merengue by Mario Gama. N'Zaji released at least four or five more records, including a single by Portuguese folk singer António Beja in support of the People's Movement for the Liberation of Angola, or MPLA

(which was re-pressed in the Netherlands by Angola Comité) and three 7″s by Pedrito (who also recorded for the similar Batuque label). The label should not be confused with Conjunto 'Nzaji, a group deep in the MPLA camp that released an LP on Eteenpäin! and self-released a 10″ in the Democratic Republic of Congo.

Ocarina
Nicaragua

A postrevolutionary label from Nicaragua, distributed by the larger state-controlled ENIGRAC. I would guess that Ocarina is to ENIGRAC as Areito is to ENGREM in Cuba. The label largely focused on Nicaraguan music, but also released nueva canción and nueva trova records and songs from Chile, Cuba, Mexico, and Uruguay.

Ohr
West Germany

A short-lived but very influential experimental music label. It released forty-five records in only four years (1970–73), but many of them have been re-pressed and rereleased multiple times. Records ranged from free jazz to krautrock to abstract experimental sound and included key didactic political releases from Floh de Cologne, and important experimental records by Ash Ra Tempel, Embryo, and Xhol.

Oihuka
Basque Country

Founded in 1987, Oihuka focuses on Basque popular music. The home of the militant Basque nationalist punk/ska band Kortatu, and their successor, Negu Gorriak. Oihuka also released LPs by political rock band Barricada and licensed and put out the first two Chumbawamba albums for a Basque audience.

OIR
Argentina

A militant nueva canción label that likely released about a dozen records in the late sixties/early seventies, including an album of Chilean resistance songs and one of Cuban trova by Carlos Puebla.

Oktober
Norway

Marxist book publisher that released a single LP in 1971 of polit-folk by the groups Front-Teatret and Visegruppa PS—*Slutt Opp, Kamerat!*

Oktober
Sweden

One of many Scandinavian radical left labels (such as Demos, Plateselskapet Mai, Forlaget Tiden, Nacksving, etc.). It released about three dozen records between 1972 and 1982, including Pete Seeger, Mikis Theodorakis, Fria Proteatern, and compilations dedicated to May Day and Swedish renditions of international socialist songs.

Old Lady Blue Jeans
USA

The personal label of trailblazing lesbian singer-songwriter Linda Shear (she performed at the first out-lesbian concert in the US in 1972), which she ran in the mid-seventies while living in Northampton, MA. Although promoted as a production and distribution system for lesbian music, it only released Shear's 1975 debut *A Lesbian Portrait: Lesbian Music for Lesbians*, and then a 1977 re-pressing with the slightly reworked title *A Lesbian Portrait: Lesbian Music for Lesbians Only*. The initial pressing is stamped with the directive, "To be shared and sold to women only," while the back cover of the second pressing states, "This music is for lesbians only!" as well as, "This album is especially dedicated to the Lesbians who have internalized the basics of the analysis called Lesbian Separatism, and who continuously strive to push their own limits."

Olivia
USA

Olivia was started in 1973 in Washington, DC and collectively run by members of the Furies Collective and Radical Lesbians. It released around fifty records in its fifteen active years, staying committed to a small stable of musicians who put out the majority of the albums (such as Meg Christian, Cris Williamson, and the Berkeley Women's Music Collective).

One Spark Music
USA

Label of the band Prairie Fire, a political folk outfit named after the manifesto of the Weather Underground. The label name references the same Mao quotation: "A single spark can start a prairie fire." Contrary to the name, the band was far more connected to the Revolutionary Communist Party than Prairie Fire, the above-ground support group for Weather. One of the main members, Mat Callahan, went on to form The Looters and the collective political music club (and early nineties cassette label) Komotion International. See also Direct Hit Records.

Oneworld Peacesongs
UK

An ad hoc label created to release the 1984 benefit LP *We Have a Dream*, an international collection of women's peace songs supporting the women's international peace movement. The artwork and songs on the album make clear reference to the long-running women-only antinuclear encampment at Greenham Common, but the LP doesn't appear to have any direct connection to Greenham.

Ons Suriname
Suriname

The label used to release a seventies LP of anticolonial and nationalist poems and songs by Surinamese political poet R. Dobru (aka Robin Ewald Raveles) titled *Strijdliederen uit Suriname* (Battle Songs from Suriname). Suriname was a Dutch colony until 1975. The label and Dobru were associated with the Partij Nationalistische Republiek, a social-democratic political party that existed until a 1980 military coup in Suriname, after which it was banned.

On The Line
Canada

Label of Canadian folk musician Arlene Mantle, who used the name to release a series of labor- and solidarity-themed LPs and singles throughout the eighties, often in collaboration with Canadian labor unions.

Open Door Records
USA

A queer-focused label run by lesbian folk and blues musician Ginni Clemmens. It released the initial pressing of the *Gay & Straight Together* compilation LP in 1980, which was re-pressed by Folkways later that year.

Opération W
France

Not a label, but a political or social project that released at least one 7″, a compilation titled *Apartheid*. It looks like it's from the sixties or seventies, but it's undated and difficult to place. I haven't been able to track down any information about what Opération W was, or the organization that apparently ran it, Mobilisation Mondiale de la Jeunesse (World Youth Mobilization), but the musicians featured are religious, which makes me think that this record was an anti-apartheid statement by a Christian charity.

Opponer
Swedish

A political progg/agit-folk band that released a couple records under their own name, including a 7″ in 1975 supporting striking Alfa Laval workers (Alfa Laval AB is a Swedish company specializing in the production of chemical solutions used in heavy industry).

L'Orchestra
Italy

Also known as Cooperativa L'Orchestra, the label was formed in 1974 as an outlet for what was thought of as noncommercial music. Very unique at the time, L'Orchestra was run by the musicians on it, including the popular experimental folk and prog band Stormy Six. (The label's first release was Stormy Six's political concept album about Italian partisans, *Un Biglietto del Tram*.) The label became a home for music that was political in both content and form, and also for the "Rock in Opposition" movement, a crew of staunchly independent prog rock groups including Stormy Six, Henry Cow (UK), and Etron Fou Leloublan (France).

Organisationen til Oplysning on Atomkraft
Denmark

Antinuclear group that organized an LP of polit-folk in 1976 with multiple acts from the Demos roster (Agitpop, Jomfru Ane) as well as other Danish political folk-rock bands like Totalpetroleum.

Origami Records
USA

The label created to release the feminist folk LP *Sweet Sorcery* by Cathy Winter and Betsy Rose.

Part of the LP centers around a nineteenth-century protofeminist character called Amazon Dixie, and the entire LP is dedicated "To the spirit of adventure, persistence and survival in all woman."

Osiris
Portugal

A small fado label whose founders were likely politicized by the Carnation Revolution in Portugal, and went on to release a small stack of political fado and folk records in the mid- to late seventies, including a couple singles extolling the virtues of, and benevolent relationship between, the left-wing military—which sparked the revolution—and the people ("Soldados e Povo").

OUT & OUT BOOKS

Out & Out Books
USA

Out & Out Books was a Brooklyn-based feminist publisher founded in 1975 by poet Joan Larkin. In 1977, it pressed an LP titled *A Sign/I Was Not Alone*, featuring poetry by Larkin, Audre Lorde, Honor Moore, and Adrienne Rich. This was the only record released by the press.

Outlet Records
Northern Ireland

A Belfast-based label that released a large volume of traditional Irish musical fair, but also pressed a series of 7"s in 1969 and 1970 that are direct responses to the Republican uprising in Derry known as the Battle of the Bogside. It also released a decent amount of recordings of Irish revolutionary songs, tunes by James Connolly, and compilations with titles such as *Rifles of the IRA*. Together with the Dublin-based Release Records, Outlet also set up the explicitly Republican R&O Records.

Out On Vinyl
UK

A Manchester-based deep house label committed to releasing music for the city's gay dance scene. It released multiple versions of Coming Out Crew's "Free, Gay, and Happy" in the mid-nineties, as well as 12"s by Hot Drum and T-Empo.

Outpunk
USA

Originally started as a fanzine by Matt Wobensmith focused on being queer and punk, in 1992 Outpunk began releasing records. The first 7" was titled *There's a Dyke in the Pit*, and featured tracks by Bikini Kill, Lucy Stoners, Tribe 8, and 7 Year Bitch. (A companion 7", *There's a Faggot in the Pit*, was released on the ad hoc label Bobo Records.) Sixteen records followed, released between 1992 and 1998, all by bands featuring prominent queer members, including God is My Co-Pilot, Mukilteo Fairies, The Need, Pansy Division, and Team Dresch.

CULTURAL ARTS SECTION
DEPARTMENT OF INFORMATION AND NATIONAL GUIDANCE
PALESTINE LIBERATION ORGANIZATION
BEIRUT, P.O.B. 5383

Palestine Liberation Organization—Cultural Arts Section
Lebanon

The Cultural Arts Section released at least one 7″ while the Palestine Liberation Organization (PLO) was based in Lebanon, a single by Zeinab Shaath titled *The Urgent Call of Palestine*.

Pan-American Records
USA

An ad hoc label used to release the LP *Sí Se Puede* in 1976, a benefit record for the United Farm Workers featuring a number of singers, all backed by a very young Los Lobos (then known as Los Lobos del Este de Los Angeles).

Palm
France

Palm was an experimental jazz label that was more often political in form rather than content, but it worked with Expression Spontanée and Disques Vendémeire, both explicitly leftist labels, to put out co-releases.

Panoptikum
West Germany

Panoptikum was a short-lived (1968–69) political comedy label, which released records by lefty comedy and cabaret performers Wolfgang Neuss, Volker Kühn, and Reichskabarett Berlin theater.

Pan African Records
UK

Pan African was the name used by Liberian singer Miatta Fahnbulleh to release her undated (though likely around 1980) liberation-themed Afrobeat LP, *The Message of the Revolution*. The record was engineered by Dennis Bovell, one of the key members of London's late seventies/early eighties dub scene and known for working with Linton Kwesi Johnson and for his collaborations with The Slits and The Pop Group.

Panther Music
West Germany

Panther was a militant krautrock band from Ahrensburg, Germany. They self-released a single LP, 1974's *Wir Wollen Alles!* (We Want Everything!) under the label name Panther Music. The band called themselves "*volksrock*," or people's rock, and were equally inspired by fellow krautrock band Ton Steine Scherben and US influences such as the MC5 and John Sinclair's White Panther Party, with its hybrid mix of rock 'n' roll, pot smoking, and armed struggle.

Paredon
USA

A fifteen-year (1970–84) and fifty-album experiment in political music. Founded by northern soul singer Barbara Dane and her husband Irwin Silber (who edited *Sing Out! Magazine*). Both Dane and Silber were part of the Line of March, a seventies New Communist group. Their commitment to both internationalism and Marxism is apparent in the label's catalog, which is one of the most diverse collections of political music assembled on vinyl. Countries represented include Angola, Argentina, Chile, China, Cuba, Dominican Republic, Ecuador, Greece, Haiti, Italy, Nicaragua, Northern Ireland, Palestine, Philippines, Puerto Rico, El Salvador, Thailand, Uruguay, the US, Mexico, and Vietnam. Early albums were packaged in the same format as Folkways Records—and produced by the same company—with cardboard sleeves wrapped with a glued-on cover sheet, and an extra piece of 12″ square cardstock slid into the cover. Another aspect of Paredon that makes it unique is that the albums were not distributed only through records stores or mail order, but were sold at tables at political events sponsored or supported by Line of March.

Participación
Peru

The name used in 1973 by the Revolutionary Government of the Armed Forces of Peru (the product of a left-wing coup in 1968) to release a 7″ documenting the Inkari Encuentro, and an LP of psychedelic-tinged pop called *Linkari*, directly inspired by the event. Inkari was a national political and cultural gathering of workers, peasants, students, and artists organized by SINAMOS (National System of Support for Social Mobilization). SINAMOS was the military government's attempt to create a mass organization that could support its goal of social democracy. A liberatory Peruvian youth culture developed out of Inkari, and the *Linkari* LP documents its musical wing.

PARTI COMMUNISTE RÉUNIONNAIS

Parti Communiste Réunionais
Réunion

The Communist Party of Réunion released two LPs in 1976 to commemorate their Fourth National Congress. Both records are collections of sega and maloya, traditional music from Réunion, a small island and French colony (or "overseas department" in today's bureaucratic lingo) to the east of Madagascar.

Partido Africano da Independência da Guiné e Cabo Verde
Guinea Bissau

The Partido Africano da Independência da Guiné e Cabo Verde (PAIGC, or African Party for the Independence of Guinea and Cape Verde) led a successful armed struggle against Portuguese colonialism, but was also the name put on a couple of records of liberation songs and poetry from Guinea-Bissau and the Cape Verde Islands. These records include an album by Kaoguiamo (the cultural group of the PAIGC) pressed in a German edition (co-released with Neue Welt) and one intended for Africa (pressed in Italy), as well as a poetry collection that appears to have been pressed in the Netherlands, but the cover lists PAIGC office addresses in both Guinea and Senegal.

Partido Socialista
Portugal

Like the Partito Comunista Italiano and Partito Socialista Italiano, the Portuguese Partido Socialista tried its hand at releasing records of both speeches and music in the mid-seventies.

Partido Socialista Obrero Español
Spain

The Spanish Socialist Workers' Party (PSOE) was forbidden under the Franco regime. Folk musician Julio Matito pressed a psychedelic polit-folk record dedicated to—and under the label name—PSOE in 1976, which was banned from distribution in Spain. See also Partito Socialisto Popular.

Partido Socialisto Popular
Spain

The Partido Socialisto Popular (PSP) was formed in 1974 and existed as an underground party in Francoist Spain, largely on college campuses. In 1977 it was legalized and quickly won a number of seats in regional elections. In 1978 it merged with the Partido Socialista Obrero Español (PSOE), and in '79 PSP founder Enrique Tierno Galván was elected mayor of Madrid.

In '77 the party released a 7″ with "Vive en la Libertad" b/w "La Internacional."

Parti Socialiste
France

The main social-democratic party in France, it released records under the names Parti Socialiste du Livre and Club Socialiste du Livre, both front groups. Releases included one by Mikis Theodorakis to encourage voters in the 1978 election, and another by Marcel Amont promoting François Mitterand's election in 1981.

Partito Comunista Italiano
Italy

The Italian Communist Party (PCI) released about a dozen records in the sixties and seventies. Many contained speeches from party leader Palmiro Togliatti, but others were songs by the travelling bard Franco Trincale. In an attempt to reach out to youth, it even put out a 7″ with the polit-folk/prog rock group Stormy Six.

Partito Socialista Italiano
Italy

Like the PCI above, the Partito Socialista Italiano

(PSI) released records as both propaganda and to build popular support. Most of these 7"s appear to have been promotional, and might have been distributed via the party's newspaper. The records often contain a speech on one side, and a folk or pop song on the other, including a track by the "Italian Beatles," Equipe 84.

Pasquinade Music Co.
USA

The label of Texas-based political comedy-folk singer Lu Mitchell. Mitchell released a handful of LPs on the label, including a 1970 live LP *Chant of the Rat Race*, with songs titled "The Inflation Lament," "Secretary's Stomp," and "Bigger is Better."

Pass-Op Produktion
German

A radical label that put out at least two records, including a compilation of antinuclear folk *Bauer Maas: Lieder Gegen Atomenergie*–Songs Against Nuclear Power) in 1977 and a pro-squatting alt-rock album (*Schoner Wohnen-Abber Fix*–Home Sweet Home-but Needs Fixing) in 1982.

Patricio Weitzel
Sweden

An ad hoc label used to release the Swedish pressing of nueva canción chilena singer

Charo Cofré's 1975 LP *El Canto del Chile* (titled *Kampsång für Chile* in Swedish). Cofré was a left-wing singer in the spirit of Isabel Parra and Victor Jara, and went into exile in Italy after the 1973 coup in Chile. The name used for the label tells an additional story. Patricio Weitzel (full name Patricio Lautaro Weitzel Perez) was a twenty-six-year-old militant of the Juventud Radical Revolucionaria (JRR) who–along with two other young men–was picked up on October 1, 1973 by the Chilean military, tortured, killed, and had his body thrown under a bridge. JRR was a socialist and antifascist youth organization, which in 1969 had split from the more conservative Juventud Radical de Chile. After the coup it became a clandestine organization. Weitzel was held up by many as an antifascist martyr.

Peace Pie
Netherlands

A folk sublabel of Xilovox, it released a number of records sung in the Brabantian dialect as well as an LP by the Dutch political theater/folk outfit Toneelwerkgroep Proloog.

Peasant's Revolt Records
UK

This was a side project of the band Chumbawamba. The label name was used to release two poll-tax resistance benefit albums featuring the band's songs: 1989's *A Pox on the Poll Tax* (with additional songs by Dan, Dog

Faced Hermans, Stretch Heads, Thatcher on Acid, Wat Tyler, and more) and 1990's *Greatest Hits: A Benefit for the Trafalgar Square Defence Campaign* (with additional songs by Stitch, Shelley's Children, Robb Johnson Band, and The Ex). While the former record is designed to look like a punk remake of a tract from the English Revolution, the latter is very slick, the entire cover filled top to bottom with a first-person narrative text, in a crisp serif font, about the Trafalgar Square riot.

Pegafoon
Netherlands

This label released a dozen far-left records from the late sixties through the late seventies, including songs from demonstrations and housing occupations, and songs in solidarity with Spain.

Peña de los Parra
Chile

Founded in 1968 by Isabel and Angel Parra—children of Chilean folk music hero Violeta Parra—and named after the space founded by their mother as a national center for folk music education and history. Starting in 1970, the label was produced and distributed by DICAP, given DICAP catalog numbers, and released music related to the Parra family as well as other Chilean musicians connected to the center. It ceased functioning in 1973 after the Pinochet coup.

Peñón Records
USA

Ad hoc label used by a Brooklyn-based solidarity group to release *¡El Salvador: Su Canto, Su Lucha, Su Victoria, Amaneciendo!* (El Salvador: Its Song, Struggle, Victory, Awakening!) by militant Salvadoran folk act Yolocamba I-Ta. The LP contains songs written by guerrilla poet Roque Dalton as well as Nicaraguan Luis Enrique Mejía Godoy.

Pentagrama
Mexico

A small eighties label, Pentagrama doesn't appear to be expressly political, but it did release an LP by the social justice-focused folk/jazz/fusion group Tribu, along with Mexican pressings of records by Cuban musicians, Billy Bragg LPs, and a double album of Mejía Godoy songs in support of the Sandinistas in Nicaragua.

The People's Music Works
USA

The People's Music Works is the house label of the band The People's Victory Orchestra and Chorus. The band is a elusive outfit from Long Island that recorded three LPs and a 7" of psychedelic blues-rock with communist sympathies in the seventies. Little is known about them, as the records contained limited or no liner notes, but seventies music aficionados have identified the key members as Carla Lund and R. Alt, who worked with a revolving collection of friends and local musicians for the band's recordings.

People's National Party
Jamaica

The People's National Party (PNP), with its leader Michael Manley, was the ruling party in Jamaica from 1972–1980 and 1989–2007. Manley pulled the PNP to the left in the seventies, using increasingly Marxist rhetoric in public speeches and joining the Socialist International. The party instituted a series of significant socialist-inspired reforms, including a minimum wage, land reform, and free public education. Manley was popular amongst the poor and working-class majority, but these reforms—and Manley's close relationship with Fidel Castro—were not popular with the US, and the CIA was involved in destabilizing his regime, including encouraging coup attempts and arming gangs of drug dealers to provoke mass violence. In 1976, the PNP released a two-album set titled *We Know Where We Are Going*, which interspersed Manley's speeches with reggae songs by the party's house band, The PNP Pioneer Band.

People Unite
UK

The label run by the UK reggae act Misty in Roots. It mostly released conscious reggae and dub, but also put out the first 7″ by political punk band The Ruts. Misty in Roots often played Rock Against Racism shows in the late seventies.

Perfect Pair Records
USA

A New Jersey–based house label that was home to The Coming Out Crew, and released multiple versions of their Pride anthem "Free, Gay, and Happy."

PGP RTB
Yugoslavia

The state record label in Yugoslavia from 1959 until its collapse in 1992. The acronym stands for "Produkcija Gramofonskih Ploca Radio Televizije Beograd." Next to Melodiya in the Soviet Union, it was likely the largest and most advanced label in the Eastern Bloc, releasing thousands of records, including a broad range of folk, jazz, classical, rock, and more. It also released many spoken word LPs by Yugoslavian leader Josip Broz Tito, and unlike other Communist state labels, it released a wide range of Western pop music for Yugoslavian audiences, from ABBA to John Coltrane, Michelle Shocked to The Jam.

Philo Records
USA

Philo was founded in Vermont in 1973 to release and distribute mostly North American folk music, and was similar to both Flying Fish and Rounder Records, other labels coming out of a second-wave revival of folk, blues, and other traditional music in the US in the seventies. What makes Philo of interest here is that it was home to Utah Phillips, the travelling bard of the Industrial

Workers of the World (IWW) and inheritor of the musical tradition of Joe Hill and other IWW singer-songwriters. Phillips released four LPs with the label between 1973 and 1983, including *We Have Fed You All a Thousand Years*, a collection of IWW songs and stories. Philo was sold to Rounder in 1982.

Physical Records
USA

Small, eclectic label that is included here because it released two LPs by Red Shadow, "The Economics Rock 'n' Roll Band." They were just that, a band made up in part of Marxist economists, with songs titled "Commodity Fetishism," "Stagflation," and "Labor is Value." The label also released the first LP by Laduvane, an all-women's Balkan folk band.

Pincén
Argentina

A small left-populist label, with a list that is split between spoken word LPs (Che Guevara, Peronist poet Alfredo Carlino, poems against the Vietnam War) and music (Uruguayan singer-songwriter Tabare Etcheverry, Argentine anarchist songs from the first half of the twentieth century).

[pi'ra:nha]

Piranha
West Germany

An independent label founded in 1987 in Berlin, with a focus on socially engaged "world music." Its first release was a compilation titled *Beat Apartheid!*, and much of its output is politicized, if not expressly political, including records by Orchestra Marrabenta Star de Moçambique, Stella

Chiweshe (Zimbabwe), and Mzwakhe (South Africa). My favorite act on its roster is Carte de Séjour, an explicitly antiracist French-Algerian group that mixes raï and post-punk styles. Sadly, like many labels that didn't start up until the late eighties and early nineties, a significant portion of their catalog is available only on CD.

Pläne
West Germany

Pläne was a prolific left-wing label from Dortmund, Germany that released at least five hundred records. It took its name (which translates as "Plans") from—and evolved out of—the banned 1930s antifascist magazine of the Youth Bund. In the fifties the magazine was revived, and in the sixties the publishing group turned towards the production of records. Although info is scarce, it seems that most of the funding for the label came through the DKP (West German Communist Party), which in turn was covertly funded by the GDR. From the beginning, the focus was on left-wing song, particularly the new German chansonniers such as Dieter Süverkrüp, as well as a recuperation of pan-European folk music that could be interpreted as antifascist, from Italian partisan chants to songs of the Spanish Civil War to the music of the French Revolution. Like many left-leaning European labels, after the 1973 coup in Chile it churned out dozens of nueva canción albums in solidarity with Latin American struggles. By the late seventies, Pläne began releasing politicized krautrock and German proto-punk (Floh de Cologne, Lokomotive Kreuzberg), and in the early eighties a small stable of African and anti-apartheid solidarity LPs (Jabula, Miriam Makeba, Bongi Makeba). There was also an interesting connection to the Anglo music world, as the label released German editions of politicized pop music from Canada and the UK, including records by Bruce Cockburn, The Parachute Club, and Robyn Hitchcock. Pläne folded in 2011.

The Plane Label
UK

A short-lived British folk label that released two LPs between 1979 and 1981, one antinuclear (*Nuclear Power, No Thanks!!?*) and the other feminist (*My Song Is My Own: Songs From Women*).

Plateselskapet Mai
Norway

A communist record label that ran from 1973–1983. More prolific and successful than many other lefty Scandinavian labels, its one-hundred-record-deep catalog is full of political folk, progg, rock, new wave, and punk, as well as solidarity records with Chile and Palestine. Plateselskapet Mai also pressed and distributed DICAP LPs in Norway, and the early records by Sami label Jår'galæd'dji. One of the label's signature bands was Vømmøl Spellmannslag, a successful Maoist folk-rock act aligned with the AKP (M-L), the Workers' Communist Party. Like many of its counterparts in the New Communist movement in the US, the AKP (M-L) sent its largely university-educated members to work in factories and become "proletarianized." The party was also connected to the publishing house and record label Oktober Forlag.

Plattlangarna
Sweden

Not a label, but a distributor and aggregator of Swedish progg and folk labels such as Amalthea, Avanti, Kofia, Nacksving, and Proletärkultur.

Pleiades Records
USA

Pleiades was set up in 1976 by lesbian singer-songwriter and jazz pianist Margie Adam to release her first LP, *Songwriter*. Almost all aspects of this initial record were created and produced by women. Adam continued to use the label to release an additional seven albums into the early 2000s.

Pluf
Netherlands

The personal label of Dutch singer-songwriter Nico Denhoorn. Denhoorn was involved with the post-Provo political and countercultural group the Kabouters (Gnomes), who took a strong environmental stance, opposed Dutch involvement in militarism, and attempted to convert Amsterdam into a car-free city. Denhoorn's first release was in 1970 with a psychedelic folk band he called Kabouter Chismus, and then in the late seventies he followed it with two solo LPs of home-recorded songs.

Poètes du Temps Présent
Poètes du Temps Présent
France

A label that released a half dozen records in the mid-seventies, all mixing politicized poetry with basic folk songs. The initial release by Uruguayan Marcos Velasquez is titled *Chants pour un people en lutte* (Songs for a people in struggle) and states on the back, "Poetry is a weapon of the future."

Pogo Plattan
Swedish

A mid- to late seventies label that released about a dozen folk and poetry LPs, with an emphasis on Swedish culture and left-leaning folk.

Polemic Records
USA

Polemic was a Bay Area hip-hop label started by Walter Riley, father of Boots Riley of the ultraleft hip-hop crew The Coup. In 1991 the label pressed The Coup's first release, *The EP* 12". In 1993 it released a cassette by local rapper Point Blankk Range, and then lay dormant until 1998. After The Coup released a couple LPs on the hip-hop indy Wild Pitch, the label was resurrected to release the group's third LP, *Steal This Album*, in 1998.

POLITIQUE
hebdo

Politique Hebdo
France

Politique Hebdo was a weekly paper that ran from 1970 to 1978. It was nonsectarian and inclusive of many left and progressive viewpoints. It briefly ran a record label—the only album I have, and possibly the only one it ever put out, is an album titled *Chants de Luttes du Chili*, a compilation of songs by nueva canción chilena artists. In addition, the magazine put on an annual gathering of music and politics called "La Fête," of which the label Expression Spontanée released a couple albums of documentation.

Portugal-Spanien-Gruppe

Portugal-Spanien-Gruppe Berlin
West Germany

A solidarity group that released a 1975 benefit LP for cooperatives in Portugal titled *Poder Popular*. It featured three Portuguese singers and a German backing band playing songs popularized during the Carnation Revolution in Portugal, including four by José Afonso. A different edition of this same LP was also released by Trikont.

Positive Action
UK

An ad hoc label that put out the antimilitarist/antipoverty *Bread Not Bombs* benefit 7" in 1986.

Power Noize Records
South Africa

One of the first punk labels from South Africa, started by members of the Durban-based group Power Age. It released records by Power Age, fellow South African band Screaming Foetus, as well as an anti-apartheid benefit 7" by US punk band White Flag.

Pragmaphone
France

Small, eclectic seventies label that released about twenty LPs. Music ranged from Spanish political chansons, Dixieland jazz, Catalan experimental folk, and a great LP of anarchist songs from the Spanish Civil War. Its black flag–based logo and catalog content make me suspect anarchists were involved in the label, but I haven't been able to confirm.

PRODUCCIONES DUPUY

Producciones Dupuy
Argentina

This label's output of about a dozen 7"s and LPs, which all appear to be from the mid- to late sixties, are all political, but are strangely split between recordings of Peronist speeches on one side, and Che speeches and Guevarist nueva trova and nueva canción on the other. It was likely connected to the musician Alfredo Dupuy, who also recorded with other Argentine left labels such as Lince and OIR.

Producciones Jaosbe
Venezuela

An ad hoc label name used to release a 1988 three-LP set titled *Martires de la Resistencia*, which narrated the story of three pro-democracy activists in Venezuela: Leonard Ruiz Pineda, Alberto Carnevali, and Andrés Eloy Blanco. All were associated with the leftist group Acción Democrática (AD), which had been key in bringing democratic practices to Venezuela but was forced underground during a decade of dictatorship between 1948 and 1958. This triple album celebrated thirty years since the party emerged from exile. Although quite radical at its beginning, by 1988 AD was riddled with corruption.

Profane Existence
USA

For a decade (1989–98), Profane Existence was the primary label and distributor of anarcho-punk in the US, securing its importance with releases by Nausea, Doom, and Hiatus, as well as with benefit compilations such as *In the Spirit of Total Resistance*, in support of the 1990 Mohawk occupation of Kanesatake. Also known as the Oka Crisis, in 1989 a golf course announced plans to expand onto land claimed by the Mohawk community in southern Québec, Canada, leading to a 78 day occupation and violent conflict between Mohawk warriors and the Canadian government. In addition, Profane Existence put out a widely distributed and epononymously-named anarcho-punk newspaper with regular information about politics in North America and autonomous social movements in Europe. The label reformed in 2000, and continues to put out records.

Progressive Labor Party
USA

The Progressive Labor Party is the oldest Trotskyist group in the US. It released two albums in the seventies. The first is called *All Power to the Working Class*, which features half pseudo–Appalachian folk and half amateur soul, most of both being cover songs with highly politicized changes to the lyrics. My favorite song is "*Challenge*, it's the Communist Newspaper!" with the song name chanted by children as the chorus. The second, titled *A World to Win*, is a more traditional lineup of classic communist and labor songs, with renditions of Joe Hill, Woody Guthrie, "Bella Ciao," and "The International." The back of this second LP states, "We've got a long way to go before our cultural work equals the advanced and correct line of our Party, but this album represents progress in that direction."

Proletärkultur
Sweden

Started in 1973 to release explicitly communist music, and broadened slightly in the late seventies/early eighties to include working-class and more general politicized records. When it began, it was the record label of the KFML(r)—the Swedish Communist Party (Marxist-Leninist) and released acts associated with the party, such as Dan Berglund and Knutna Nävar. In the 1980s, records are more sparse and also less ideologically focused, with folk and world music releases. Distributed by Plattlangarna.

Promauca
Sweden

A group of Chilean exiles in Sweden who self-released an LP of political nueva canción chilena in 1978, simply called *Chile*.

Promecin
Venezuelan

Promecin was largely a Venezuelan production house for Chilean records originally released by DICAP. It pressed records in the late sixties and early seventies by Los Curacas, Inti-Illimani, Victor Jara, Angel Parra, Quilapayún, and more.

Pueblo
France

An eclectic folk, chanson, and zouk label that released about twenty records from 1970 to 1975. Many weren't overtly political, yet their first release was a 7″ by Los Argentinos in homage to Che Guevara.

Québékiss
Québec

Also the title of a popular seventies Québécois separatist song by Marie Savard, *Québékiss* is the name used on a 1971 LP of separatist songs and poems. The album was released by the Québec label Les Disques Zodiaque (beyond this record, not specifically political), but the cover indicates that this was intended as the initial release of a larger project, giving an address for Québékiss as an entity. The cover is also very unique, a double-sided printed sheet, folded and placed over a blank, brown record sleeve. No other releases on Les Disques Zodiaque came this way, so it is possible this was intended as a self-released project but was then picked up by the larger label. I don't believe future records were ever released. The same album was released in 1977 in France by Vendémiaire under the title *Québec: 200 Ans de Résistance*.

R & O RECORDS

R&O Records
Ireland

Joint label of Release and Outlet Records, which put out about a half dozen hardcore

Irish Republican LPs in the early seventies, including *Smash Internment and Injustice*, which was recorded live in Long Kesh Prison and smuggled out.

Radical Wallpaper Records
UK

An early eighties label that released five 7″s of political spoken word, poetry, and experimental sound, including records by punk poetry act Attila the Stockbroker, dub poet Benjamin Zephaniah, and Little Brother (aka Jon Langford of The Mekons and The Waco Brothers). The label also released a record by International Pen Pals, a group featuring Red Saunders, one of the founders of Rock Against Racism.

Radioactive Records
USA

Radioactive is the name used on a 1978 LP produced by a group of people protesting the construction of Black Fox Nuclear Power Plant in Oklahoma. The collection, titled *Black Fox Blues: Music from the Movement*, is all local folk, country, and blues-rock acts, and the record was sold as a benefit for the campaign. Initiatives like this record, as well as large-scale occupations of the land slated for construction, led to the cancelling of the project in 1982.

RÁDIO MOÇAMBIQUE

Rádio Moçambique
Mozambique

The state radio agency of postcolonial Mozambique, it worked with the label Ngoma to release a series of albums, including field recordings from the Lusaka Accord (which formalized Mozambican independence in 1974), a couple of 7″s of revolutionary songs by the a cappella group Coral das Forças Populares de Libertação de Moçambique, and a documentary history of FRELIMO (Frente de Libertação de Moçambique, or Mozambique Liberation Front).

RAG BABY

Rag Baby Records
USA

Initially started as a magazine, Rag Baby was a project of Country Joe McDonald. In 1965, he released the "Talking Issue" of the magazine as a lead-up to a Bay Area, California protest against the draft. The issue took the form of a 7″ with two songs by McDonald and his jug band The Fish (including the antidraft protest song "I-Feel-Like-I'm-Fixing-To-Die Rag") and two by Pete Krug. The cover states that these are "Songs of Opposition." The issue was a success, and a year later the first Country Joe and The Fish single was released under the Rag Baby moniker. A third single, simply called *Resist!*, featured a cover illustration of a protest fist hitting a military helmet (drawn by Jane Fonda). The label lay dormant for eight years, until the name was revived by McDonald in 1979 as an outlet for his music. Although a lot of this later output wasn't particularly protest oriented, a small number of serious political records were released, including McDonald's 1985 double LP, *Vietnam Experience*.

Rainbow Snake Records
USA

A small Massachusetts-based folk label connected to the lefty folk band Bright Morning Star. Between the late seventies and mid-eighties it put out about ten LPs, all politically progressive folk and pop with pro-queer, antinuke, and Latin American solidarity songs.

Raizer X Records
USA

A small San Francisco–based label that released records by political punk bands The Witnesses and The Looters (featuring former Prairie Fire member Mat Callahan), and a compilation documenting the political performance venue Komotion International (with tracks by Beatnigs, Peter Plate, and the Yeastie Girlz).

Raubbau
West Germany

A folk, krautrock, and early punk label from the Hamburg area, it released a couple dozen records in the early eighties, including political vinyl by Antropos and Slime (one of the most celebrated German punk bands).

Raven Records
USA

Raven is the label of Paul Metsa, a Minneapolis-based singer-songwriter who plays a Midwestern bluesy folk-rock with a labor consciousness at its core. Metsa used the label to release his 1984 LP *Paper Tigers* (named after Mao's description of the United States, I assume), and his 1985 7" "59 Coal Mines" b/w "Stars Over the Prairie." Locally he is known for happily performing at (and organizing) benefit concerts for a wide range of political issues.

Raw Ass Records
UK

An ad hoc label name used to release the 1989 benefit 7" *Smash the Poll Tax!*, with all proceeds going towards community resistance to the much-hated tax. A play on corporate benefit records, the band was called Punk Aid and was a "supergroup" consisting of members of popular anarcho-punk bands, including Active Minds, Chumbawamba, Oi Polloi, and more. The logo is a clear reworking of the masthead and graphic style of the anarchist newspaper *Class War*.

Rē Records
UK

Both Rē and Recommended are labels set up in 1978 by Chris Cutler, socialist and key member of the prog band Henry Cow. Along with Italy's

Stormy Six, Cutler and Henry Cow were the main players in the political prog rock entity Rock In Opposition, organized against the mainstream record industry. Rē was set up for Art Bears releases (Cutler's band, post–Henry Cow). Also known as ReR Megacorp.

Rebellion Records
Canada

Rebellion is the name used by early "world music" band Compañeros to release their 1979 LP *Blazing Frontiers*. The group was largely composed of Chilean and Greek musicians in exile in Canada, and their songs spoke to international solidarity and the immigrant experience.

Recommended Records
UK

Founded by Chris Cutler at the same time as Re Records, Recommended was used primarily to release music by bands he wasn't in, but in practice there was a lot of overlap. The output of both labels tends to be more avant-gardist than vanguardist, but there are definite overtly political gems, like a 12″ dedicated to striking miners in 1984.

Recordiau Anhrefn

Recordiau Anhrefn
Wales

A Welsh label founded in 1983 by Rhys Mwyn to release records by his punk band Yr Anhrefn (The

Disorder). It released fifteen records between 1984 and 1988, all by Welsh antiauthoritarian counterculture groups performing in the Welsh language, including punk, indie rock, and the first Welsh hip-hop act, Llwybr Llaethog. The label released multiple benefit records for both the UK Anti-Apartheid Movement and Cymdeithas yr Iaith Gymraeg, a militant nationalist campaign for Welsh-language education.

Recordiau Ar Log
Wales

A very small Welsh label that released two records, a 1984 LP by folk act Ar Log, and a 1985 compilation 7″ titled *Dwylo Dros y Môr* (Hands Off the Sea), a charity record to benefit Ethiopian famine victims.

Records Against Thaatchism!!!
Netherlands

An ad hoc label used to release a Dutch benefit LP for the UK miners' strike. The music, by The Ex, Morzelpronk, and Zowiso, was all recorded live in 1984. The record came with info and a poster in support of the strike. In all likelihood, Records Against Thaatchism!!! (or RAT) was another moniker for Ex Records, and this LP was probably put out by the band.

R-Edition
Denmark

Active in the late seventies through the early eighties and focused on releasing militant Latin American and Latin American–inspired folk music, including Karaxu (Chile), Pablo Milanés (Cuba), and Yolocamba I-Ta (El Salvador).

Redwood Records
US

A Bay Area–based folk label founded by Holly Near in 1972. It released all of Near's political albums, including *Hang In There*, created in support of the North Vietnamese), as well as releases by the Chileans Inti-Illimani and Victor Jara.

Refill Records
UK

Refill is the label set up by The Desperate Bicycles. Along with Crass, The Desperate Bicycles were the pioneers of the do-it-yourself spirit of punk, their motto being "it was easy, it was cheap—go and do it!" And they believed that forming a band and putting out records was just the first step in youth taking back their lives from corporate control. In order to prove how easy a record could be produced, they listed the costs on the back of their first 7". Between 1977 and 1980 the band self-released six 7" singles (one under the alternate band name The Evening Outs) and an LP on the Refill label.

Reigning Records
USA

Label of Seattle-based folk singer Dana Lyons, used to release his 1985 antinuclear 12" of the song "Our State is a Dumpsite."

Relevant Records
USA

Label name used by Matt Jones to release his music: an undated seventies funk rock 7" ("Hell No! I Ain't Gonna Go!" b/w "Supersam") and an undated eighties folk LP, *Matt Jones: Then and Now*. Jones had been a SNCC organizer and director of the Freedom Singers during the Civil Rights Movement.

Résistance
Québec

Released a series of compilation LPs in the early seventies under the title *Poèmes et Chants de la Résistances*, featuring a wide range of francophone chanson, poetry, stand-up comedy, and free jazz.

Resistance Records
Ireland

Not to be confused with the white-supremacist label of the same name, this is the label of the militant Northern Ireland nationalist group Men of No Property (who also released an LP with Paredon). In the mid-seventies it released a series of LPs with titles such as *Ireland: The Fight Goes On* and *England's Vietnam*.

Revolum
France

A Toulouse-based folk outfit that ran from the early seventies through the mid-nineties. It largely focused on music rooted in the different cultural traditions of southern France, including Basque and Occitan. The politics of the label are a product of the struggles for regional autonomy and independence in Europe. For example, the label released an early LP by Catalan singer-songwriter Jacmelina (Jacqueline Conte) that features a song dedicated to Salvador Puig Antich, a Catalan anarchist murdered by the Franco regime (in addition to a song in protest of the right-wing coup in Chile).

Ricordu
Corsica

This label released a broad collection of music recorded in the Corsican language (a significant portion of it pop music without discernable politics). Founded in the mid-seventies, it did release a number of records focused on Corsican autonomy and freedom.

Rise Up Records
USA

A label of the Afrocentric jazz band Spirit of Life Ensemble from Jersey City, New Jersey. In 1986 it released the now-much-sought-after LP *Journey into Freedom Music*, which features songs such as "Ronnie Got a Ray-Gun" and "Soweto."

Rival
Québec

Ad hoc label used to release a single record in 1975, the compilation *Le Disque L'Automne Show/On va passer à travers* (The Autumn Show Album/We will go through), documenting a concert put on for striking workers at United Aircraft in Longueuil, Québec.

Robin Hood
Netherlands

Appears to have put out a single album—*Christiania-Vores Musik*—a solidarity compilation from 1977 supporting Christiania, the squatted free town in the center of Copenhagen.

Rock Against Records
Netherlands

An early Dutch punk label that released about a dozen political punk records from 1980 to 1983, including a compilation of feminist punk bands titled *Rock Tegen de Rollen* (Rock Against Rolls/Roles) and multiple records whose sales benefited squats and squatting actions.

Rock Gegen Rechts
West Germany

Rock Against Racism in the UK released its *Greatest Hits* LP with big-name bands and major distribution in 1980, but a smaller German group from Hannover with a similar name actually beat them to the punch. In 1979, Rock Gegen Rechts (Rock Against the Right) released a document of a solidarity concert held that same year featuring anti-Nazi tracks from Misty in Roots as well as a bunch of local political prog, krautrock, and proto-punk bands. It also appears to have become an open-source label name of sorts, with multiple German punk and rock bands self-releasing records and listing "Rock Gegen Rechts" on the vinyl, probably due to the popularity of the sentiment expressed in the name.

Rock Against Racism
UK

At a concert in August 1976, Eric Clapton drunkenly told his audience to "keep Britain white"; this came on the heels of his first major hit, a cover of Bob Marley's "I Shot the Sheriff." In response, Roger Huddle (a member of the UK Socialist Workers Party), Red Saunders (an agitprop theater performer), and David Widgery (an author, organizer, and SWP member) wrote a letter to the *New Musical Express* denouncing Clapton and calling for a new movement: Rock Against Racism (RAR). A series of concerts was launched, always with an active balance of "white" and "Black" acts, as well as some of the few racially integrated bands, like The Specials. Big-name bands like The Clash, Elvis Costello, The Buzzcocks, and Aswad attracted up to a hundred thousand people to these gigs. In 1979, the Stevenage chapter of RAR (thirty miles north of central London) pressed a split 7" by Restricted Hours and The Syndicate. Two additional 7"s quickly followed: another split, this one by Proles and The Condemned; and a solo single by Alien Kulture, one of the few British punk bands with Asian members. In 1980, the central RAR branch compiled and released a *Greatest Hits* LP featuring fourteen bands that had played RAR gigs and supported the movement, including The Clash, Gang of Four, Tom Robinson Band, Elvis Costello, Steel Pulse, and X-Ray Spex. Although self-released on RARecords, the LP was distributed by Virgin. Versions were pressed in a half dozen countries, in collaboration with local political labels in some places (for instance, Nacksving in Sweden).

Rock Radical Records
France

Very early and short-lived French punk label started by members of The Brigades. Between 1982 and 1984, Rock Radical put out nine releases, including records by Bérurier Noir and most of The Brigades records, including the *Riot and Dance* 7" and the *Bombs n' Blood n' Capital* 12".

Røde Mor Musikforlag
Denmark

The popular communist band Røde Mor (Red Mother) released most of their albums on the collective label Demos, but in 1976, when that label had a political split, they began putting out their records themselves.

Rosetta Records
USA

Produced a number of LPs in the early eighties, primarily compilations of female jazz and blues performers. It was founded by Rosetta Reitz, who was part of many feminist groups, including NY Radical Feminists. The concept behind the label was to showcase forgotten women musicians and to give them their rightful place in history.

Rough Trade
UK

Rough Trade is both a label and a distributor of other independent UK record labels. It began as a record shop in London in 1976, and started pressing records in 1978. While its focus was on a broad range of independent music and styles, Rough Trade released key records by political punk and post-punk bands such as Stiff Little Fingers (who ended up writing a song about their experience with the label called "Rough Trade"), Angelic Upstarts, Scritti Politti, The Slits, Pop Group, Robert Wyatt, and Zounds. Not sticking to just Western pop, it also put out records by Tapper Zukkie and Thomas Mapfumo.

Rounder Records
USA

Rounder has released a broad array of US roots music, as well as a smattering of international records. Founded in 1970 by Ken Irwin, Bill Nowlin, and Marian Leighton Levy (Nowlin was active in the US anarchist movement in the sixties and seventies), Rounder in many ways stepped in to replace Folkways, particularly as the main outlet for blues, bluegrass, Appalachian, and other folk styles rooted in social commentary. It also put out a couple of anti-apartheid LPs: a document of the ANC pirate station Radio Freedom and a compilation of South African punk and new wave against military conscription called *Forces Favourites* (originally released on the South African label Shifty). Rounder also briefly (1985–87) had a UK-based sublabel called Rounder Europa that pressed and distributed its releases in Europe (in the late nineties this was relaunched in the Netherlands as Rounder Europe).

RPM
USA

A San Francisco–based jazz label from the eighties, RPM released a half dozen LPs, including two by Asian-American pianist Jon Jang and two by political free jazz group United Front (who gave their songs titles such as "There is Nothing More Precious than Independence and Freedom" and "Ballad of the Landlord," the latter based on a Langston Hughes poem).

R Radical
USA

Punk label run by Dave Dictor of MDC (Millions of Dead Cops/Millions of Damn Christians). It not only released MDC records throughout the eighties, but also D.R.I, B.G.K., and the influential antinuclear benefit compilation *P.E.A.C.E.* (It appears Dictor had a love of acronyms.)

Rugger Bugger
UK

A highly politicized punk label founded in the late eighties, but unlike most of its predecessors, Rugger Bugger refused to take itself too seriously. Much more pop-based bands, such

as Snuff and Wat Tyler, make up the bulk of the roster, as well as Chumbawamba-associated acts like Credit to the Nation, Danbert Nobacon, and the Passion Killers. The label ran until about 2003, but after 1995 or so it became a more general mash-up of less overtly political pop punk and new and rereleases of older eighties punk bands such as The Mob, The Subhumans, and Zounds.

Rundfunk der DDR
GDR

A label run by the state radio station in the GDR. Like other East German labels (Amiga, Eterna, etc.), the catalog is diverse and not entirely politically focused. The label did release a number of international solidarity LPs, including one documenting an Angela Davis speech in Berlin in 1973, and another, simply titled *Solidarität* and also from '73, which features a range of East German singers addressing Vietnam, Angela Davis, and solidarity.

Ruptura
Venezuela

A label that released one LP in 1970, a collection of songs in memory of the Venezuelan guerrilla leader Fabricio Ojeda, who cofounded the Venezuelan FALN (Fuerzas Armadas de Liberación Nacional, or Armed Forces of National Liberation) in 1963 and died in state custody in 1966.

SAFCO Records
USA

The label of the South African Freedom Committee, which released one LP–*Liberation: South Africa Freedom Songs*, a star-studded South African jazz record featuring Abdullah Ibrahim (Dollar Brand) and Sipo Mzimela. Ibrahim was central to organizing the album.

Šafrán 78
Sweden

This label was founded by Czech exiles Jiří Pallas and Jaroslav Hutka as an outlet for pressing records by other exiled or banned musicians and writers from Czechoslovakia. Šafrán translates as "Saffron" in Czech, and the label was set up in 1978. The label released about two dozen records between 1978 and 1985, including a radio play by Václav Havel, five LPs by Karel Kryl (a singer-songwriter who emerged out of the Prague Spring and was exiled in West Germany after his first LP was banned), and a number of records supporting the Polish Solidarność movement.

SALAAM

Salaam Records
USA

A sixties label connected to the Nation of Islam that released 7″ singles by Louis X (aka Louis Farrakhan) and other Nation-affiliated musicians.

"SALAMANSA RECORD'S"

Salamansa Records
Netherlands

The name used to release the Dutch version of an LP by Cape Verdean musician Nhô Balta. While the original LP was released by A Voz de Cabo-Verde and titled *Mel d'abelha* (A bee's honey), this edition is much more politicized, with the artist's name on the LP written as "Nhô Balta ma Voz d'Pove" (Voice of the People), the LP title changed to *Terra Livre* (Land and Freedom), and a cover image of Amílcar Cabral, a leader in the PAIGC (Partido Africano da Independência da Guiné e Cabo Verde, or the African Party for the Independence of Guinea and Cape Verde).

Salsa
USA

A New York City-based "Latin" music label that ran from 1971–82. As common for the period, much of the music featured loose themes of freedom and liberation, as well as references to Puetro Rican independence. The real standout on the label is the group, the Ghetto Brothers. Evolving out of gang culture, this crew of seven teenagers mashed up salsa, funk, and rock, creating a sound recognized as a precursor to hip-hop. Associated with the Puerto Rican Socialist Party, their music fluctuated between independence-themed salsa jams ("Viva Puerto Rico Libre," the rock-tinged "Ghetto Brothers Power," and the kinds of lyrics you'd expect from a crew of high school kids ("Girl from the Mountain").

Samspill
Norway

Early seventies leftist label with a strong focus on keeping Norway out of the European Economic Community, the forerunner of the European Union. Ultimately merged with, or evolved into, Plateselskapet Mai.

S and M Records
USA

Label name used to release a seventies Black nationalist jazz-poetry single by the Shahid Quintet, "Invitation to Black Power."

Saoirse Records
Northern Ireland

This label was used to release a single 7" in 1973, the James Connolly Folk Group's "Ballad of Joe Cahill/Lynch's Merry Men." Joe Cahill was a founder of the Provisional IRA, and was arrested in '73 for importing weapons into Northern Ireland.

save the mountain

Save the Mountain Album Project
USA

An ad hoc label created to release a local folk compilation album in 1980 as part of the political campaign to defend a mountain in Minnewaska State Park Preserve, in New York's Hudson Valley, from destruction and development by the Marriot hotel chain.

Ṣawt al-'Āṣifa (صوت العاصفة)
Egypt

The label of the Palestinian radio station of the same name (which roughly translates as "The Sound of the Storm"), run by the Fatah wing of the Palestinian Liberation Organization and based in Cairo. It released a series of 7" records in 1969, all with songs by the male choral group الفرقة المركزية (al-Firqa al-Marakziyya). The records were produced and distributed by Sono Cairo.

Ṣawt al-'Awda (صوت العودة)
Lebanon

Ṣawt al-'Awda was a label set up by the Popular Front for the Liberation of Palestine—General Command (PFLP-GC). Ṣawt al-'Awda roughly translates to "Talk Back." In 1968, the PFLP-GC split with the main Popular Front for the Liberation of Palestine over questions of militancy, with the GC demanding less talk and more action. It appears that only one 7" was ever released, a song called "Department of Redemption" with music by Nayef Ali and lyrics by poet Samih Hamada sung by someone called "Wadad." The record is undated, but was released in Lebanon, so is most likely from the period of the Lebanese Civil War, when the PFLP-GC was one of the militias fighting.

Scarab Records
USA

Scarab was the label of The Pharaohs, a Chicago jazz/funk group that grew out of the Afro-Arts Theater (run by Phil Cohran). The group was part of the Chicago jazz scene created by the Association for the Advancement of Creative Musicians and the Art Ensemble of Chicago. Although more pop oriented, the band maintained a strong Afrocentric vibe, featuring songs titled "Tracks of My Tears," "Black Enuff," and "Freedom Road."

Scarface Records
USA

Scarface was a Bay Area independent hip-hop label run by Black nationalist and leftist rapper and producer Paris. Paris was profoundly influenced by the Black Panthers and African liberation movements, and used his label to groom other political-leaning rap, including the Conscious Daughters.

Schneeball
West Germany

Schneeball (Snowball) was the successor to kraut/prog label April (the name was changed

in 1977). It released similar music, much of it politicized krautrock by the likes of Ton Steine Scherben, Checkpoint Charlie, and Brühwarm (about seventy five records between 1977 and 1990). It still exists, although since 1990 it has primarily focused on rereleasing its catalog on CD.

SDPL:N POHJOISUUDENMAAN AJ RY

SDPL:N Pohjois-Uudenmaan Aluejärjestö Ry
Finland

Otherwise known as the Union of Pioneers of the Democratic Society of Finland, SDPL:N was a Communist youth organization originally set up right after World War II, in part to root fascism out of the education system. In 1984, the group released an LP of children's marches titled *Ystävyyden Silta* (Friendship Bridge).

Sea Wave Records
USA

The label used by Jeriann Hilderley to release her 1978 new age folk LP *Jeritree's House of Many Colours*. Hilderly was part of the New York City women's music scene and had performed on the 1973 LP *A Few Loving Women*. This LP was distributed by Wise Women Enterprises.

Sedim Records
UK

This label released an undated 10″ (most likely in the late sixties) by Palestinian composer Youssef Khasho. The record, *Two Ouvertures:*

Palestine 1917–1947/El Fatah, is comprised of two works by Khasho, performed by the Symphony Orchestra of Rome. The first song is dedicated to the Palestinian people and the Nakba (catastrophe), the Palestinian name for the 1948 expulsion of Palestinians from their native land by Israeli forces; the second song is dedicated to Fatah and the Palestinian Liberation Organization, seen by Khasho as the Palestinians' only hope. This is possibly the only record released on the label.

S'EIGE ZEIGE

S'Eige Zeige
France

An ad hoc label used to release the French edition of *Marckolsheim/Wyhl: Lieder Im "Frendschaft's Huss"/Chansons Dans La "Maison De L'Amitié,"* a compilation LP of folk songs in support of the struggle opposing a nuclear power plant in Wyhl, which sits right on the border between Germany and France. The collection was put together by the group Les 31 Comités de Défence Badoises et Alsaciennes, and two versions were released, this one in France and one in Germany (by Trikont). Both versions were bilingual.

Servire il Popolo
Italy

The label of the Unione dei Comunisti Italiani (M-L), a small Italian far-left party that merged members of the Roman student movement, the PSIUP (Partito Socialista Italiano di Unità Proletaria), and other Trotskyist elements. They released one LP, *Alla Riscossa!* (To the Rescue!), that imagines the UCI (M-L) as the solution to all the problems of the Italian working class—"L'Italia sarà presto rossa!" (Italy will soon be red!)

Shanachie
USA

Started in 1976 as a home for Celtic fiddle music, it quickly branched out into other international music, much of it featuring social protest or commentary, including Black Uhuru, Ladysmith Black Mambazo, Linton Kwesi Johnson, and Fela. It also released an anti-apartheid record in celebration of the work of Bishop Desmond Tutu.

Shifty Records
South Africa

Named after a recording studio of the same name, it was started in part by Ivan Kadey of the punk band National Wake, and one of the engineers was Warric Swinney, who recorded under the name Kalahari Surfers. It released an amazing cross section of South African music from the eighties, from traditional Zulu worker choirs to political punk, dub poetry, reggae, and Afrobeat.

Significant Other Records
USA

Significant Other was the personal label of AIDS activist and singer-songwriter Michael Callen. It released a small number of CDs, and one LP, 1988's *Purple Heart*, which featured a number of his songs about living with AIDS and the AIDS crisis ("Living in Wartime," "How to Have Sex").

Silence
Sweden

Silence is an independent pop/rock/folk/progg label. I don't think it has a specific political leaning, but it released records by Tillsammans (a prolific polit-folk-rock band), a concept LP about social welfare by Troels Trier of Røde Mor, a couple collections of feminist songs, and multiple compilation albums against nuclear power and weapons.

Silhouttes in Courage
USA

An ambitious aural education project, in 1969–70 this label released three double LP box sets and one single LP box set narrating the history of Africans in America. In addition, it released a kids' funk LP recorded with the students of Public School 186, an elementary school in Harlem.

Simple Machines
USA

An early "indie rock" label founded by Jenny Toomey and Kristin Thomson. Although little of its musical output was explicitly political, one of the first things the label released was a popular handbook on how to press your own records and start your own label, updating and rejuvenating the DIY impulse of early punk bands like Crass and Desperate Bicycles.

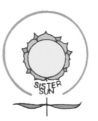

Sister Sun Records
USA

The record label of political and lesbian folk singer Joanna Cazden, which she used to produce five solo albums, including 1977's *Hatching*, which was widely distributed by Olivia Records, and 1984's *Rebel Girl*, named after and featuring a rendition of the song by Joe Hill. Cazden also co-penned the theme song for the 1983 LA Pride Parade.

Sisters Unlimited
USA

Sisters Unlimited was the label of lesbian singer-songwriter Carole Etzler. She used this name to release a half dozen records between 1976 and the mid-nineties, some with cellist Brenda Chambers.

Sky & Trees
UK

This is the largely cassette-only label of the anarcho-punk-*cum*-dance-band Chumbawamba, where they put out just shy of a dozen releases between 1983 and 1985. They used this label for informal releases prior to—and after—the creation of their more formal Agit-Prop imprint. Sky & Trees did release a vinyl LP, Danbert Nobacon's alternative kids' record *The Unfairy Tale*.

ſmokeſtax recordſ

Smokestax Records
USA

Smokestax was an ad hoc label used to release a single 7″ in 1979 by La Banda del Pueblo (The People's Band), a nueva canción/blues fusion band made up of Indiana steelworkers. The band played at union events across the Midwest in the seventies and early eighties, but this is their only vinyl release.

Socialdemokraterna
Sweden

The Swedish social-democratic labor party, which released *Vårt Vapen Heter Solidaritet* (Our Weapon is Solidarity), an LP of historical and traditional labor songs in 1975 with the help of A Disc.

Solidarity with Solidarity
UK

An ad hoc label set up to release a 7″ in support of the Polish Solidarity union movement in 1982. The record featured "Solidarity Defiant," a contemporary Polish workers anthem by Andrzej Smoleń.

Solomonic
Jamaica

The record label of Bunny Wailer, of Bob Marley and the Wailers fame. It released Wailer's

political albums *Struggle* and *Protest*, as well as singles like "Anti-Apartheid/Solidarity" by Peter Tosh.

Somodiscos
Mozambique

Somodiscos was a vinyl pressing plant set up in the early sixties in Mozambique by the Portuguese. After decolonization it was used by FRELIMO (the Mozambique Liberation Front) to press records by government agencies such as Rádio Moçambique and the Instituto Nacional do Livro e do Disco, as well as a double LP dedicated to its leader, Samora Machel, which simply lists Somodiscos as the label.

Sonorama
Costa Rica

A small label used by Nicaraguan exiles to record music in support of the Nicaraguan Revolution. Both Carlos Mejía Godoy and Grupo Pancasán released pro-Sandinista albums in the 1970s on Sonorama, and both would eventually record for the postrevolution Nicaraguan state label ENIGRAC.

Sound House Records
USA

The label used to release two folk compilation LPs to benefit the Hudson River sloop *Clearwater*. Founded by Pete Seeger and his wife in 1966, the group, the sloop, and an annual music festival are all focused on protecting the Hudson River. In part because of the work of Seeger and the *Clearwater*, a large amount of attention has been brought to General Electric's dumping of PCBs into the river throughout the mid–twentieth century, and parts of the upper Hudson have been designated as a Superfund cleanup site.

Sozialdemokrat Magazin

Sozialdemokrat Magazin
West Germany

A German social-democratic magazine that released a single LP in 1977: *". . . erkämpft das Menschenrecht": Lieder von Freiheit, Gerechtigkeit und Solidarität* (". . . fight for Human Rights": Songs of Freedom, Justice and Solidarity), a collection of labor and solidarity classics sung by polit-folk stalwart Lerryn.

Sozialistische Deutsche Arbeiterjugend
West Germany

Also known by its acronym SDAJ, the German Socialist Youth Workers functioned loosely as the youth wing of the German Communist Party. The group released at least two records in association with the label Pläne: a document of a 1974 benefit concert for Chile, and a 1980 promotional

7" featuring the folk song "Mach mit bei uns in der SDAJ" (Join us in the SDAJ).

SMI

Sozialistische Musiker Initiative
Switzerland

An experiment in creating an explicitly communist music project, the Sozialistische Musiker Initiative (SMI) released a single album in 1977, an experimental recording of text and sound by Max E. Keller and Martin Schwarzenlander. The record included a manifesto for the SMI: "Art (music) is the aesthetic form of social consciousness, which is class-specific in capitalist society. Bourgeois music, also in its avant-garde form, reflects the interests of the bourgeoisie. By contrast, the Socialist Musicians Initiative promotes and produces those musical works that seek to consciously and manifestly engage the people against oppression and socialism."

Spanischer Kulturkreis

Spanischer Kulturkreis
West Germany

The organization Spanischer Kulturkreis (Spanish Culture Circle) released one double LP in 1977, *Leben/Kämpfen/ Solidarisieren* (Living/Fighting/ Building solidarity). The record documents a massive international solidarity concert in Essen in 1976 with musicians and representatives from a wide swath of movements, including Andres Carmona (Basque ETA), Franco Trincale from Italy, Marcos Velasquez and Quintín Cabrera from Uruguay, and the ZANU-Gruppe from Zimbabwe. Another document of this same concert, with the same title but different songs, was released by Trikont in 1976.

Special Records
Canada

A blues-rock label that released the amazing 1972 political prog/jazz concept album *On the People's Side*, the sole record by the group Horn.

Spiderleg
UK

The label of the anarcho-punk band Flux of Pink Indians (who got their start on Crass Records). In addition to Flux records, from 1981–84 it released vinyl from like-minded groups such as Amebix, Kronstadt Uprising, and The Subhumans (UK).

Spiral Records
USA

Small mid-nineties punk label from California, notable because its second release was a benefit for the Denver General Hospital Sexual Assault Volunteers. It was also the label of Resist and Exist, an anarcho-punk band heavily influenced by anti-imperialist politics and the Black Panthers. Resist and Exist founder Jang Lee is from South Korea, and Korean political history informs the band (their first LP is called *Kwangju*, named after the city that saw a massive popular revolt against military rule in 1980).

Spring Records
Northern Ireland

Spring was started in 1982 by Colum Sands, of the popular lefty Northern Ireland song group The Sands Family. He used the label to release records related to The Sands Family, most with at least some content related to working-class Irish life and the Troubles.

ST. PANCRAS RECORDS

St. Pancreas Records
UK

This was the label Scritti Politti used to release their initial three records (*Skank Bloc Bologna* 7″ in 1978, *Work in Progress* 7″ in 1979, and *4 "A Sides"* 12″ in 1979, the latter two in association with Rough Trade). They went on to become a major-label pop phenomenon, but these early recordings catch the band as the discordant Marxist art students they started out as. The initial 7″ in particular is an attempt to engage politics through music—the band begun as a self-described leftist collective, inspired equally by seeing the Sex Pistols live in 1976 and reading Italian Marxist theorist Antonio Gramsci (which is where they copped the name).

Sterile Records
UK

Sterile was an early industrial music label founded by Nigel Ayers of the band Nocturnal Emissions. Along with fellow UK industrialists Test Dept., Nocturnal Emissions sat squarely on the left wing of a musical movement that often flirted (and still flirts) with the Right and fascism. Sterile put out about thirty releases between 1980 and 1986, with fourteen of those on vinyl. The label released the Nocturnal Emissions LPs

Songs of Love and Revolution and *Shake Those Chains, Rattle Those Cages*, as well as recordings by SPK and Lustmørd, and many compilations, including 1985's *Here We Go*, a benefit for the UK miners' strike going on at the time ("All proceeds to the miners!").

STICHTING ISARA

Stichting Isara
Netherlands

I haven't been able to find any information about this label beyond what's on an undated LP I have titled *Daarom ben ik bereid te sterven* (Why I am ready to die). The A side has extracts from a recording of Nelson Mandela's speech at the 1964 Rivonia Trial, and the B side contains six songs by an unattributed South African Zulu jazz band. A UK version of this same album was released on Ember Records in 1964. Ember otherwise almost exclusively rereleased R&B records from the US.

STOPP APARTHEID-86

Stopp Apartheid-86
Norway

This was an ad hoc label (and band) set up to release a 1986 anti-apartheid 7″ conceived and recorded by Rolf Aakervik, Abuwa Edeshowo, and a collection of Norwegian musicians. All proceeds were donated to the African National Congress.

Strata-East
USA

Musician-run avant-garde jazz label (founded by Charles Tolliver and Stanley Cowell) with a heavy

dose of Black nationalist and socially conscious free jazz and soul funk. Gil Scott-Heron, Jayne Cortez, Mtume Umoja Ensemble, The Ensemble Al-Salaam, and Oneness of JuJu all recorded for the label.

Stroppy Cow Records
UK

An explicitely feminist label, Stroppy Cow was home to Ova, Jam Today, Siren, and other women-only groups. It put out about a dozen LPs in the 1980s, and each record contained a variation of the same mission statement: "We are anti-commercial—we aim to make a living as musicians rather than a profit as a business."

STUDENT
NON-VIOLENT
COORDINATING
COMMITTEE
SNCC-101

Student Nonviolent Coordinating Committee
USA

The Student Nonviolent Coordinating Committee (SNCC) was one of the major Civil Rights organizations in the US in the sixties. SNCC put out one of the first vinyl records in support of the movement, 1962's *Freedom In the Air*.

Subverskivbolaget
Sweden

A play on words, the name roughly translates as "Subversive Record Company." It released about a dozen records in the seventies, mostly folk plus a left antimilitarist prog rock LP by Subgruppen.

SUDDEN RECORDS

Sudden Death Records
Canada

Punk label founded by Joey Shithead of the band D.O.A. From 1978–86, it released a half dozen records by or featuring D.O.A., including the *Right to Be Wild!* 7″—a benefit for the campaign to free five anarchist political prisoners then facing life in prison for environmental, feminist, and antinuclear direct actions. It also released the anti-apartheid single *Expo Hurts Everyone*, and a 7″ of D.O.A.'s song "General Strike," in support of a proposed 1983 general strike by British Columbia's Solidarity Coalition against government austerity measures.

SudNord Records
Italy

Late eighties/early nineties label that released a diverse catalog of Italian folk and global music, including two LPs by the Palestinian band Handala.

Suomen Työväen Musiikkiliitto Ry
Finland

The Suomen Työväen Musiikkiliitto (Finnish Workers' Music Association) functioned as a music publishing company until 1980, when it began releasing a series of Nordic folk and polka records under its own name, including multiple double LP sets in honor of the organization's sixtieth and seventieth anniversaries (in 1980 and 1990, respectively), which collected songs from throughout its history.

Survival Alliance
USA

An antinuclear organization that released a single record, a folk/blues album by a group of musicians calling themselves Meltdown Madness. The record contains songs such as "The Radiation Blues," "The Abandoned Reactor Jig," and "The Ballad of Karen Silkwood."

Survival Records
USA

The record label of Rashied Ali, who ran a free jazz loft space called Ali's Alley from 1973–79 in Soho, NYC. The label released a dozen records between 1973 and 1976, the majority of them by Ali and his Quintet (Ali relaunched the label in 1999 and ran it until he passed away in 2009). Most of the early recordings have a heavy Black nationalist bent, and were engineered by Marzette Watts.

Svenska Chilikomittén
Sweden

One of many Scandinavian solidarity committees, the Swedish Chilikomittén was a broadly anti-imperialist solidarity group that existed for twenty years, from 1971–91. It helped produce a single LP: *Chile-Kampen Går Vidare* (Chile-The Fight Goes On), a 1975 Scandinavian edition of the album *Canción para los Valientes* (Song for the Brave) by Venezuelan nueva canción singer Ali Primera. The LP was co-released with the organization's Finnish counterpart, Soumi-Chile-Seura (Finnish-Chile-Club).

Swords Into Plowshares
USA

This Philadelphia-based peace organization worked with Folk Tradition Records to release the 1985 double album *Swords Into Plowshares: Songs of Freedom and Struggle*, featuring Pete Seeger, Tom Paxton, Roy Brown, Bright Morning Star, Si Kahn, the Kim and Reggie Harris Group, and a dozen additional folk performers.

Sveriges Socialdemokratska Ungdomsförbund
Sweden

More popularly known as the SSU, the Sveriges Socialdemokratska Ungdomsförbund (Swedish Social Democratic Youth League) is the youth wing of the Swedish Social Democratic Party (Socialdemokraterna). Originally founded in 1917, in the sixties and seventies the SSU took on an internationalist position, focusing particularly on opposition to the Vietnam War. While a couple records were released under the SSU name, the group primarily used its publishing wing, Frihets Förlag (Freedom Publishers), for vinyl output. The output of SSU, Frihets Förlag, and Socialdemokraterna is blurry and overlapping, with many releases listing more than one of the organizatons as the label.

Taï-Ki
France

The ad hoc label name used to release early pressings of *Magny 68/69*, an LP by political chanteuse Colette Magny. A document of the May '68 uprising in France, the record is an assemblage of field recordings, poetry, and singing, with Magny building her songs on top of recordings made by William Klein and Chris Marker during the revolt. The title of the extended piece on the A side of the record is "Nous Sommes le Pouvoir" (We are the power), taken from a slogan on a poster produced by the Ateliers Populaire, a radical printing group active during the uprising.

SWAPO
Namibia

SWAPO (South West African People's Organization) was the main organization and political party that led the independence movement for Namibia (formerly known as South West Africa) in 1990. One of the party's musical groups, the SWAPO Singers, released a single with Robert Wyatt (on Rough Trade, but co-listed as a SWAPO release) and an LP (*One Namibia, One Nation*) in association with the Netherlands-based solidarity organization Angola Comité.

Tammi
Finland

Tammi was a short-lived sixties label that released around a half dozen records, including an LP by leftist poet Arvo Turtiainen, a 7" of Brecht and Eisler songs by Kaisa Korhonen, and an LP by communist avant-garde composer Kaj Chydenius (who also founded the KOM Theater).

Les Temps des Cerises
France

This label's name translates as "Season of the Cherries," and is taken from one of the most famous chanson songs in French history, originally written in the 1860s but popularized by its use during the Paris Commune in 1871. The label put out a half dozen records in the mid-seventies, almost all far-left free jazz by the bands Intercommunal Free Dance Music Orchestra and Fanfare Bolchévique de Prades-Le Lez.

Teachers Action Caucus
USA

This group released an LP in 1972 titled *Angela Must Be Free!* that features songs by the Rev. Frederick Douglass Kirkpatrick and speeches by left and communist members of the New York City Teacher's Union such as Celia Zitron.

Terrapin Records
USA

A Chicago-based label that released Sirani Avedis's 1979 LP, *Tattoos*. Avedis was a feminist and lesbian singer-songwriter with an all-women backing band called Kid Sister.

El Teatro del Triangulo
Venezuela

One of the more mysterious records I've come across, a political theater group calling itself El Teatro del Triangulo self-released a great anti-imperialist nueva canción LP by its musical wing, Grupo del Triangulo. The record, called *Otra Vez...*, was released sometime in the sixties or seventies, and features an amazing cover illustration by Alexis Matamoros. There is almost no information on the record about when and where it was pressed, and research has turned up little else, but the songs include a mix of originals and genre classics by Héctor Numa Moraes (Uruguay), Judith Reyes (Mexico), and Atahualpa Yupanqui (Argentina). One of the group's members, Luis Suaraz, also played on records by Venezuelan nueva canción singers Ali-Ko and Alí Primera.

Terz
West Germany

A small mid-eighties Hamburg-based label that released an eclectic set of about a dozen records, including a 7" of the song "Fighting for Nelson Mandela" by the rock group HH 19, a nueva canción LP by exiled Chilean group Amauta, and a joint LP by German and Turkish protest singers Frank Baier and Mesut Çobancaoglo. The label was distributed (and possibly manufactured) by Pläne.

Théâtre de l'Aube
France

I can find almost nothing about this theater ("l'Aube" means "Dawn"), but in 1979 it released an LP titled *Aux Infants de Soweto*, a recording of a musical performance by Abia Mukoko based on Cameroonian author Paul Dakeyo's poetry in response to the 1976 Soweto Uprising in South Africa.

Le Théâtre de l'Ouest Parisien
France

Le Théâtre de l'Ouest Parisien was founded in 1968 and was administered by Mohammed Boudia until its forced closure in the early seventies. Boudia, an Algerian playwright and journalist who had been an active member of the Front de Libération Nationale (FLN) and then a militant with the Popular Front for the Liberation of Palestine (PFLP), used the theater as a front for recruiting revolutionaries from immigrant communities and the formerly incarcerated. The theater staged a number of political productions, including a 1971 run of Henri-François Rey's 1954 play *La Bande à Bonnot* (about the anarchist bank robbers the Bonnot Gang). Boudia was killed in June 1973, although it is unclear if he was assassinated by Mossad or accidently blown up by a bomb he made and was carrying in his car. Palestinian supporters pressed a record under the label name TOP (Le Théâtre de l'Ouest Parisien) in homage to Boudia. The record documents a memorial event for Boudia held at the Theater.

Third World Records
USA

A label set up to release records by Clifford Thornton—jazz trumpet player, member of the Sun Ra Arkestra, and cornet player on Archie Shepp's *Attica Blues*. It released his 1969 free jazz LP *Freedom & Unity*, which included the tracks "Free Huey" and "Uhuru."

Thunderbird Records
USA

Thunderbird is the name used on *¡Viva la Causa!*, a 1966 LP documenting the Delano grape pickers strike organized by the United Farm Workers (UFW). The first side of the LP features songs and skits by El Teatro Campesino, and the second side features field recordings of the strikers themselves. The name of the label is likely derived from the UFW symbol of a black Aztec eagle inside a white circle on a red background.

Thunderbird Records
USA

An ad hoc label name used to release the 1973 feminist folk and country LP *Virgo Rising: The Once and Future Woman*. The record featured women-centric and labor-oriented songs by Nancy Raven, Malvina Reynolds, Janet Smith, and others. The record was produced and bankrolled by Mollie Gregory, who has written multiple books and made a number of films about the role of women in Hollywood.

TINGLUTI FORLAG

Tingluti Forlag
Denmark

The record label of Danish folk singer Fin Alfred Larsen, a member of the political progg group Den Røde Lue, which released a string of records opposing Denmark's participation in NATO, entry into the European Union, and in support of striking workers.

Toma lá Disco
Portugal

The first truly independent Portuguese record label, founded as a musician's collective in 1975. Released music by a wide range of supporters of the 1974 Portuguese revolution and the broader Portuguese Left, including José Jorge Letria (a member of the Portuguese Communist Party [PCP]), José Carlos Ary dos Santos (who was originally a member of the PCP, but became more militant during the revolution and joined the Maoist armed group the União Democrática Popular [UDP]), Júlia Babo, and Paulo de Carvalho (one of the founders of Toma lá Disco, and writer of the anthem of the social-democratic Partido Popular Democrático).

Ton Cooperative Hannover
West Germany

A small recording studio based in Hannover

that recorded a wide range of musicians, but only released two records under its own name. Both are by the Arbeiter-Musik-Assoziation, are overtly political, and were distributed by Trikont. The first is from 1973, a 7" called *MC Talking Blues*, featuring songs about George Jackson, Joe Hill, and Sacco and Vanzetti. The second is an undated LP titled *Lieder des Internationalen Proletariats*, which is exactly that, a collection of workers' songs from around the world, including "Die Internationale," "Bella Ciao," and "Which Side Are You On?"

topic

Topic
UK

A British traditional folk label that had a catalog similar to the folk and blues part of Folkways. It featured US artists like Woody Guthrie, Peggy and Pete Seeger, and Sonny Terry alongside UK acts like Dominic Behan, The Exiles, and Ewan MacColl. The label also released dozens of collections of traditional music from Britain, Scotland, and Ireland. A decent amount of its output includes workers' songs, prisoner songs, Irish resistance tunes, and similar fare.

Trades Union Congress

Trades Union Congress
UK

A federation of unions across the UK, the Trades Union Congress (TUC) released a 7" (produced and distributed by Rough Trade) in 1985 featuring Robert Wyatt (of Soft Machine fame) with The Grimethorpe Colliery Brass Band, with all proceeds going to the TUC Miners' Hardship Fund (this was during the UK miners' strike).

Tribal War
USA

Anarcho-punk label with a twenty-year run, putting out over fifty records from 1991–2010. It released vinyl by Anti-Product, Aus-Rotton, and Resist and Exist. Not just a label, founder Neil Robinson (who also played in the anarcho-punk band Nausea) could be found at every nineties Sunday punk matinee show at New York City's ABC No Rio with a giant table of records he was distributing for dozens of small, DIY labels from around the world.

Tribe Records
USA

Tribe was a collectively run jazz label from Detroit. Founded by Phil Ranelin and Wendell Harrison in 1972, it was operated by a dozen or so musicians for its five year existence. It released just shy of a dozen records by multiple constellations of musicians who made up the Tribe family (including Doug Hammond, David Durrah, Jimmy McCloud, Marcus Belgrave, Harold McKinney, as well as Harrison and Ranelin). The label had a pronounced Black nationalist and spiritualist perspective, with Afrocentric motifs in both album cover art and songs, including the tracks "The Time is Now for Change," "Ode to Africa," "Farewell to the Welfare," and "Wake Up Brothers."

Tribune Socialiste
France

In the seventies, *Tribune Socialiste* was the weekly paper of the United Socialist Party (PSU) in France. The paper released one 7″ of songs dedicated to the Vietnamese struggle by socialist chanson singer Simone Bartel. Politically, the PSU was akin to the left wing of France's Socialist Party (social democratic but with support for workers' self-management).

Tricontinental
Cuba

The record label of the Organization of Solidarity with the Peoples of Africa, Asia, and Latin America. OSPAAAL is best known for its internationalist political posters and its magazine *Tricontinental*, but it also released one LP, a collection of national anthems from countries in the Global South that the organization worked in solidarity with.

Trikont
West Germany

Trikont, also known as Trikont Unsere Stimme, is the music wing—founded in the early seventies—of the radical German publisher Trikont

Verlag. "Unsere Stimme" means "Our Voice," and the "Trikont" part of the name is derived from the concept of the tricontinental—the political centrality of the three continents of the Global South: Africa, Asia, and Latin America. Although it did release records from the Third World (in particular an album by Karaxu, the group of young Chilean exiles that actively supported the armed struggle group MIR, and three LPs by the Liberian funk rock group Kapingbdi), its focus was mostly on German polit-folk and krautrock. It also had an interesting focus on marginal US folk styles—from the release of a slew of Cajun records to a series of Native American folk and country LPs. In addition to record production, the label also did a significant amount of distribution, in particular of other like-minded labels from around the world, including I Dischi del Sole, Expression Spontanée, Folkways, and Paredon.

Franco Trincale
Italy

Franco Trincale was a musician trained in the Sicilian storytelling tradition. He started out in the early sixties writing popular tunes about news events for the large Milan-based Fonola record company. In the seventies, Trincale merged two traditions, Italian storytelling and protest folk, to forge what he called "*giornalismo cantato*," or journalism through song. He came from the working class, and saw himself as a voice for his people. By telling their stories, he denounced injustice, championed their struggles, and called out politicians and capitalists for their greed and corruption. As the working-class struggle in Italy became more militant in 1969 ("Hot Autumn"), he began performing live in and outside factories during strikes, crafting songs about workers' struggles and bringing workers with him to perform in the next factory, and so on. From 1969 through the mid-seventies he pressed a series of self-released records documenting all

these songs, including *Cantiamo insieme* (Let's Sing together), *Canzoni in Piazza!* (Songs in the Public Square), *Canzoni di Lotta* (Songs of struggle), and *Canzone Nostra* (Our Song). Trincale didn't use a separate label name or moniker on his self-released albums, which is why I've included his name here *as* the label name.

TSL
Finland

A socialist folk label that released a half dozen records in the late seventies and early eighties. Its output is a mix of Finnish folk and workers' songs, along with an early punk rendition of "L'Internationale" by Rytmimusiikkiyhtye Heippa, and a couple 7"s of international field recordings from Africa and Asia.

TURC
UK

Coventry-based label that appears to be the private press of the Banner Theatre, a political and activist theater troupe. I haven't been able to figure out what the acronym TURC stands for, but the 7" I have (catalog number "TURC 2") is a benefit for "jailed and sacked" striking miners from the Keresley Pit in Coventry, so I suspect the T and U stand for "Trade Union."

TVD
West Germany

Thomas-Verlag Düsseldorf, a publisher and record label founded by Uwe Seidel, a member of a religious sect that follows the teachings of Thomas à Kempis, the author of *The Imitation of Christ*. In the seventies and early eighties, TVD functioned as a home for records rooted in liberation theology, including albums in solidarity with Chile, Nicaragua, and South Africa.

Two Tone
UK

Started in Coventry by Jerry Dammers of The Specials, Two Tone was left-leaning and staunchly antiracist. Unlike many of the labels that were part of the Rock Against Racism scene, it was unique in its attempt to merge Black and white musicians into the same bands, rather than simply putting out both punk and reggae records side by side, but never touching. The label also released "The Boiler," Rhoda Dhakar's harrowing musical account of being date raped. Dammers went on to become a key organizer in the UK Anti-Apartheid Movement and champion of the cultural boycott of South Africa. The Specials track "Free Nelson Mandela" became both the most popular anti-apartheid song of the eighties, and an unofficial theme song for the movement.

UAW Records
USA

The label of the United Auto Workers, historically one of the largest and most powerful unions in the US. The name was used on and off from the sixties into the nineties, mostly for labor-themed folk music, including compilations with titles like

Rise Again: Union Songs for the '80s and *Songs for a Better Tomorrow*.

Ugat Tunog Ng Lahi
Philippines

The name of this label translates as "Root Sound Race." It started as a compilation of pinoy music on Vicar Music (one of the main Filipino record companies) and was quickly spun off as its own label. In 1978 it released the first album by the group Asin, one of the first records in the Philippines to mix traditional folk styles with rock elements and emancipatory politics. It also released multiple records by political folk star Freddie Aguilar between 1978 and 1980.

Uitgeverij Polypoepka
Netherlands

A record-producing collective founded in 1981, which ran for about five years. It had a duel focus: putting out records by radical Dutch bands, such as RK Veulpoepers BV (anarchist folk-rock); and putting out solidarity records with leftist militant music groups from El Salvador (Banda Tepeuani, Yolocamba I-Ta).

Ulo
Greenland

Greenland's first significant record label, founded in 1977 by Danish producer Karsten Sommer.

Sommer was introduced to music from Greenland while producing Sume's *Sumut* LP for Demos. Sume was Greenland's first political folk-rock band, and Sommer worked with them to release two LPs for Demos, before moving to Greenland and setting up Ulo. The first record released was Sume's third LP, followed by more than a hundred records over the next twenty years, most focused on preserving Greenland's musical culture.

Ultimatum
Netherlands

Ultimatum was the name of a Netherlands-based Latin American info and action center. It was a main proponent of the eighties "Weapons for El Salvador" campaign, which raised money to buy weapons for leftist guerillas in El Salvador. In 1989, Ultimatum teamed up with the punk band The Plot to release a benefit 7″ for the campaign, pressed by the punk/alternative label ADM, with all proceeds going to El Salvador. "Weapons for El Salvador" is also the name of a song by the Dutch political punk band The Ex.

Undercurrent Records
USA

Record label of the Black United Front in Kansas City. Throughout the eighties it released a series of annual *Frontliners* compilation LPs of Afrocentric soul, spoken word, and jazz, including tracks by Haki R. Madhubuti, Sonia Sanchez, and Serious Bizness, among others.

Unga Örnar
Sweden

Unga Örnar is Swedish socialist youth organization that is part of the International Falcon Movement–Socialist Educational International (IFM-SEI), which includes the Rote Falken in Germany and Switzerland. Different chapters in Sweden have released records since the early seventies, mostly pop and folk children's songs. (In addition, it is a sister organization to the International Union of Socialist Youth [IUSY], which is also included in this encyclopedia.)

Ungkommunistens Förlag
Sweden

The name translates to "Young Communist Publishing" and the label released only a small number of records, including a much sought after double 7″ by the communist progg group Knutna Nävar titled *Vi slåss för vår framtid* (We fight for our future) and a garage-y proto-punk LP by Röda Ropet titled *Spänn Bågen* (Tighten the Bow) in 1975.

UGT

União Geral de Trabalhadores
Portugal

A union that released one 7″, *Hino da UGT*, sometime in the late seventies. The União Geral de Trabalhadores (UGT), or General Union of

Workers, is generally aligned with Portuguese Socialist Party.

UNI/CI/TÉ

UNI/CI/TÉ
France

Short for "Unité Cinéma Télévision," the label was run by Communists who worked in the media industry to support the French Communist Party. Most of the records are speeches or educational, with little or no music.

Union des Étudiants Vietnamiens en France
France

A student organization that released one single in the sixties, *Vietnam Chant*—a collection of Vietnamese songs against French colonialism and in support of national liberation.

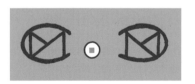

Union des Populations du Cameroun
Cameroon

The Union des Populations du Cameroun (UPC) is a Communist political party in Cameroon, initially founded by trade unionists in 1947 as part of the anticolonial movement. In 1953, it encouraged and participated in a widespread revolt against the French; by 1955 the revolt was suppressed and the party banned. The UPC went underground and fought a guerilla war until the early seventies. While in hiding and exile in the late seventies and early eighties, the party released at least two LPs of Pan-African

folk music. The one I have is titled *Chanson du Manidem/Manidem Songs*, "Manidem" being shorthand for "Mouvement Africain pour la Nouvelle Indépendance et la Démocratie," a faction of the UPC that would eventually split off in the nineties.

Union of God's Musicians and Artists Ascension
USA

The Union of God's Musicians and Artists Ascension (usually referred to by its acronym, UGMAA) was a musicians collective formed by Black nationalist jazz piano player and band leader Horace Tapscott and his Pan-Afrikan Peoples Arkestra. Based in Los Angeles, the UGMAA was part political concept, part artists' union (it helped Black musicians find gigs), and part educational project—providing music lessons for poor and working-class kids in the city.

Unitarian Universalist Records
USA

The Department of Education and Social Concern of the Unitarian Universalist Church in Boston set up this label (and the Worship Arts Clearing House, its distribution wing) in 1970 to release records by left-wing Christian folk musician Ric Masten. Throughout the seventies, seven Masten records were pressed by the label, most from the Boston church, but at least one was produced by the First Unitarian Church of Pittsburgh.

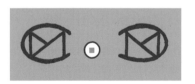

A B C D E F G H I J K L M N O P Q R S T U V W X Y Z

United Steel Workers of America
USA

The largest industrial union in North America, the USWA put out an LP in the early eighties which was distributed to its rank-and-file membership. *Songs of Steel and Struggle* is a fifteen-song concept album by Joe Glazer, in which he takes the listener through a tour of the history of the Steelworkers. While it includes classics such as "Solidarity Forever," the bulk of the LP consists of songs specifically written for this project.

Uniteledis
France

Founded by the French Socialist Party in 1973, in part as a training facility in media making for party organizers. Throughout the rest of the decade it released a limited yet interestingly eclectic catalog, including albums and singles by Archie Shepp, Mikis Theodorakis, Quilapayún, Carlos Puebla, and speeches by party leader François Mitterand.

Universidad Autonoma de Sinaloa
Mexico

Small in-house label of the Autonomous University of Sinaloa in Mexico. Not very active, but it released two LPs of politicized folk/nueva canción by León Chávez Teixeiro. Teixero was involved in both the labor and 1968 movements in Mexico, and often performed live at protests and marches. The two albums released by UAS in 1979 and 1981 were reissued later in the eighties by Pentagrama.

UP
Chile

The record label of Chile's Unidad Popular party, the coalition that brought Salvador Allende to power in 1970. Distributed (and likely produced) by DICAP to promote UP in the 1970 election, a single 7″ was released under the label name—a collection of nueva canción chilena, including Victor Jara performing "Venceremos," the UP campaign song.

Upright
UK

A London-based indie label from the eighties which has a small and eclectic catalog, including records by the leftist dub poet Benjamin Zephaniah, the anarcho-feminist punk band Poison Girls, and *The Pope is a Dope* 7″ by The Living Legends, featuring Ian Bone, who would go on to form the anarchist organization and newspaper *Class War*.

Uprising
Trinidad and Tobago

The label of Brother Resistance and his genre of

rapso, a politicized mixture of rap, reggae, and soca developed in the late eighties and early nineties in Trinidad.

URC
Japan

The URC (Underground Record Club, アング ラ・レコード・クラブ) was one of the first independent Japanese record labels and was initially run as a subscriber-based vinyl club. It was founded in 1969 by Yoshio Hayakawa, songwriter for the early psychedelic folk group Jacks. The initial records released by the label are compilations of field recordings of Tokyo "folk guerrillas," or street musicians. The covers feature photos of protests and demonstrations. URC was the home of Japan's most well-known protest singer, Nobuyasu Okabayashi, as well as much of the early seventies Japanese folk revival. It also released a 7″ by Vietnamese antiwar poet and singer Trịnh Công Sơn and a rendition of "The Ballad of Ho Chi Minh" by Japanese folk singer Tomoya Takaishi.

URGENT
RECORDS

Urgent Records
USA

The record label of singer-songwriter Dave Lippman, who used it throughout the eighties to release a series of increasingly satirical rock/ new wave records. The first 7″ is the most didactically political, with a cover featuring Jimmy Carter, Ronald Reagan, Henry Kissinger, and Uncle Sam in fatigues with assault rifles marching in front of the Ku Klux Klan as they burn a cross on the lawn of the White House.

Utility
UK

The London-based label that was home to Billy Bragg, including his album *The Internationale*.

Valentim de Carvalho
Portugal

Portuguese pop label that had a pressing plant in Angola and produced and distributed much of the musical output of the Portuguese colonies in Africa, including the Angolan labels N'Gola and MPLA/DIP, as well as pro-Portuguese revolutionary folk after the leftist coup in 1974. In 1983, it merged with the Portuguese wing of EMI.

Vancouver Folk Music Festival Recordings
Canada

The Vancouver Folk Music Festival is an annual three-day outdoor music festival begun in 1978. The festival has often featured highly politicized folk and international acts. As an extension of the festival itself, Canadian folk label Aural Tradition Records worked with the organizers to release over a dozen LPs in the eighties and early nineties, including Utah Phillips's album of IWW songs, *We Have Fed You All a Thousand Years* (released on Philo in the US), two LPs by militant Salvadoran band Yolocamba I-Ta, a compilation of folk songs in solidarity with Central America called *Bullets and Guitars*, and a couple albums of Japanese folk music by Takeo Yamashiro.

VARAgram
Netherlands

The record label of the radio station VARA, which started in 1925 with strong ties to the Social Democratic Workers' Party in the Netherlands. Although it went on to release a really broad collection of records, it also showed its left-leaning origins, putting out a large number of Latin American artists who supported popular struggles in their countries (particularly Nicaragua), a fair number of anti-apartheid records, and a small list of Dutch political folk music, including worker and antifascist songs.

Venceremos
Netherlands

A small label dedicated to releasing Cuban nueva trova records to a Dutch audience. I only have one compilation LP–*La Nueva Trova*–and it's difficult to tell from the record and catalog number whether other albums were released as well.

Vendémiaire
France

Founded in 1977 by experimental Corsican musician Jean-Pierre Graziani. Although the focus is on experimental and free jazz records (by groups like L'Intercommunal Free Dance Music Orchestra), the label had a strong anti-imperialist and antifascist streak, with a diverse list of albums that includes *Chant et Danses d'Erythree* (Eritrean Songs and Dances), *Argentine Solidarité*, *Chants Revolutionnaires d'Oman*, and an antiprison concept album dedicated to the Red Army Faction.

Ventadorn
France

The record label of the Institut d'Estudis Occitans, Ventadorn ran for a decade (1971–81) and released about one hundred records, the vast majority folk music in the Occitan language. Although the music was not always political, many of the prominent artists on the label, such as Marti and Patric, developed out of the leftist nueva canción tradition of reviving regional popular song.

Vento de Leste
Portugal

Vento de Leste, which means "East Wind," was a name used to release a couple records in 1977: the East Timorese independence LP *Hinos e*

Canções da Revolução do Povo Maubere (Hymns and Songs of the Revolution of Maubere People), which was released in concert with the political groups Fretilin and Comité 20 de Novembro; and a 7″ of a version of "L'Internationale" sung by the group Coro Popular "O Horizonte é Vermelho" ("The Horizon is Red" People's Chorus), a communist song group that emerged from the Carnation Revolution in Portugal and also released records on Alvorada and their own Viva o Povo! label.

Verlag Jürgen Sendler
West Germany

A short-lived label of the seventies that released solidarity records in support of Third World liberation organizations, including ZANU (Zimbabwe African National Union), PAIGC (African Party for the Independence of Guinea and Cape Verde), and the Vietminh in Vietnam. VJS was also a publisher of antifascist and communist books.

VERLAG NEUER WEG

Verlag Neuer Weg
West Germany

Neuer Weg (New Way) was the publishing house and record label of the Kommunistische Arbeiterbund Deutschlands (KABD, or Communist Workers' Union of Germany), a left splinter off the KPD, West Berlin's traditional Communist Party and political puppet of the GDR. In the mid-seventies it released a series of at least three 7″s of international *rote lieder*, or "red songs," (from China, Palestine, Angola, Chile, and more) recorded by the Stuttgarter Chor, the Orchester des KABD, and Roter Zünder (Red Detonator), the propaganda wing of the KABD.

Vermiform
USA

The label started in 1990 by Born Against singer Sam McPheeters. Tottering between, on the one hand, anger and cynicism about living under the right-wing policies of Ronald Reagan and George Bush, and on the other, hopefulness about building an alternative through do-it-yourself ethics, Vermiform staked out a new sound and politics for hardcore kids. Through bands like Born Against, Citizens Arrest, Rorschach, Man is the Bastard, and Econochrist, it gave voice to a generation of punk youth who rejected the macho posturing of straight-edge, youth-crew hardcore and wanted a return to the darker side of political punk.

VICTORIA RECORDS

Victoria Records
Puerto Rico

I've only seen two albums on Victoria, both re-presses of nueva trova LPs originally released on Areito in Cuba. It's possible that Victoria was a Puerto Rican conduit for Cuban music, or that it released other records as well and I just haven't been able to find them.

Viva o Povo!
Portugal

This ad hoc label released a single record in the wake of the 1974 Portuguese Carnation Revolution—*Viva a Bandeira Vermelha* (Long Live the Red Flag) by the group Coro Popular "O Horizonte é Vermelho" ("The Horizon is Red" People's Chorus).

The Voice of Friendship and Solidarity
Libya

A Libyan propaganda label that released a half dozen or more LPs of Maltese synth-pop and light disco dedicated to Muammar Gaddafi, his *Green Book*, the Libyan working class, and a free Palestine. The Voice of Friendship and Solidarity (VOFS) was also the name of a Libyan-run Maltese radio station. The label has some connection to the New Dawn Production Company (NDPC), another Libyan propaganda outfit with very similar recorded output, but the VOFS records are recorded and produced in Italy, as opposed to Malta.

VOICESPONDENCE

Voicespondence
Canada

Voicespondence was started by Clive Robertson in the mid-seventies as a cassette magazine,

putting out poetry and spoken word releases that functioned much more as art than music. By 1979, Robertson turned towards more traditional record production, putting out the album *Electric Eye* by Toronto art punks The Government (the album was a live recording of the band playing the soundtrack to a video performance). The label ran through the mid-eighties, releasing another dozen records of Robertson's political sound poetry, other art-rock (including a 7" by feminist post-punks Fifth Column), as well as Canadian dub poets and steel bands.

" LA VOIX DU PARTI COMMUNISTE FRANÇAIS "

La Voix du Parti Communiste Français
France

An early label of the French Communist Party, it released vinyl recordings of speeches by party leader Maurice Thorez in the late fifties.

Het Voorlichtingscentrum van de Partij van de Arbeid
Netherlands

This organization's name translates to "Labor Party Information Center," and it released a 1968 7" by De Stem des Volks (The Voice of the People), an Amsterdam-based socialist choir that existed as part of the Dutch labor movement for over one hundred years, from 1898-2002.

Vox Pop
Switzerland

Active from the late seventies into the early

eighties with a decidedly leftist bent, this eclectic label released political folk and rock from Europe (pro-labor, feminist, klezmer) and Latin America (including Numa Moraes from Uruguay and Amerindios from Chile), as well as a couple early Swiss punk records. In addition, it distributed and/or coproduced a selection of records with Eigelstein Musikproduktion.

A Voz de Cabo-Verde
Cape Verde

A long-running label with a focus on the music of the former Portuguese colonies in Africa, in particular the Cape Verdean Islands. Because the Portuguese never built a pressing plant in Guinea-Bissau or Cape Verde (they did build plants in Angola and Mozambique), records on the label were pressed in multiple countries; early records from the late sixties and early seventies in particular seem to have been pressed in either Portugal or Angola. Angolan artists like David Zé and Conjunto Evolução Àfrica cut records with VCV, but the core of the catalog is Cape Verdean artists such as Bana, Black Power, Luis Morais, and the band Voz de Cabo Verde, which recorded in a variety of musical styles, from cumbia to merengue to morna. (The band even released a funk-tinged LP on the label; entitled *Independencia*, the album features songs dedicated to Amílcar Cabral and the PAIGC [African Party for the Independence of Guinea and Cape Verde.])

Vozes Na Luta
Portugal

Vozes Na Luta (Voices in the Fight) was the label of Grupo de Acção Cultural (GAC, or Cultural Action Group), a collective of musicians that formed in the immediate aftermath of the 1974 Carnation Revolution in Portugal. GAC focused on reviving singing and folk music as a revolutionary tool, recording songs and releasing records that directly supported the struggles of people organizing on the ground, including in the Portuguese colonies in Africa. After multiple splits, the group (and the label) broke up in 1978.

Vrije Muziek
Netherlands

Although independent from DICAP, Vrije Muziek was almost solely focused on being the Dutch distributor for nueva canción chilena, releasing albums by Inti-Illimani, Quilapayún, Tiempo Nuevo, and more. (Many of these records maintained their DICAP catalog numbers, even though they have specific and often unique Vrije Muziek covers and labels.) In addition, the label released a series of solidarity records about the Chilean struggle, and a single 7″ about Puerto Rico, which might imply a plan (that apparently never came to fruition) to put out more pan–Latin American political music.

VVR
Netherlands

VVR stands for "Vrienden van de Vrije Radio" (Friends of Free Radio Foundation), an organization and label supporting pirate radio. This was not the type of pirate radio popular today in the US, however. Instead, VVR documented and supported popular music stations that were based on offshore boats—a tactic for working around the corporate control over broadcasting rights in different European countries. The label released a "Pirate-Memories" series of 7″s documenting the jingles and call signs of popular offshore stations such as Radio Caroline (UK) and Radio Atlantis (Belgium).

Wagenbachs Quartplatte
West Germany

A small label run by Klaus Wagenback in West Berlin. It started as an extension of his publishing outfit, releasing spoke word and poetry, then in the late sixties put out records by Wolf Biermann, a dissident GDR singer-songwriter, and Austrian avant-gardist Ernst Jandl. In the seventies, the label turned towards almost exclusively releasing records by the political children's theater group Grips.

Wake Up!
UK

This label only put out one record, a 1987 benefit EP for the UK miners' strike. Artists included Billy Bragg, Redskins, and Attila the Stockbroker.

Way Out
Italy

One of a series of sublabels of Vedette Records (along with Albatros and I Dischi dello Zodiaco), Way Out generally leaned towards explicitly political folk, with albums dedicated to Italian anarchist and socialist songs, as well as a document of a communist folk concert. It also released the LP *Canzoni degli Schiavi Americani* (American Negro Slave Songs), which doesn't really fit the pattern, so I'm not entirely sure what the full concept of the label was. Because it shares the same Vedette catalog numbers as all the sublabels, its hard to know exactly how many records Way Out released.

Web Women's Music Co-Operative
New Zealand

The label and organization of the Web Women's Collective, a feminist folk/country/rock crew that included the lesbian sister duo the Topp Twins.

Which Side Records
UK

An ad hoc label name used to release a 1985

------

folk-music benefit compilation in support of the UK miners' strike, including new renditions of labor classics by Ewan MacColl, Woody Guthrie, and Aunt Molly Jackson. The record sleeve was crammed with information about how to support the strike, as well as a large solidarity poster.

WOGA
Wiener Organisation gegen Atomkraftwerke in der Initiative Österreichischer Atomkraftwerksgegner

Wiener Organisation Gegen Atomkraftwerke
Austria

This Austrian antinuclear organization pressed a 7" record sometime in the seventies (it is undated) by the song group Gruppe Dreschflegel (which also released an LP on Extraplatte in 1979). The record is titled *Da habt ihr euch verrechnet: Lieder gegen Atomkraftwerke* (Since you have miscalculated: Songs against Nuclear Power Plants), and features four tracks. Two are traditional folk songs reinterpreted, and two are originals by this polit-folk act with a schlager-heavy sound.

Wiiija
UK

An indie rock label started in 1988 out of the Rough Trade record shop in West London. While much of its output isn't of interest here, in the early nineties it functioned as the main outlet for the UK riot grrrl scene, releasing records by London riot grrrl bands Huggy Bear and Skinned Teen, as well as putting out UK editions of records by Bikini Kill. In addition, Wiiija also put out Cornershop's first four LPs. Cornershop was an outspokenly antiracist and politicized indie rock band merging South Asian music with reggae, disco, and other dance music.

WINDBAG
RECORDS

Windbag Records
USA

The label of the Berkeley Women's Music Collective. It was distributed by the larger lesbian-feminist sister label Olivia Records.

Wise Women Enterprises
USA

A lesbian label with a small stable of artists, similar in some ways to Olivia, but based in New York. It ran from the mid- to late seventies, and released a half dozen albums, including some under the name Urana Records.

ANY WOMAN'S BLUES

Women's Prison Concert Collective
USA

This political group released an LP titled *Any Woman's Blues* in 1976. The record, which lists no label moniker, documents an all-women's folk and blues concert recorded live at the Women's Jail in San Bruno, California in December 1975. Musician's included Holly Near, well-known lesbian folk singers Cris Williamson and Pat Parker, and others. I believe the title of the record is taken from a Bessie Smith song of the same name.

Women Strike for Peace
USA

The largest women's peace organization in the US, Women Strike for Peace peaked in the sixties, leading marches of up to fifty thousand women against nuclear weapons. In 1967, it released a compilation LP titled *Save the Children: Songs from the Hearts of Women* that included songs by Joan Baez, Barbara Dane, Odetta, Malvina Reynolds, Buffy Sainte-Marie, and more. The cover design is build around an image by Käthe Kollwitz.

Women's Wax Works
USA

The label of New York City singer-songwriter Alix Dobkin, one of the trailblazers of lesbian folk music. Dobkin used the label first in 1973 to release her LP *Lavender Jane Loves Women*, which was re-pressed at least a half dozen times in the seventies. *Lavender Jane* featured fellow lesbian musicians Kay Gardner (who went on to record a couple LPs with both Urana Records/Wise Women Enterprises and Ladyslipper) and Patches Attom, but is sometimes attributed to Dobkin because of her outsized presence in women's and lesbian music history. Dobkin went on the use the label to release three more vinyl LPs, a 12" single, and a number of cassettes and CDs.

Words of Warning
UK

A Bristol-based political punk label, it began releasing records by anarchist bands like Oi Polloi, Hex, and Resist in 1989, and had a breakout release in 1992 with the hugely popular LP *United Colors of Blaggers ITA* by the antifascist oi/rap/dance band Blaggers ITA (who would sign a deal with EMI a year later). Words of Warning went on to release music by similar punk/dance crossover bands such as Dub War and Scum of Toytown.

Worker Records
USA

A Washington, DC label started by labor folk singer Joe Uehlein. It released at least a couple LPs: 1979's *Groundwork: Songs of Working People*, Uehlein's collection of renditions of classic folk and country songs by Joe Glazer, Woody Guthrie, Joe Hill, Ewan MacColl, and Merle Haggard; and 1982's *Solidarity Day*, a documentary compilation of a folk concert in support of workers.

Workers' Music Association
UK

Not so much a label, but a British music publishing company used in the fifties and sixties for labor-related releases on Topic Records, then in the sixties and seventies by the Dubliners for their UK releases. It most recently resurfaced on Robert Wyatt's 1982 *Nothing Can Stop Us* LP as the publishing company for the song "Red Flag."

Xntrix
UK

Label run by Vi Subversa of the anarcho-punk band Poison Girls. It was the main outlet for the Poison Girls once they left Crass Records, and also released records by bands featuring Vi's kids Gem Stone and Pete Fender.

Xtra
UK

A British folk and blues label in the tradition of Rounder or Topic, with a heavy catalog of folkies Woody Guthrie, Pete Seeger, Ewan MacColl, bluesmen Sonny Terry and Memphis Slim, plus a half dozen albums of nueva canción chilena.

Yangki
UK

This interesting label was an early project of Current 93's David Tibet. It was set up in 1985 to release *Devastate to Liberate*, a compilation LP, with all proceeds going to the Animal Liberation Front. The record is a collection of bands coming from both the experimental wing of anarcho-punk (Crass, Annie Anxiety) and the social wing of industrial (Legendary Pink Dots, Nurse with Wound). The label name would later be used for a couple Current 93 pre-releases and sampler records.

YE.T
Turkey

A small label that released albums by Ömer Zülfü Livaneli, one of Turkey's most popular—and political—musicians. Since the sixties, Livaneli's music has been sung in the street at protests by students and others, and he has performed with Mikis Theodorakis, Inti-Illimani, and Joan Baez.

Youth Against Racism in Europe
Europe

Youth Against Racism in Europe is a pan-European organization founded by the Trotskyist Committee for a Workers' International in 1992 to fight the rise of the Right across Europe. In the UK the group took up the mantel of Rock Against Racism and in 1993 released a double LP compilation of diverse alternative pop, rock, and hip-hop acts, including Chumbawamba, Björk, Cornershop, Saint Etienne, Jamiroquai, and Credit to the Nation.

YTF
Sweden

The record label of the Yrkestrubadurernas Förening, the Swedish union of singers and songwriters. Founded in Stockholm in 1971, it works to advocate for musicians, builds relationships with other trade unions, and supports the development of Swedish popular music. The label put out close to one hundred albums. Many are not overtly political, yet it released a solidarity LP in support of Spanish political prisoners as well as multiple polit-folk records (including one of antifascist songs by Chilean exile Francisco Roca).

ZANU
Zimbabwe

ZANU (Zimbabwe African National Union) was one of the two major guerrilla groups fighting for national independence for Zimbabwe (then Rhodesia). In the late seventies it released an LP titled *Chimurenga Songs: Music of the Revolutionary People's War in Zimbabwe*; "chimurenga" means "struggle" in Shona, and is the popular term for the guitar-based fusion of Zimbabwean folk and Western rock and blues that was a core element of the independence struggle. (Chimurenga music has been popularized globally by Thomas Mapfumo.) The same LP was released in Germany by Verlag Jörgen Sendler.

Zhongguo Changpian (China Records)
China

The state record company of the Chinese Communist regime, set up in 1954. Releases range from recordings of operas (*The East is Red*; *Red Detachment of Women*), political songs (*Beloved Chairman Mao, You Are the Red Sun that Shines in our Hearts*), regional folk music, classical (*Lu Chunling and His Magic Flute*), and marching bands (the ever popular classic *We Are Marching on the Great Road* by the Chinese People's Liberation Army Band).

Zida
Lebanon

A very short-lived Beirut-based label that released multiple records by Khaled al-Habre, a Lebanese musician with strong communist sympathies who lived amongst Palestinians in Southern Lebanon and set the poems of Mahmoud Darwish to music.

Zip-Zip
Portugal

This label emerged from the Portuguese television show of the same name, which aired for six months in 1969. The first variety/talk show in the country, the program was groundbreaking for pushing the political envelope under an arguably fascist regime. The label began as an extension of the show, releasing recordings of guest interviews, skits, and theme songs, but quickly began releasing fado and folk music critical of the regime. In 1974–75, Zip-Zip put out a stream of revolution-themed 7″s, their covers festooned with fists, hammer and sickles, and carnations.

Zulu Records
USA

Zulu is the mid- to late sixties label run by Phil Cohran, who played with Sun Ra and was a founder of the Association for the Advancement of Creative Musicians (AACM) in Chicago. The label released a half dozen records, including Cohran's *The Malcolm X Memorial (A Tribute in Music)*.

GLOSSARY OF MUSICAL STYLES

Afrobeat is both used as a catch-all term for music that fuses various traditional African folk styles with Western R'n'B, rock, and sometimes reggae styles, and more specifically for the sound promoted most popularly by Fela Anikulapo Kuti, merging Nigerian highlife with jazz and funk.

Big band, as used in this book, is a form of jazz—sometimes known as swing—played by a large ensemble of musicians. Usually at least ten instruments are involved, including saxophones, trumpets, trombones, as well as a guitar (or banjo) and bass.

Bluegrass is a form of US roots music which developed in Appalachia in the 1940s, mixing African-American blues and jazz traditions with British and Celtic ballads and jigs. Originally acoustic, it was popular with Appalachian workers and miners, and often fused quirky storytelling with political commentary.

Bossa nova is a Brazilian musical style created in the 1950s and popularized in the early sixties, becoming hugely successful with youth. Translating to "new wave," it swept through Brazil with its mix of classical guitar and jazz percussion. Largely romantic in lyrical content, the mid- to late sixties saw it used as the musical base for the newer música popular brasileira (MPB), which featured much more politicized lyrics (although often coded to escape censorship from the military dictatorship).

Calypso music was created in Trinidad and Tobago in the 19th century and spread throughout the Caribbean and parts of Latin America in the 20th century. It mixed social commentary, originally sung in patois and eventually in English, with rhythms from West Africa, and became massively popular with the Caribbean working class. It is considered the root of much of Caribbean music, including ska, soca, and kaiso.

Chaabi, or sha'bi, literally means "folk" in Arabic, and is a name used to describe a broad-range of North African traditional music. Across Morocco, Algeria, and Egypt, chaabi began as popular street music, with lyrical content often narrating the struggles of rural peoples migrating to urban areas. It is at the root of youth-based styles that emerged in the 1960s and 1970s, including raï and the trance-based chaabi/gnawa fusion of Nass El Ghiwane.

Chanson has its origins in Medieval times, but was the most popular form of French music thoughout most of the 19th and 20th centuries. It is lyric-driven, and thus a popular form for political engagement and critique. It is polyphonic, and although it can be "pop," it follows the sounds of the French language, not English like most Western pop music. The term *chansonnier* (one who sings chanson) is sometimes more broadly used to describe any European singer-songwriter that performs in a structured folk form.

Chimurenga is the guitar-based fusion of Zimbabwean folk and Western rock and blues traditions. It was a core element of the independence struggle in Zimbabwe in the 1970s, surpassing rock music in popularity both because of its more native roots and because it was sung in Shona, and thus hard for white Rhodesians to understand. The word chimurenga means struggle in Shona, and the music was popularized globally by Thomas Mapfumo throughout the eighties and nineties.

Corridos are Mexican narrative ballads rooted in social commentary. Their original heyday was during the period from Independence to the Revolution (roughly 1810–1910), but they are still massively popular in Mexico and the southwest of the US today.

Cumbia began as a Colombian form of working class song and dance style in the early 20th century. It is known for its fusion of Spanish lyrical style, Indigenous rhythms and instrumentation, and African percussion. By the mid-19th century it had spread across the rest of Latin America, often mixing with more local musics to create new forms.

Dub is broadly understood as a wide-array of electronic musical forms that evolved out of reggae production in the 1960s. It began when Jamaican DJs stripped the lyrics off reggae tracks and remixed them for extended instrumental B-sides, often with a heavy focus on the drums and bass. It quickly evolved into an art form of its own, with early progenitors King Tubby and Lee "Scratch Perry" building successful careers off their dub production. In the seventies, the aesthetics of dub spread from reggae into other musical genres, including disco, rock, and early hip-hop.

Éntekhno is a Greek orchestral music that incorporates Greek folk melodies and elements of Western folk and classical traditions. Often composed in cycles with lyrics based on classical Greek poetry, it seems an odd genre to find popularity with the Greek urban working class in the 1950s, but that is exactly what happened. Composers such as Mikis Theodorakis played open air concerts to large crowds, sneaking anti-Junta messages into the music. Éntekhno developed parallel to the rebetiko revival in the sixties and seventies.

Fado is a Portuguese folk music which follows a traditional structure and historically features mournful lyrics related to living life in poverty. In the 18th and 19th centuries it was solidified as the music of the Portuguese working class, and in the mid-20th century a new generation of musicians began using fado as a tool to critique the dictatorship. After the Carnation Revolution in 1974, fado was merged with other European folk traditions to fuse a protest music that roughly corresponded to the nueva canción genre developed in Latin America in the fifties and sixties.

Free jazz is a form of jazz developed in the late 1950s by musicians who felt that existing jazz was too structured and limiting. While jazz musicians had been creating new, unconventional sounds and had begun to reject written scores earlier, some argue it was the emergence and evolution of the Civil Rights Movement and its demands for "freedom" that gave Black musicians the drive to push their art into forms increasingly liberated from existing structures. While European musicians have prefered the term "improvisational," the political idea of freedom was central to the creation of the genre in the US, and it has been important to have the word "free" associated with it.

Gnawa music developed out of Muslim spiritual songs in Morocco. In it, both musical and lyrical phrases are repeated over and over to create epic, drone-like songs. In the 1960s, Western rock musicians became interested in gnawa, and starting in the 1970s, young Moroccan musicians began experimenting with the merging of gnawa with other traditional music. Not only did they begin playing it with Western instruments, but also moving the lyrical content from the spiritual to the political and social. These fusions by bands such as Nass el Ghiwane and Jil Jilala became massively successful, creating a new popular music.

Highlife originated in Ghana in the early 20th century, primarily by merging traditional Fante rhythms with Western and Caribbean influences. It was originally played by large bands, primarily for wealthy Ghanian elites under British colonialism, but in the 1940s the genre split, with the development of a guitar-driven highlife that could be played by much smaller bands. Much easier to play (with bands that could travel cheaply), this stripped-down highlife became hugely popular with both urban and rural populations, and quickly spread across Anglophone West Africa, creating new evolutions of the form in Nigeria, Liberia, and elsewhere.

House music is a form of electronic dance music which developed out of the queer Black music scene in Chicago in the 1980s. Rooted in disco, house DJs would mix in jazz, various Latin genres, synth-pop, and early hip-hop at underground parties. A similar, harder-edged sound would develop in Detroit, which was dubbed techno.

Jive, in the context of this book, is South African jive. It is also known as township jive, because of its origin in apartheid-era African townships outside of Johannesburg, as well as mbaqanga. Developing in the 1960s and 70s, it draws on both gospel and traditional South African music, but mixes in fast, choppy guitar and a strong bassline. While it was discouraged and even banned at certain points by the apartheid government because of its popularity amongst Black South Africans, it was also plugged into the international music scene very early, with many artists signing to major multinational labels and fueling the "worldbeat" phenomena of the eighties.

Kabyle is a Berber language used by the Kabyle people largely in Algeria. It also the term used for the folk music of the Kabyle people, popularized in the 1970s by the musician Idir (Hamid Cheriet). The Kabyle style has been popular with politicized musicians who are part of the Berber nationalist movement.

Klezmer is a musical form developed by Jews in Eastern Europe between the 16th and 18th century, but was generally referred to as Yiddish music until the 1970s. Although originally based on religious music, klezmer is largely secular, and speaks to the experiences of working class Jews concentrated in ghettos in Europe.

Krautrock is a term coined in the 1970s to describe a form of rock music that emerged in Germany in the sixties. Although generally used to refer to bands such as Can or Kraftwerk that eschewed the blues elements of rock music and replaced them with electronics and propulsive, repetitive percussion, it has also be used to describe a group of highly politicized bands that emerged out of the West German student movement and squatting scene in the late 1960s and early seventies. Bands such as Ton Steine Scherben and Floh de Cologne actually embraced the blues-y proto-punk of US bands like the MC5, but importantly sung in German (very rare at that time) and embedded ultraleft politics into their lyrics.

Merengue first emerged in the Dominican Republic in the mid-nineteenth-century, and from the beginning contained an element of social commentary. Initially performed with string instruments, it is now popularly performed with an accordian. It has also fused with other Latin music styles, and elements of it can be found in Cuban and Puerto Rican musical styles.

New wave was created by musicians influenced but the liberatory qualities of punk, but who wanted to move away from a blues and rock core. Initially new wave bands incorporated synthesizers, and eventually absorbed aspects of disco and other popular musics anathema to punks. Although often thought of as apolitical, many early new wave acts (such as Scritti Politti) had members who studied Marxism in art school, and incorporated political theory into their lyrics.

Nueva canción, or new song, emerged in Latin America (and Spain) in the late 1950s and early 1960s. A renewal of Latin American folk traditions, the music was largely guitar-based, and updated the songs of the poor, women, prisoners, and the working class for a contemporary youth audience. Its politics and popularity led to its suppression in a number of countries, including Argentina, Uruguay, and most acutely, Chile. In Chile in particular, the music became politically militant, becoming the sound of both communist youth and the insurgent Popular Unity government of Salvador Allende.

Nueva trova, or new trova, developed in Cuba as an explicitly political music style after the Revolution. Trova is a guitar-based Cuban folk music, and the nueva trovadors (the most well known being Pablo Milanés and Silvio Rodríguez) and of the sixties and seventies took this root, as well as influences from nueva canción, and crafted an updated style intended to be the popular soundtrack of the unfolding Cuban Revolution.

Oi! is a subgenre of punk that developed in the UK in the late 1970s. A direct rejection of the experimentation found in post-punk, oi! bands centered their music around the blues rock roots of punk, and their culture around ideas of working class pride and the skinhead aesthetic. Although in its origin most oi! was not particularly ideologically left or right, it has often been used as a tool by far right organizers to recruit young working class youth into white supremacist organizations. At the same time bands such as Angelic Upstarts were explicitly leftists.

Polit-folk is simply a catch-all term to describe the more ideologically driven elements of the folk revival that emerged across Europe in the sixties and seventies. Many communist youth groups, unions, and other socially-engaged community organizations developed musical groups that performed under the banner of polit-folk.

The name withstanding, **post-punk** emerged roughly the same time as punk in the mid- to late 1970s, but eschewed the more brash and straightforward elements for a sound that was often more angular, layered, and at its core, experimental. Unlike new wave, post-punks embraced punk's do-it-yourself ethos, as well as its antiauthoritarian tendencies, although these were often channelled into more cerebral politics tempered by Marxist theory.

Progg is a Scandinavia-specific genre popular in the 1970s that shared commonalities with prog rock, but the shortened term for "progressive" here often had more to do with political content than the formal qualities of the music.

Raï music developed in the first half of the 20th century in western Algeria. The region was heterogenous, with Arabic, French, Jewish, and Spanish areas, and out of this fusion rose a class of bawdy female singers known as cheikas. Poor and marginalized, these Muslim women mixed street slang and dance elements into traditional music which became the foundation of raï. In the 1950s, these women were the first musicians to use their songs to support the FLN and the Algerian armed struggle against France. After liberation, the government attempted to suppress the more explicit elements in the music, and push for a more respectable national culture. In the 1970s, Algeria had a massive population of disaffected youth, drawn to the taboo aspects of raï, its rebellious history, and its vocalization of the difficulties of life for the poor.

Rebetika is a series of folk traditions coming from the poor and working class of Greece in the 19th and first half of the 20th century. In the 1960s, it was used as the foundation for a new generation of musicians to revive popular, political folk music is Greece, often called the rebetiko revival (rebetiko is the singular of the plural rebetika).

Riot grrrl was both a cultural movement and a musical genre. In the early 1990s, fed up with a misogynist and male-dominated punk scene, more and more women began playing in punk bands, and forming all-female acts. Bikini Kill is often considered the progenitor of the movement, and they were involved in all aspects of it, from music, to zine creation, to the setting up of discussion groups amongst young women in both Olympia, WA and Washington, DC (in many ways successors to the consciousness raising groups of second wave feminism). As a musical style, there was little that held all the bands together other than a leaning towards loud, easily played punk with strong pop sensibilities.

Sahrawi is a term used broadly to describe the culture of the people of the Western Sahara, and more specifically the music created by supporters of the Polisario Front and independence for Western Sahara. It is largely a mix of North African music traditions, including gnawa and the desert blues of the Tuareg people.

Salsa is a popular Latin music genre that developed in the 1960s in New York City, largely in the Cuban and Puerto Rican communities. At its core it is largely a mixture of Cuban son music and jazz, with bits and pieces of guaracha, bomba, bolero, and even rock and funk thrown in. Initially its lyrical content was structured by an urban working class and immigrant consciousness, as well as an inclusive desire to create a pan-Latino sound, but in the eighties and nineties it became a global pop phenomena, losing almost all of its political content.

Soca is an evolution of calypso music, created by Lord Shorty in Trinidad in the 1970s. He successfully mixed calypso with the more popular sounds of reggae, funk, and soul to reinvigorate the genre. Lord Shorty also reinjected politics into the music.

Synth-pop is a term used to describe Western popular music in which the dominant instrument is the synthesizer. It was first used to describe a subgenre of new wave, but has found broad usage for any music driven by synthesizers, drum machines, and other forms of electronic sequencing.

APPENDICES

RECORD LABELS BY REGION OF ORIGIN *

The United States and Canada

3rd Street Records, 13
African Methodist Episcopal Church, 14
Afrikan Poetry Theatre Records, 15
Afro Records, 15
Afro-American Museum, Inc., 15
Afrikings, 15
AFSCME, 16
AIDS Action Committee, 17
Alacran Productions, 17
Alternative Tentacles, 18
American Civil Liberties Union, 19
Americanto, 19
Anti-Corporate Speak Records, 21
Apir, 21
Aquifer Records, 21
ARF Shant, 24
Ars Pro Femina, 25
Ascension Records, 25
Asch Records, 25
SHA Recording Co., 26
Asian Improv, 26
Bamboo Records, 28
Better Youth Organization, 29
Big Crossing Records, 29
Big Toe, 30
Black Artists Group, 30
Blackbeard Records, 30
Black Family Records, 30
Black Fire, 30
Black Forum, 31
Black Jazz Records 31
Bola Press, 31
Boží Mlýn Productions, 31
Bread and Roses, 32
Broadside, 32
Broadside Voices, 32
Brotherhood Records, 32
Canadian Communist League (M-L), 34
Candy-Ass Records, 34
Carolsdatter Productions, 36
Cassandra Records, 36
Celluloid, 38
Center for the Study of Comparative
    Folklore and Mythology, 38
Chainsaw Records, 38
Chol Soo Lee Defense Committee, 40
Clergy and Laymen Concerned, 41
Clouds Records, 42
CMS, 42
Collective Chaos, 43
Collector Records, 43
Comité Québec-Chili, 45
Context Music, 47
The Council for United Civil Rights
    Leadership, 47
Crazy Planet Productions, 49
Credo, 49
Cutty Wren Records, 50
CW Records, 50
Dare to Struggle, 50
Del-Aware, 51
Delta Records, 51
Direct Hit Records, 54
Dischord, 55

Discos Coquí, 56
Discos Lara Yarí, 56
Discos Sanjuancito, 57
Disques Sol 7, 59
Distributive Workers of America, 60
Dubious Records, 61
East/West World Records, 61
En Lutte, 65
ESP-Disk, 61
The Fellowship of Reconciliation, 68
Femme Records, 68
Final Call Records, 68
Finnadar Records, 69
Fire on the Mountain, 69
First Amendment Records, 69
Flying Fish, 70
Folkways, 71
Friends Records, 73
Front Page Entertainment, 74
FSM Records, 74
Full Circle Productions, 74
FUSE Music, 74
Golden Triangle Records, 75
Great Leap, 76
GR Records, 77
GYN Records, 78
Healing Earth Productions, 78
Hermonikher, 78
Hide, 79
High Hopes Media, 79
Hilltown Records, 79
Hippycore, 80
Hot Wire, 80
Im-Hotep Records, 81
Index Records, 82
Indian Records, 82
Institute of Positive Education, 83
JCOA Records, 85
Jihad Productions, 86
John Paul Records, 87
June Appal, 87
Kill Rock Stars, 89
Komotion International, 90
KPFA, 91
Ladyslipper, 92
Lengua Armada Discos, 92
Leona Records Corporation, 92
Lesbian Feminist Liberation, 93
Liberation Music, 93
Liberation Support Movement, 93
Lima Bean Records, 94
Lion's Roar Records, 95
Live Oak Records, 95
Local 1199 Drug and Hospital Union, 95
Longview Records, 95
Mary Records, Inc., 97
Menyah, 98
Michga, 99
Michigan Interchurch Committee on
    Central American Human Rights, 99
Mobilization for Survival, 101
Monitor, 101
More Record Company, 101
Muhammad's Mosque of Islam, 103

A Muslim Sings, 104
New Clear Records, 106
New Morning Records, 106
New Vista Arts, 106
Nexus Records, 107
Nimbus West, 108
Nonantzin Recordings, 108
Non Serviam Productions, 108
Noona Music, 109
Old Lady Blue Jeans, 112
Olivia, 113
One Spark Music, 113
On The Line, 113
Open Door Records, 113
Origami Records, 114
Out & Out Books, 115
Outpunk, 115
Pan-American Records, 116
Paredon, 117
Pasquinade Music Co., 119
Peñón Records, 120
The People's Music Works, 120
Perfect Pair Records, 121
Philo Records, 121
Physical Records, 122
Pleiades Records, 123
Polemic Records, 124
Profane Existence, 125
Progressive Labor Party, 125
Québékiss, 126
Radioactive Records, 127
Rag Baby Records, 127
Rainbow Snake Records, 128
Raizer X Records, 128
Raven Records, 128
Rebellion Records, 129
Redwood Records, 130
Reigning Records, 130
Relevant Records, 130
Résistance, 130
Rise Up Records, 131
Rival, 131
Rosetta Records, 133
Rounder Records, 133
RPM, 134
R Radical, 134
SAFCO Records, 135
Salaam Records, 135
Salsa, 135
S and M Records, 136
Save the Mountain Album Project, 136
Scarab Records, 137
Scarface Records, 137
Sea Wave Records, 137
Shanachie, 138
Significant Other Records, 138
Silhouttes in Courage, 139
Simple Machines, 139
Sister Sun Records, 139
Sisters Unlimited, 139
Smokestax Records, 140
Sound House Records, 141
Special Records, 142
Spiral Records, 142

* I've done my best to place labels into the region they themselves identify with, rather than where they would be placed by their history of colonialism. For instance, Puerto Rican labels are located in Latin America and the Caribbean, as opposed to North America.

173

Latin America and the Caribbean

Western Europe

Southern Europe

Nikos Productions, 107
NR Produzioni, 110
Oihuka, 112
L'Orchestra, 114
Osiris, 115
Partido Socialista, 118
Partido Socialista Obrero Español, 118

Partido Socialisto Popular, 118
Partito Comunista Italiano, 118
Partito Socialista Italiano, 118
Servire il Popolo, 138
SudNord Records, 144
Toma lá Disco, 147
Franco Trincale, 150

União Geral de Trabalhadores, 152
Valentim de Carvalho, 155
Vento de Leste, 156
Viva o Povo!, 158
Vozes Na Luta, 159
Way Out, 160
Zip-Zip, 164

UK, Northern Ireland, and Ireland

1 in 12 Records, 13
7:84 Theater Company, 13
Action Records, 14
AD Records, 14
African National Congress, 15
Agit-Prop, 17
Alliance, 18
Alternative Energy, 18
Arc, 23
Ardkor Records, 23
Artists Against Apartheid, 25
Axum, 28
Biafra Choral Society, 29
Blackthorne, 31
Catch 22, 37
Chebel Records, 39
Children of the Revolution, 39
CirCus, 41
Club Sandino, 42
C. Miner Records, 42
CNT Productions, 43
Corpus Christi, 47
CounterAct, 47
Crass, 48
Cutting Records, 50
Delyse, 52
Derry Records, 52
Deviant Wreckords, 53
Dolphin, 60
Earthworks, 61
Edição Fora do Comércio Oferta dos
    Comunistas Brasileiros a Seu
    Amigos, 62

Flat Earth Collective, 69
Forward Sounds International, 71
Friends of Bogle Records, 73
Fuse Records, 75
Greenbelt Records, 76
Groucho Marxist Record Co:Operative, 77
HHH Productions, 79
IDAF Records, 80
Jabula, 85
Jobs for a Change, 86
Jumbo, 87
Liberation Records, 93
Loony Tunes, 96
Love Conquers All, 96
Manchester Greenham Common
    Women's Support Group, 97
Miner Hits Records, 99
Ministry of Power, 100
Mortarhate, 101
Music for H-Block, 103
Nadiya, 104
New Army Records, 105
Oneworld Peacesongs, 113
Out On Vinyl, 115
Outlet Records, 115
Pan African Records, 116
Peasant's Revolt Records, 119
People Unite, 121
The Plane Label, 123
Positive Action, 124
R&O Records, 126
Radical Wallpaper Records, 127
Raw Ass Records, 128

Re Records, 128
Recommended Records, 129
Recordiau Anhrefn, 129
Recordiau Ar Log, 129
Refill Records, 130
Resistance Records, 130
Rough Trade, 133
Rugger Bugger, 134
Saoirse Records, 136
Sky & Trees, 139
Solidarity with Solidarity, 140
Spiderleg, 142
Spring Records, 142
St. Pancreas Records, 142
Sterile Records, 142
Stroppy Cow Records, 143
Topic, 148
Trades Union Congress, 148
TURC, 150
Two Tone, 151
Upright, 154
Utility, 155
Wake Up!, 160
Which Side Records, 160
Wiiija, 161
Words of Warning, 162
Workers' Music Association, 162
Xntrix, 163
Xtra, 163
Yangki, 163
Youth Against Racism in Europe, 162

Scandanavia

A Disc, 14
Afrogram, 16
Agitpop, 16
Amalthea, 19
Arbeidernes Opplysningsforbund i Norge, 22
Arbejderkultur KA (M-L), 22
Arbejdernes Oplysningsforbund, 22
Arbetarkonferensen, 23
Arbetarkultur, 23
Arbetarrörelsens Bokcafé med Tidens
    Bokhandel, 23
Avanti, 27
Befria Südern, 29
Bruksskivor, 33
BT Klubben, 33
Centerns Ungdomsförbund, 38
Chile-Kommittén, 39
Clarté, 41
Clarté ML, 41
Cuba Records, 50

Danmarks Lærerforening, 50
December 7, 51
Demos, 52
EKO, 65
Eteenpäin!, 66
Folkebevægelsen Mod EF, 70
Folksång, 71
Forlaget Tiden, 71
Fredsång, 72
Frihets Förlag, 73
Greenpeace Records ApS, 76
International Physicians for the
    Prevention of Nuclear War, 83
Intersound, 84
Jår'galæd'dji, 85
Källan, 88
Kansankulttuuri Oy, 88
Kofia, 90
Kommunistisk Ungdom, 90
Lilla Raven Records, 94

Love Records, 96
Manifest, 97
MNW, 100
Musikpres, 104
Nacksving, 104
Narren, 105
Nørrebro Beboeraktion, 109
Oktober (Norway), 112
Oktober (Sweden), 112
Opponer, 114
Organisationen til Oplysning on
    Atomkraft, 114
Patricio Weitzel, 119
Plateselskapet Mai, 123
Plattlangarna, 123
Pogo Plattan, 124
Proletärkultur, 126
Promauca, 126
R-Edition, 130
Røde Mor Musikforlag, 133

Eastern Europe

Sub-Saharan Africa

The Middle East and North Africa

Asia and Oceana

RECORD LABELS BY MUSICAL STYLES

African, MENA, Indigenous, and Asian folk and pop

classical and experimental

jazz, soul, funk, blues, and hip-hop

North American and European folk

nueva canción, nueva trova, and other Latin music

AD Records, 14
A Disc, 14
Aksie Latin Amerika, 17
"Aktionskomitee Chile" Köln, 17
Alacran Productions, 17
Albatros, 18
Amalthea, 19
Americanto, 19
AMIGA, 19
Apir, 21
Arauco, 22
Arbeiterkampf, 22
Arbetarrörelsens Bokcafé med Tidens Bokhandel, 23
Archivi Sonori, 23
Areito, 24
Arzobispado de Santiago, 25
Avanti, 27
Ayuí/Tacuabé, 28
Balkanton, 28
Barlovento Discos, 28
CA de RE, 34
Cantares del Mundo, 35
Canto Libre, 35
Canzoniere il Contemporaneo, 35
Canzoniere Internazionale, 35
Caracola, 36
Casa de las Américas, 36
CEAL, 37
Ceibo, 37
Center for the Study of Comparative Folklore and Mythology, 38
Cercle du Disque Socialiste, 38
Le Chant du Monde, 39
Chile-Kommittén, 39
Chile Solidarität, 40
Cigarrón, 40
CirCus, 41
Club Sandino, 42
Collettivo Teatrale la Comune, 44
Comitato Vietnam-Milano, 44
Comite Promotor de Investigaciones del Desarrollo Rural, 44
Comité Québec-Chili, 45
Comité Solidarité Salvador, 45
Committees for the Defense of the Revolution, 46
Context Music, 47
Cuba Records, 50
Demos, 52
DIAP, 53
DICAP, 53
I Dischi dello Zodiaco, 55
I Dischi del Sole, 55
Disco Libre, 56

Discos America, 56
Discos Lara-Yarí, 56
Discos NCL, 56
Discos Pueblos, 57
Discos Vipar, 57
Discovale, 57
Disques Alvarès, 58
Disques Perspective (ASBL), 59
Disques Sol 7, 59
Disque Terra Nostra, 59
DOM, 60
DT64 Polit-Song, 61
Edição Fora do Comércio Oferta dos Comunistas Brasileiros a Seu Amigos, 62
Ediciones América Hoy, 62
EGREM, 64
ENIGRAC, 65
Eteenpäin!, 66
ETERNA, 66
Expression Spontanée, 67
Folk Internazionale, 71
Folkways, 71
Fotón, 71
France Amérique Latine, 72
FSLN, 74
Gong, 76
Guimbarda, 78
Imprenta Nacional de Cuba, 82
Indisha, 82
Instituto Cubano de Amistad con los Pueblos, 83
International Union of Students, 84
IRT, 84
Italia Canta, 84
Jota Jota, 87
Karaxu, 89
KKLA, 90
Leona Records Corporation, 92
Lince Producciones, 94
Love Records, 96
Macondo, 96
Mascarones, 98
Melodiya, 98
Menyah, 98
Misereor, 100
Mobilization for Survival, 101
Monitor, 101
Mundo Novo, 103
Narren, 105
Nonantzin Recordings, 108
Le Nouveau Chansonnier International, 109
Nuestro Canto, 110
Nueva Trova, 110

Nueva Voz Latino Americana, 110
Un Nuevo Amanecer del 30 de Agosto, 111
Nuevo Arte, 111
Ocarina, 111
OIR, 112
L'Orchestra, 114
Pan-American Records, 116
Paredon, 117
Participación, 117
Patricio Weitzel, 119
Peña de los Parra, 120
Peñón Records, 120
Pentagrama, 120
Pincén, 122
Pläne, 122
Plateselskapet Mai, 123
Poètes du Temps Présent, 123
Politique Hebdo, 124
Pragmaphone, 124
Producciones Dupuy, 125
Promauca, 126
Promecin, 126
Rebellion Records, 129
R-Edition, 130
Redwood Records, 130
Ruptura, 134
Smokestax Records, 140
Sonorama, 140
Sozoalistische Deutsche Arbeiterjugend, 141
Spanischer Kulturkreis, 141
Svenska Chilikommittén, 144
El Teatro del Triangulo, 146
Terz, 146
Thunderbird Records, 147
Toma lá Disco, 148
Trikont, 149
TVD, 150
Uitgeverij Polypoepka, 151
Uniteledis, 154
Universidad Autonoma de Sinaloa, 154
UP, 154
Vancouver Folk Music Festival Recordings, 155
Varagram, 156
Venceremos, 156
Vendémiaire, 156
Victoria Records, 157
Vox Pop, 158
Vrije Muziek, 159
Xtra, 163
YTF, 163

reggae, soca, and calypso

A&B Records, 13
AD Records, 14
Alliance, 18
Amiga, 19
Amnesty International, 20
Artists Against Apartheid, 25
Ateliers du Zoning, 26

Axum, 28
Disques Espérance, 58
Friends of Bogle Records, 73
Greenpeace Records ApS, 76
Gridalo Forte Records, 77
Karibe, 89
Kronchtadt Tapes, 91

Michga, 99
Milkyway, 99
Misereor, 100
MNW, 100
Monitor, 101
Music is Life, 103
A Muslim Sings, 104

rock (prog/progg/kraut/punk)

spoken word, martial music, children's songs, and field recordings

RECORD LABELS BY LABEL TYPE

traditional record label*

Acousti — Yuri Korolkoff, 14
Action Records, 14
Afro Som, 16
Agitat, 16
Alternative Tentacles, 18
Amalthea, 19
Antagon, 20
Archivi Sonori, 23
Argument-Verlag, 24
Ar(i)ston, 24
Asch Records, 25
Asian Improv, 26
Ateliers du Zoning, 26
Avanti, 27
Barlovento Discos, 28
Batuque, 29
Black Fire, 30
Black Forum, 31
Black Jazz Records, 31
Broadside, 32
Canto Libre, 35
Caracola, 36
C B, 37
CDA, 37
CEAL, 37
Ceibo, 37
Celluloid, 38
Center for the Study of Comparative
    Folklore and Mythology, 38
Le Chant du Monde, 39
Children of the Revolution, 39
Cigarrón, 40
Le CLEF, 41
CMS, 42
CNT Productions, 43
Collective Chaos, 43
Cramps, 48
Credo, 49
CSM, 49
Cuba Records, 50
Cutty Wren Records, 50
Delta, 51
Delyse, 52
Derry Records, 52
Diapasão, 53
Dickworz Bladde, 54
Dikanza, 54
Disaster Electronics, 54
I Dischi dello Zodiaco, 54
I Dischi del Sole, 55
Discófilo, 55
Discos America, 56
Discos Coquí, 56
Discos NCL, 56
Discos Vipar, 57
Discoteca Polo Norte, 57
Discovale, 57
Disques Alvarès, 58
Disques Espérance, 58
Disques Cyclope, 58
Disques Pavé, 59
Disques Perspective (ASBL), 59
Disques Sol 7, 59

Disque Terra Nostra, 59
DNG, 60
Dolphin, 60
DOM, 60
La Do Si Discos, 60
Earthworks, 61
Ediciones América Hoy, 62
Editions Borgson, 62
Edizioni di Cultura Popolare, 64
Edizioni Lotta Poetica, 64
Eigelstein, 65
ESP-Disk, 65
Eteenpäin!, 66
Expression Spontanée, 67
Extraplatte, 67
Flying Dutchman, 70
Flying Fish, 70
Folk Freak, 70
Folk Internazionale, 71
Folkways, 71
Forward Sounds International, 71
Fotón, 71
Friends Records, 73
Friends of Bogle Records, 73
Fuse Records, 75
Gala Gala, 75
Golden Triangle Records, 75
Gong, 76
Gougnaf Mouvement, 76
Greenbelt Records, 76
Gridalo Forte Records, 77
Guilda da Música, 78
Guimbarda, 78
Herri Gogoa, 79
Indisha, 82
Intersound, 84
IZ Disketxea, 85
Jumbo, 87
Kalakuta Records, 88
Källan, 88
Kill Rock Stars, 89
Le Kiosque d'Orphée, 89
KomistA, 90
Konkurrel, 91
KPFA, 91
Larrikin Records, 92
Leona Records Corporation, 92
Liberation Records, 93
Lince Producciones, 94
Linea Rossa, 94
Loony Tunes, 96
Love Records, 96
Love Conquers All, 96
Macondo, 96
Manifest, 97
Manifesto, 97
Il Manifesto, 97
Merengue, 98
Metro-Som, 99
Michga, 99
Milkyway, 99
Minos, 100
Misereor, 100

MNW, 100
Monitor, 101
More Record Company, 101
Movimento, 102
al-Mu'assasa al-Fanniya al-'Alamiya, 103
Mundo Novo, 103
Musangola, 103
Musikant, 104
Musikpres, 104
Nacksving, 104
Neue Welt Schallplatten, 105
New Wave Records, 106
Nexus Records, 107
N'Gola, 107
Ngoma, 107
Nicole Going to Africa, 107
Nikos Productions, 107
Nimbus West, 108
Nourphone, 109
Le Nouveau Chansonnier International,
    109
Le Nouveau Clarté, 109
Nuestro Canto, 110
Nueva Voz Latino Americana, 110
N'Zaji, 111
Ohr, 111
Oihuka, 112
OIR, 112
Oktober (Sweden), 112
Osiris, 115
Outlet Records, 115
Palm, 116
Panoptikum, 116
Paredon, 117
Peace Pie, 119
Pegafoon, 120
Pentagrama, 120
Perfect Pair Records, 121
Philo Records, 121
Physical Records, 122
Pincén, 122
Piranha, 122
Pläne, 122
The Plane Label, 123
Plattlangarna, 123
Poètes du Temps Présent, 123
Pogo Plattan, 124
Polemic Records, 124
Pragmaphone, 124
Profane Existence, 125
Promecin, 126
R&O Records, 126
Radical Wallpaper Records, 127
Raizer X Records, 128
Raubbau, 128
Recordiau Ar Log, 129
R-Edition, 130
Résistance, 130
Revolum, 131
Ricordu, 131
Rock Against Records, 132
Rough Trade, 133
Rounder Records, 133

* Since much of the information about these labels is based on limited and initial research, for labels that I am unsure of
    how they were organized, I've defaulted to listing them under the "traditional" category.

antinuclear, antidevelopment, antimilitarist, and/or environmental-focused

cooperative, collective, or musician run

identity-based focus (Black, lesbian, women, minority-linguistic group, etc.)

Im-Hotep Records, 81
Imparja Records, 81
Index Records, 82
Indian Records, 82
Institute of Positive Education, 83
Jihad Productions, 86
June Appal, 87
Ladyslipper, 92
Lesbian Feminist Liberation, 93
Lim Bean Records, 94
Manchester Greenham Common
    Women's Support Group, 97
Movimento Democrático de Mulheres,
    102
Movimento Femminista Romano, 102
Muhammad's Mosque of Islam, 103

A Muslim Sings, 104
Nonantzin Recordings, 108
Noona Music, 109
Old Lady Blue Jeans, 112
Olivia, 113
Open Door Records, 113
Origami Records, 114
Out & Out Books, 115
Out On Vinyl, 115
Outpunk, 115
Rosetta Records, 133
Salaam Records, 135
Sea Wave Records, 137
Silhouttes in Courage, 139
Sister Sun Records, 139
Sisters Unlimited, 139

Stroppy Cow Records, 143
Student Nonviolent Coordinating
    Committee, 143
Third World Records, 147
Thunderbird Records, 147
Tribe Records, 149
Undercurrent Records, 152
Union of God's Musicians and Artists
    Ascension, 153
Ventadorn, 156
Which Side Records, 160
Windbag Records, 161
Wise Women Enterprises, 161
Women's Wax Works, 162
Zulu Records, 164

international solidarity organization

Afrogram, 16
Aksie Latin Amerika, 17
"Aktionskommitee Chile" Köln, 17
Americanto, 19
Amilcar Cabral Gesellschaft, 20
Amnesty International, 20
Angola Comité, 20
Anti-Apartheids Beweging Nederland, 20
Antiimperialistisches Solidaritätskomitee,
    21
Anti-War Action, 21
Arauco, 22
Arbetarrörelsens Bokcafé med Tidens
    Bokhandel, 23
Artists Against Apartheid, 25
Association des Femmes Vietnamiennes
    en France, 26
Avrupa Türkiyeli Toplumcular
    Federasyonu, 27
Befria Södern, 29
Biafra Choral Society, 29
CASI, 36
Chile-Kommittén, 39
Chili Aktie, 40
Club Sandino, 42
CNSLCP, 42

Comitato per i Soccorsi Civili e Umanitari
    al Popolo Greco, 44
Comitato Vietnam-Milano, 44
Comité Québec-Chili, 45
Comité Solidarité Salvador, 45
Confederation of Iranian Students
    (National Union), 47
Defence and Aid Fund, 51
Edição Fora do Comércio Oferta dos
    Comunistas Brasileiros a Seu
    Amigos, 62
Edição Instituto Caboverdeano de
    Solidariedade, 62
Fédération Espagnole des Déportés et
    Internés Politiques, 68
France Amérique Latine, 72
IDAF Records, 80
KKLA, 90
Landelijk Vietnamkomitee, 92
Liberation Support Movement, 93
Manchester Greenham Common
    Women's Support Group, 97
Medisch Komitee Angola, 98
Michigan Interchurch Committee on
    Central American Human Rights, 99
Music for H-Block, 103

Nationales Vietnamkomitee, 105
Noise Against Repression, 108
Opération W, 114
Patricio Weitzel, 119
Peñón Records, 120
Portugal-Spanien-Gruppe Berlin, 124
Records Against Thatchism!!!, 129
Robin Hood, 131
SAFCO Records, 135
Salamansa Records, 135
Solidarity with Solidarity, 140
Somadiscos, 140
Spanischer Kulturkreis, 141
Stichting Isara, 143
Stopp Apartheid-86, 143
Survival Alliance, 144
Svenska Chilikomittén, 144
Tricontinental, 149
Ultimatum, 152
Union des Éstudiants Vietnamiens en
    France, 153
Venceremos, 156
The Voice of Friendship and Solidarity,
    158
Vrije Muziek, 159

political party, organization, or state label

African National Congress, 15
AIDS Action Committee, 17
American Civil Liberties Union, 19
AMIGA, 19
Arbejderkultur KA (M-L), 22
Areito, 24
Arzobispado de Santiago, 25
Association des Stagiaires et Etudiants
    des Comores, 26
Aurora, 27
Avrupa Türkiyeli Toplumcular
    Federasyonu, 27
Balkanton, 28
Belgische Socialistische Partij, 29
Blackbeard Records, 30
Bund Demokratischer Jugend, 33
Bürgeraktion Küste, 33

Canadian Communist League (M-L), 34
Casa de las Américas, 36
Centerns Ungdomsförbund, 38
Chol Soo Lee Defense Committee, 40
Circolo Ottobre, 40
Clarté, 41
Clarté ML, 41
Clergy and Laymen Concerned, 41
Comité Anti-Militariste, 44
Comite Promotor de Investigaciones del
    Desarrollo Rural, 44
Comité Révolutionnaire d'Agitation
    Culturelle, 45
Committees for the Defense of the
    Revolution, 46
Les Communistes de la Radio et de la
    Télévision, 46

The Council for United Civil Rights
    Leadership, 47
CounterAct, 47
Deutsche Kommunistische Partei, 52
Deutsche Schallplatten Berlin, 53
Dihavina. 54
Disco Libre, 56
Les Disques ICEM-CEL, 59
Dislaohaksat, 58
DT64 Polit-Song, 61
Edição da Comissão Organizadora das
    Comemorações do 25 de Abril, Dia
    da Liberdade, 61
Edições Avante, 62
Editions Syliphone Conakry, 63
Editori Riuniti, 63
Edizioni Circolo Culturale Popolare

union or labor-related

INDEX

7 Seconds, 18, 29

Aboriginal, 30, 81, 92
Afonso, José, 21, 53, 61-62, 94, 106, 109, 124
Africa, 5, 6, 8, 14, 15, 38, 71, 104, 107, 149,
    149-150, 150; famine relief in, 81, 103-104;
    Francophone, 5, 41, 63, 153; Ghana, 15;
    independence and nationalism, 3, 63; liberation,
    30-131, 85, 93, 110, 137; music in, 18, 25,
    40, 58, 61, 93, 98, 99, 167, 168; North, 28, 38,
    58, 71, 167, 172; the Sahel, 71, 81; southern,
    6, 7, 16, 20, 51, 61, 80, 93, 98; Stern's Africa,
    61, 88; Union of Comoros, 26. See also African
    National Congress; Angola; Mozambique; MPLA;
    Namibia; PAIGC; Pan-Africanism; South Africa
African National Congress (ANC), 5, 15, 16, 31, 89,
    96, 98, 107, 133, 143
Afro Records, 15
Afrobeat, 62, 88, 116, 138, 167
Afrocentric, 1, 13, 15, 30, 31, 108, 131, 137, 149, 152
AIDS, 6, 17, 138
AIDS Action Committee, 17
Alarcón, Rolando, 94, 96
Algeria, 19, 65, 86, 147
Allende, Salvador, 17, 22, 34, 40, 59, 98, 154, 170
Amandla, 15, 16, 98
AMIGA, 19-20, 28, 53, 54, 61, 66, 134
anarchism, 1, 3, 4, 13, 17, 23, 35, 43, 44, 48, 54, 55,
    58, 63, 64, 65, 66-67, 70, 71, 80, 89, 90, 94,
    100, 104, 108, 122, 131, 133, 144, 147, 151,
    154, 160, 162; and punk, 1, 17, 38, 39, 43, 47,
    48, 66-67, 69, 77, 80, 90, 96, 101-102, 104,
    105-106, 119-120, 125, 128, 139, 142, 144,
    149, 154, 162, 163
Angola, 5, 6, 15, 20, 23, 29, 37, 42, 53, 54, 55, 57,
    66, 71, 75, 82, 83, 84, 86, 93, 98-99, 102,
    103, 107, 111, 145, 155, 157, 159
Angola Comité, 6, 15, 19, 86, 111, 145
animal liberation, 80, 102-103, 162
anti-apartheid, 3, 5, 7, 14, 15, 16, 19, 20, 25, 31,
    49, 51, 76, 77, 80, 85, 91, 98, 104, 114, 122,
    124, 129, 133, 140, 143, 144, 151, 156, 169;
    Sharpeville Massacre, 14; Bishop Desmond Tutu,
    104, 138; UK Anti-Apartheid Movement, 25, 129,
    151. See also African National Congres; Nelson
    Mandela; Soweto
anticolonialism, 4-5, 6, 7, 14, 16, 26, 42, 43, 54, 57,
    73, 75, 83, 86, 102, 103, 107, 109, 113, 116,
    117, 153, 155, 159
anticommunism, 3, 26, 31-32, 80
antifascism, 23-24, 34, 44, 66, 69, 95, 96, 97, 109-
    110, 119, 122, 137, 156, 157, 162, 163-164
anti-imperialism, 1, 3, 17, 21, 29, 34, 36, 39-40, 47,
    58, 93, 98, 142, 144, 146, 156
antimilitarism, 17, 21, 27, 36, 41-42, 44, 73, 97, 101,
    123, 124, 127, 133, 143
antinuclear movement and organizations, 29-30, 50,
    69, 79, 81, 88, 127, 138, 144, 161. See also

Greenham Common; nuclear; Three Mile Island
antiwar. See antimilitarism
Areito, 24, 65, 74, 110, 111, 157
armed struggle. See guerrilla struggle
Armenia, 4, 23, 24, 60, 66
Asian-American, 26, 28, 40, 61, 69, 76, 134
Association for the Advancement of Creative Music
    (AACM), 137, 164
atomkraft. See antinuclear; nuclear
avant-garde, 33, 48, 64, 129, 141, 143, 145-146, 160
Aztlan, 17, 93

Baez, Joan, 37, 46, 162, 163
Baldwin, James, 42, 49
Bambaataa, Afrika, 15, 38
Baraka, Amiri, 31, 86
Basque, 4, 77, 79, 85, 109, 112, 131, 141
"Bella Ciao" (song), 6, 125-126, 148
benefit concerts, 20, 81, 128, 129, 141
benefit records, Africa, 16, 29, 81, 91, 103-104,
    124, 125, 129, 132, 142, 144; antinuclear
    movements, 69, 88, 113, 127, 134, environmental
    movements, 76-77, 80, 141; labor movements,
    71, 87-88, 116, 124, 129, 143, 150, 160-161;
    Latin America, 45, 141, 152; Poll Tax resistance,
    105-106, 119-120, 128; Pride parades, 39, 53;
    other, 20, 21, 61, 91, 103, 119-120, 124, 129
Berber, 4, 25, 28, 81, 169
Berlin, 19-20, 21, 24, 34, 61, 72, 116, 122, 124, 134,
    157, 160
Bikini Kill, 89, 115, 161, 170
Black Arts Movement, 30, 31
Black Panthers, 31, 93, 101, 137, 142, 147
Black Power, 13, 31, 136
Bobo Records. See Outpunk
Bragg, Billy, 19, 79, 86, 120, 155, 160
Brathwaite, Edward Kamau, 18, 36
Brecht, Berthold, 14, 27, 33, 40, 41, 87, 104, 145-146
Breton, 4, 37, 58

Cabral, Amílcar, 20, 43, 102, 109, 110, 135
Cage, John, 48, 69, 90
calypso, 5, 13, 42, 68-69, 104, 167
Campos, Pedro Albizu, 36, 56
Canzoniere delle Lame, 35
Cape Verde Islands, 5, 42, 43, 60-61, 62, 105, 116,
    135, 157, 159
Capra, Juan, 18, 38
Carnation Revolution, 43, 46, 48, 53, 56, 57, 61-62,
    78, 93-94, 99, 102, 115, 124, 148, 155, 156-
    157, 158, 159, 164, 168
cassettes, 1, 4, 8, 21, 23, 24-25, 62, 106, 124,
    162; cassette labels, 90, 90-91, 91, 113, 139;
    cassette magazines, 79, 90-91, 158; cassette-
    only releases, 4, 24, 27, 36, 39, 63, 81, 92
Catalan, 4, 28, 36, 59-60, 122-123, 131
CDA Records, 37, 98, 102, 107
CDs, 1, 4, 7, 8, 10, 17, 21, 26, 30, 36, 54, 57, 81, 97,

191

Josh MacPhee is a designer, artist, and archivist based in Brooklyn, NY. He is a founding member of the Justseeds Artists' Cooperative (Justseeds.org) and cofounded and helps run Interference Archive, a public collection of cultural materials produced by social movements (InterferenceArchive.org).

MacPhee is the author and editor of a half dozen books, including *Signs of Change: Social Movement Cultures 1960s to Now* (coauthored with Dara Greenwald; AK Press, 2010) and *Celebrate People's History: The Poster Book of Resistance and Revolution* (Feminist Press, 2010). He is also the coeditor (with Alec Dunn) of *Signal: A Journal of International Political Graphics and Culture.*

Since 2003, MacPhee has been publishing an ongoing series of zines under the title *Pound the Pavement*. The book you are holding originated as *Pound the Pavement* #16. He is currently working on issue #21.

Common Notions is a publishing house and programming platform that advances new formulations of liberation and living autonomy. Our books provide timely reflections, clear critiques, and inspiring strategies that amplify movements for social justice.

By any media necessary, we seek to nourish the imagination and generalize common notions about the creation of other worlds beyond state and capital. Our publications trace a constellation of critical and visionary meditations on the organization of freedom. Inspired by various traditions of autonomism and liberation—in the US. and internationally, historically and emerging from contemporary movements—our publications provide resources for a collective reading of struggles past, present, and to come.

Common Notions runs a sustainers program where you can support our work and in return receive copies of all our books. Please visit: https://www.commonnotions.org/sustain

Other Common Notions titles:

Towards the City of Thresholds
Stavros Stavrides

A pioneering, ingenious study of new forms of emancipatory urbanism emerging in these times of global crisis and resistance–a look at the spaces to be crossed from cities of domination and exploitation to a common world of liberation.

5.375" x 8.375", 272 pp, $20

Grupo de Arte Callejero:
Thought, Practices, and Actions
Grupo de Arte Callejero

An indispensible reflection on what was done and what remains to be done in the fields of art and revolution through the story of social militancy in Argentina over the last two decades.

6" x 9", 320 pp, $22

Abolishing Carceral Society
Abolition Collective

Abolishing Carceral Society renews and boldly extends the tradition of "abolition-democracy" espoused by W.E.B. Du Bois, Angela Davis, and Joel Olson. Through study and publishing, the Abolition Collective supports radical research happening both in movements and in the communities with whom they organize.

6" x 9", 256 pp, $20